LONG-TERM CARE
OF
OLDER PEOPLE

A Practical Guide

Elaine M. Brody

with two guest chapters by Stanley J. Brody

HUMAN SCIENCES PRESS

72 Fifth Avenue / 3 Henrietta Street
NEW YORK, New York 10011 / LONDON, WC2E 8LU England

Library of Congress Catalog Number 77-5944

ISBN: 0-87705-274-3

Copyright © 1977 by Human Sciences Press
72 Fifth Avenue, New York, New York 10011

Printed in the United States of America
789   987654321

Library of Congress Cataloging in Publication Data

Brody, Elaine M
    Long-term care of older people.

    (Gerontology series)
    Bibliography: p.
    Includes index.
    1. Old age homes. 2. Aged—Care and hygiene.
    3. Extended care facilities. 4. Social work with the aged. I. Title.
II. Series.
HV1451.B74   362.6′15   77-5944

This book is dedicated
to my very special parents
Dr. William J. and Mrs. Frieda R. Breslow
who exemplify
long-term caring

Gerontology Series

Research Planning and Action for the Elderly
Kent, D.P., Ph.D., Kastenbaum, R., Ph.D., and Sherwood, S., Ph.D.

Retirement
Carp, F.M., Ph.D.

Sound Sex and the Aging Heart
Scheingold, L.D., M.A., and Wagner, N., Ph.D.

Time, Roles, and Self in Old Age
Gubrium, J.F., Ph.D.

Long-Term Care of Older People
Brody, E., M.S.W.

Toward a Theology of Aging (Special Issue of Pastoral Psychology)
Hiltner, S., Th.D.

CONTENTS

PREFACE

The first version of this guide was written in 1971 under a contract awarded to the Philadelphia Geriatric Center by the National Institute of Mental Health. Published in 1974 by the United States Government Printing Office, the edition was quickly sold out, necessitating a second printing almost immediately.

By that time, events in the field of long-term care of older people had moved swiftly. There was growing public and professional awareness of the plight of the institutionalized elderly and of their increasing numbers. Efforts to enforce standards and to define "quality care" accelerated. A growing number of professionals, practitioners, and researchers were attracted to the field. Paralleling that stream of activity was a thrust to develop services outside of institutions for those older people who could continue to live in the community if supportive long-term care services were developed.

During those years, the Philadelphia Geriatric Center also grew. Its physical growth included the completion of its new Weiss Institute (120 long-term care beds for the impaired elderly), its Friedman Hospital (a 56-bed fully accredited geriatric hospital), and its Community Housing for the Elderly (27 efficiency apartments in renovated one-family homes). Added to its existing long-term care facilities and high-rise apartment buildings, those new facilities brought to over one thousand the total number of older people living and being cared for on its campus in a spectrum of living arrangements. Through additional experimentation with programs and additional research projects, the center continued its efforts to contribute to knowledge about serving older people.

Events in the larger community and in the center's own community combined to make the original guide outdated in some respects even before it was published. An additional factor that encouraged me to rewrite the book was the fact that many professionals other than social workers were finding it useful.

On beginning what was expected to be a relatively simple task of "updating" the guide, I was amazed at how much needed to be done to it. There had been many new developments and much new information had accumulated. In retrospect, this should not have been surprising. The field of long-term care is still in the earliest phases of growth and knowledge. A book of this kind never really will be finished. That is as it should be, if it is to be responsive to change and to the needs of people.

Nevertheless, major rewriting was necessary. Many of the chapters were rewritten, several entirely new ones were added, and those remaining were revised, with new material being added.

One aspect of a book like this is a constant in the midst of much change. That is the fact that there are many people who contribute, directly and indirectly. The Philadelphia Geriatric Center is a unique, adventurous, and wonderful place. I am fortunate to have spent more than twenty years working in a facility that offers such a favorable climate for caring for the social needs of older people and their families, and that emphasizes the development of knowledge through practice and research as well as values. That climate was created by the center's first executive vice-president, Mr. Arthur Waldman, and by the current executive vice-president, Mr. Bernard Liebowitz. Without the leadership and support of those two remarkable men, nothing could have happened.

It is impossible to name all of my colleagues at the center who contributed to the thinking expressed in the guide. In the area of professional practice, the largest measure of appreciation is due to the incomparable Mrs. Rose Locker, the associate director of the Department of Human Services. The dedicated and creative service of the social work staff resulted in many of the procedures and programs described. The case material in the guide credits the workers who developed it. The forms, protocols, and procedures were arrived at in the course of close collaborative efforts with all departments of the center. There is no way to describe adequately the contribution of superb secretarial support such as that given by Mrs. Gertrude Stein, chief of secretarial staff of the department, and Mrs. Anita Roffman, my personal secretary.

The contributions of Dr. Morton H. Kleban and Dr. M. Powell Lawton are acknowledged with gratitude. Over the years Dr. Lawton directed the development of the assessment measures in use at the center to evaluate the functional capacities of older people. Dr. Kleban for many years has been my research "partner." It would be unthinkable for me to initiate research without consultation and involvement of these two men—formally on large federally funded studies, and informally via curbstone consultations on internal and departmental studies.

The visible portion of the contribution by my husband Steve Brody, his two guest chapters, speak for themselves. They bring to bear the wisdom accumulated in years of public service for the Commonwealth of

Pennsylvania and the United States Government, and the years of teaching as a professor in the University of Pennsylvania's School of Medicine. Less visible are his patience and support and the stimulation of his creative thinking for more than three decades.

A special thanks is due Mrs. Marie L. Blank, Consultant, Center on Mental Health of the Aging at the National Institute of Mental Health. It was she who was a major stimulant to the production of the first guide.

Finally, when thanks are due, there is always a bottom line. In this case, it is the many thousands of applicants to and residents of the center and their families who over the years shared their lives and placed their trust in us.

Elaine M. Brody

Part I

INTRODUCTION

Chapter 1

WHAT IS LONG-TERM CARE?

The phrase "long-term care" is relatively new in the vo-
cabulary of professionals, researchers, the public, and
governmental agencies. It has in the past referred
primarily to care in institutions of various types. More
recently, it is being used in a broader sense to encompass various types of care and services provided on a
long-term basis. The individuals receiving care may reside in their own homes, with relatives or friends, or in
group facilities such as housing for the elderly and
boarding homes. Or, they may reside in institutional
facilities under voluntary, governmental or proprietary
auspices such as sectarian homes for aged, county
homes, and proprietary nursing homes. Though a firm
generally accepted definition has not been formulated,
in this book *long-term care refers to one or more services provided on a sustained basis to enable individuals whose functional capacities are chronically impaired to be maintained at
their maximum levels of health and well-being.*

The underlying values are that all people share certain basic human needs that they have a right to services designed to maximize their own and their families' capacities to meet those needs, and to be furnished services when needs cannot be met through their own resources (social, emotional, physical, financial). This book is about meeting the constellation of needs inherent in the dictionary definition of "life" as *animate* existence, that which imparts spirit or vigor. Those factors are often subsumed under the phrase "quality of life" or are described as *social needs*—that is, needs for interpersonal contacts and relationships, recreational and occupational activities, maintenance of roles, and a sense of mastery, autonomy, and some degree of self-determination or control over one's own life.

It is recognized that the need for long-term care occurs in different population groups such as the developmentally disabled, those who experience impairments during early and middle phases of life, and the elderly. Though many of the principles involved relate to all of those groups, the focus here is specifically on older people.

The book is concerned primarily with those older people who find their way into congregate facilities of an institutional nature. It is artificial, however, to dichotomize long-term care into institutional care and community care. Long-term care should constitute a continuum; institutions should be part of the community, and there is a strong trend toward institutions delivering services to older people who do not actually live in those facilities. Further, it is of primary importance that the choice of living arrangement be based on thorough exploration of options. Such an exploration requires knowledge of needs and of resources to meet those needs, whether those resources are available to maintain the individual in his/her own home, in congregate facilities, or in facilities providing less comprehensive care. Information about long-term care in the community and about the components of the decision-making process is therefore included.

The focus throughout this guide is on the social aspects of care. The overall goal is to improve services to older people residing in long-term care facilities and to their families through understanding of their social needs. A how-to-do-it section spells out the role of social work knowledge and skills in doing so.

Some of the material included appeared first in *A Social Work Guide for Long-Term Care Facilities* (Brody and Contributors, 1974). The latter was written under a contract awarded by the National Institute of Mental Health to the Philadelphia Geriatric Center "to develop and prepare a social work guidebook for long-term care facilities for the elderly." Implicit in the charge was recognition of the importance of the social needs of the institutionalized elderly and of the role of social work in meeting those needs.

In the five years since the previous guide was written, there have been significant developments that indicate the need for this book. Those years have witnessed the accumulation of new relevant information, the introduction of much new legislation (some of which has passed), and the creation of new services and programs. There has been a tremendous increase in the long overdue interest in the field of aging in general. Within that context, long-term care has become one of the burning national social issues of our time. It is a focus of attention among professionals, the public, and government. There is growing awareness of the severe deficits in community care services on the one hand and abuses and deficits in long-term facilities on the other. One measure of the public concern about it is the fact that the United States Senate Subcommittee on Long-Term Care of the Senate Special Committee on Aging has issued a major report titled *Nursing Home Care in the United States: Failure in Public Policy,* plus nine Supporting Papers. Another is that a *Long-Term Care Facility Improvement Study* has been undertaken by the Office of Nursing Home Affairs of the Public Health Service (U.S. Department of Health, Education, and Welfare). Its *Introductory Report* was issued in July, 1975.

The dimensions of long-term care are emerging in true perspective. The twentieth century has been witness to a dramatic numerical and proportionate increase in the aging population. At the turn of the century, those sixty-five and over represented about 4 percent of the total population (about 3 million individuals) compared with 10 percent (about 22 million individuals) by 1975. One of the major social consequences of this phenomenon has been the increase in the number and proportion of elderly people who reside in long-term care facilities. The proportion seems small: about 5 percent of people sixty-five and over are in institutions of all kinds. However, when translated into human terms, the statistic represents more than a million elderly individuals. The introductory report in the Senate series points out that "there are now more nursing beds (1.2 million) in the United States today than general and surgical beds (1 million)." The impact of the situations of these older people is felt by family members of every generation. Furthermore, the 5 percent estimate is based on cross-sectional data—that is, the number of people in institutions on any given day. There is some evidence to suggest that one in five of all people sixty-five and over may enter a long-term care facility at some point during their lives. The increasing cost of such care is another factor drawing attention to the need to ensure that public and private dollars are being used to best advantage in the interests of the older people whose care is being purchased.

It is less easy to count those who are not in institutions but who do require long-term care, either in institutions or via community care services. Some surveys estimate that a minimum of one-third of all older people not in institutions require one or more long-term care services. A conservative estimate, adding both groups, is that currently the target population is about 8 million individuals.

Projections indicate that by 1990 40 percent of the more than 28 million elderly (sixty-five years or over) people will be seventy-five or over. Since those in the latter group are the most vulnerable to the social and functional disabilities requiring long-term care, by that year the target population may well be more than 11 million individuals. That projection does not take into account potential breakthroughs in bio-medical research. Most scientists (but not all) discount possible discoveries that would result in the capability of altering the biological clock of aging, thus enabling large numbers of people to live well into a second century of their lives. They are more hopeful of findings that will defeat the major killer diseases of old age such as cardiovascular disease and cancer. If the latter occurs, thus lengthening life-expectancy a few years, the likelihood is that there will be an even larger group of people who reach advanced old age, swelling the numbers of those who require long-term services because of chronic disabilities.

Hundreds of thousands of workers representing many different backgrounds are involved in the decision-making and referral processes and actual provision of care and services: administrators, physicians, nurses, social workers, and many others. They work not only in long-term care facilities, but in hospitals, family agencies, senior citizens centers, public agencies, and home-care and home health agencies, to name just a few.

One of the main objectives of the book is to provide information to those workers about the social needs of the older people who require long-term care, about how the decision-making process should be managed, and about ways of meeting the social needs. A second set of objectives is to identify the role, function, and value of professional social work services in long-term care; to provide specific material that can be the basis for social work practice in decision-making and service delivery; and to enable adminstrators and health personnel in facilities to understand the potential of social work and to use it in enhancing the care and treatment of the institutionalized elderly.

It is hoped that the guide will meet the need for specific, concrete information on how social work services should be provided in long-term care facilities. It is recognized that the vast majority of facilities do not actually have full-time social workers on staff or even part-time professional consultants. I believe firmly that the provision of such services is a critical goal if quality care is to be provided. However, just as health care is provided by many types of professionals and nonprofessionals (including families), so too are social needs met from diverse sources. The same analogy can be drawn with respect to the professional providers: there is no substitute for skilled physician, nurse, or professional social worker. Nevertheless, the understanding and methods can be used by many.

One section of the guide is based on the social work model in use at the Philadelphia Geriatric Center. That model is still evolving in response to new knowledge and the development of new services and facilities. It is offered not as perfect and immutable but in the hope that in part or in whole it can be adapted and put to practical use by others—whether the "others" be agencies and personnel who make referrals to long-term care, who do screening, or who actually provide care in congregate facilities.

Apart from ethical considerations regarding society's responsibility to the institutionalized elderly, congregate care facilities are significant because:

• The image of the institution in the eyes of the community and the treatment accorded the residents affects the mental health of all old people who live daily with the knowledge that they too many some day need congregate care. Neglect or maltreatment of their institutionalized peers can only reinforce the anxiety with which older people and their families regard such a prospect even when there clearly is no alternative.

• The therapeutic pessimism that characterized attitudes towards the institutionalized elderly in the past is dissipating. Clinical reports and the research literature have shown that a philosophy of custodial care is outmoded. Old people in long-term care facilities, even those who are severely impaired, can and do respond to therapeutic and rehabilitative efforts.

• The institution, because it serves those who have experienced a convergence of social, mental, and physical assaults, occupies a unique vantage point. Study of the elderly who arrive at the institution's doors provide clues to the paths that led them there and the preventive and supportive community services that were lacking and should be developed. Therefore, in addition to serving the institutionalized population the institution can provide information valuable for broad social planning.

• The request for admission is made more often than not at a time of extreme stress to the older person and his/her family, and it often is their first contact with the long-term care system. Since admission may or may not be the plan of choice, the institution can play a pivotal role. Handled responsibly, the services offered can involve exploration of the nature of the problems, referral to more appropriate resources, and mobilization of existing supportive services. Admission to institutions may be avoided or delayed by "boosting" the applicant into the system of community care.

• Institutions can maximize the utilization of their resources by functioning as bases for the operation of services often thought of as "community care." Services such as out-patient diagnostic and evaluation services, day-care for the mentally impaired, short-term care for treatment and rehabilitation, and short-term care to permit vacation relief for families, are a mix of congregate and community care. They increase the options which constitute a continuum of care and permit the matching of services to need of older person and family at a given point in time.

• Some institutions for the elderly provide concentrations of professionals with expertise in all aspects of aging. They are therefore excellent sites for training, research, and educational programs that can serve the general community as well as the institutional community.

The professional literature and the popular press are replete with documentation of the sad plight of many of the institutionalized elderly. Undeniably, in some facilities, the provision of care and treatment is at a level which should not be tolerated. This guide will not deal with the obvious abuses that fortunately have captured public attention: profiteering, fire hazards, unsanitary conditions, lack of health care, inadequate food, and even cruel treatment. It is accepted as a given that such abuses must be eliminated. However, the adverse effects of such institutions have been generalized without justification to include all institutions and have been used as a rationale for denigrating institutions as a potential positive resource for care. The issue is not that of institutional care versus community care. The relevant issues are *to identify those for whom long-term care is appropriate and to determine the nature of the services and the qualities of the environments that would maximize their well-being.*

In short, for the right person and family at the right time, a long-term care facility can be the right service. It should serve a specific target population; it need not and should not be a poor alternative to community living.

Much remains to be done if institutions are to reach that positive goal of maximizing the functioning level and well-being of the elderly residents. As knowledge has accumulated regarding the potential detrimental effects of applying for admission, waiting on a list, actual relocation, admission, and life in the institution, so too have research and practice offered clues as to constructive methods of managing such experiences. In other words, it cannot be assumed that negative effects are intrinsic and that nothing can be done. On the contrary, studies and observation support the view that it is possible to capitalize on available information to modify positively the existing programs and environments.

One of the broadest areas of neglect in institutions has been the psychosocial needs of the elderly residents. It is recognized by professionals that the frontiers of care must be pushed beyond subsistence, survival, and the treatment of disease to dignity and enjoyment. Awareness of medical and nursing needs has resulted in increasing pressure to include such essential services. While a good deal has been written about the devastating impact of lack of attention to the social and psychological needs on the institutionalized, implementation of this understanding via programs and services patterns has lagged. Similarly, though there is widespread recognition of the need for social work services as an integral part of the programming of long-term care facilities, their full development has not taken place.

Apart from ethical considerations, there are practical reasons for administrators to increase attention to social needs of their residents and to employ professional social workers.

The expectations of older people, their families, governmental bodies, and the public are increasing in relation to long-term care. There is a heightened awareness of the importance of social factors. This trend will continue. The new groups of people who are constantly being graduated into the aging phase of life have experienced better education, better standards of living, and will be more sophisticated and articulate in their demands. The groundswell of consumerism has given impetus to this trend. Older people have a heightened awareness of the need for advocacy. Families of those in long-term care and activist groups of older people in the community increasingly will lend support to the social needs of those in long-term care who cannot act on their own behalf. As options become more available and long-term care facilities more readily accessible, administrators and owners of facilities will need to attend carefully to the quality-of-life ingredients of care.

The field of long-term care is undergoing major changes. Government legislation and regulations not only are subject to change but vary widely from region to region, state to state, and in some instances, even from county to county. The population served also is constantly changing. In the course of every five years, there is a turnover of about 35 percent of the aging population. Some die. Newcomers enter the ranks who are progressively better educated, have had access to better health care and a higher standard of living, and whose expectations are higher. We hope that new services and programs will develop that will reflect new knowledge. Therefore, the guide will require adaptation and modification. Basic human needs, however, are a constant.

The guide is designed in the main to provide needed information to professionals. It is hoped that it will in some small measure improve the lot of older people and their families. After all, that is what it is all about.

ORGANIZATION OF THIS GUIDE

The guide is organized as follows:

Part I explains what is meant by long-term care.

Part II sets the context for meeting social needs of older people requiring long-term care: Chapter 2 gives a historical perspective of the development of long-term care. Factors accounting for the growth of facilities of different types are reviewed, as are the reasons for the current lack of clarity about what such facilities should be like. Data about the number and proportion of older people in various types of facilities are included. Chapter 3 discusses how decisions are made for referral and use of various types of long-term care. It describes the elements of an orderly process of assessment and evaluation, including the role of various scales and measures to assess both individual functioning and the social/health supports available. Chapter 4 states the goals and describes the target population of long-term care services in the community. It offers a detailed inventory of services and programs that can be mobilized to help maintain the elderly community dweller at a maximum level of health and well-being. Chapter 5 summarizes demographic, health, social characteristics, and reasons for admissions, since the characteristics of the older people in long-term care facilities determine the nature of services required.

In Part III, the reader is taken step by step through the processes of institutionalization from the first inquiry about admission through the period of residence and death or discharge. Case material and various forms and protocols are used illustratively and research findings are summarized and integrated throughout where they have implications for practice. The chapters deal with meeting social needs of residents and families and specifically with the role of social work. Chapter 6 states the theoretical and philosophical basis of the following 7 chapters, including the view of the institution as essentially a living arrangement. Chapters 7, 8, 9, 10, and 11 are focused on individual and group services to applicants, residents, and their families. Chapter 12 deals with discharge and after-care, and Chapter 13 with death and dying. The social work role in research, training, and policy determination, and social work administrative considerations are the subjects of Chapters 14 and 15 respectively. Chapter 15 details the format and content of case records, the nature of the statistics that should be compiled, the kinds of reports that should be developed, and job descriptions for different levels of social work personnel. Though the guide will set up a model for practice, it recognizes that services and procedures require modification in different types of settings.

Part IV is concerned with issues of care and treatment and broad social issues. Some of the issues of institutional care discussed in Chapter 14 are what the nature of facilities should be, the identification of people who should live in them, the mix of services, the mix and match of residents; the size, locale, and design of facilities; new roles for the institution vis-a-vis the community; other types of congregate facilities; and personnel training. Chapter 17 summarizes and discusses various types of experimental treatment programs that have been tried. Chapter 18 addresses the social issues that are relevant to long-term care. It also suggests goals for the future.

Finally, Chapter 19, *A Word to Family and Friends—and to the Older People Themselves,* is written as friendly advice given directly to those with whom this book is concerned. In planning, in practice, in research, in controversy, in legislation, their perceptions of needs are not always sought. The chapter suggests what to look for in selecting a long-term care facility, what to expect in terms of service and care, and how to articulate one's own needs.

Part II

THE CONTEXT

Chapter 2

THE DEVELOPMENT AND CURRENT STATUS OF LONG-TERM CARE FACILITIES

A major difficulty in discussing "long-term care" is that it does not have a generally accepted definition. The phrase generally calls to mind institutions of various types. However, there has been increasing recognition of the fact that long-term care should constitute a continuum of services and facilities in and out of institutions. That is, long-term care services can be given to people in their own homes on the one hand, or in institutions on the other. Still other people can benefit from long-term services that are a mix or blend of institution or community, such as day care for the impaired, or temporary institutional care to permit family vacations or for relief in family emergencies. Further, many different types of congregate facilities have been evolving. There has been, for example, major growth in what have been called "quasi-institutions" or "unofficial institutions," such as boarding homes and high-rise apartment buildings for older people that offer various kinds of services.

Even if one looks only at the long-term care facilities that are institutional in nature, there is a lack of clarity about definitions. There is no orderly value system or conventional wisdom about them. There is no universally accepted nomenclature. Distinctions are blurred, and different institutional names mean different things to different people in different places at different times.

A few of the names used in referring to institutions that provide long-term care are homes for aged, homes or hospitals for chronically ill, nursing homes, geriatric centers, rehabilitation hospitals, county homes, veterans' homes, and psychiatric hospitals. Such different titles may reflect the nature of the auspice (sectarian, governmental, nonprofit, profitmaking), the goals of the institutions, the philosophy of care, the characteristics of the residents, or the kinds of services provided. Or they may reflect the perceptions of the third party payors as to the appropriate functions to which reimbursement mechanisms are keyed. Examples of titles reflecting reimbursement are: skilled nursing facility, intermediate care facility, health-related facility, personal care home. Often there are regional variations in nomenclature, and levels of reimbursement are uneven regionally.

In order to understand how the present somewhat chaotic situation came about, it is necessary to look at institutions in historical perspective. That perspective also casts light on popular perceptions of institutional care, since those perceptions often are vestiges of attitudes toward different types of institutions and their residents that have been carried over from earlier times. This chapter will therefore provide a brief overview of the development of long-term care facilities. (Long-term community care services will be discussed in Chapter 3).

One of the major influences coloring attitudes toward institutions and the people cared for in them has been the fact that earliest forms of such care were for outcasts and paupers. Thus, for example, in the fourth century hospitals existed for the care of lepers, cripples, the blind, and the sick poor. By the twelfth century, medical care was practiced in home or office, with only hopeless and homeless cases finding their way to hospitals. The evolution of the hospital as the place for temporary care of acute disease appears to have occurred in the eighteenth and nineteenth centuries.

Cohen states that long-term care in the United States has had six distinct periods: the colonial period (seventeenth and eighteenth centuries); the nineteenth century and twentieth up to 1920 (which he characterizes as the American version of the 1834 English Poor Law); 1920–1935, the rise of the eleemosynary institution for care of the elderly; 1935–1945, a period of reaction to public financing of long-term care; 1945–1965, the postwar boom in private proprietary (for profit) nursing homes and development of private and public fiscal support mechanisms; and the post-1965 period with development of "extended care," incorporation of intermediate care into medical assistance, and the major theoretical emphasis on alternatives to institutional care (Cohen, 1974).

The concern for "paupers" which characterized earliest long-term care in the United States is important to understand because vestiges of those attitudes still persist. The concept of "charity" has been tenacious, carrying with it the expectation that the recipient of care be grateful and submissive (Brody, 1973). Early county homes and almshouses were tied to the "pauper" concept—that is, the assumption by the public of responsibility for the undeserving and abandoned who could not care for himself and had no family to do so. Included in those categories were groups such as the disabled, handicapped, aged, widows with children, orphans, the feebleminded, the deranged, the chronically ill, and the unemployed.

The colonial period also included programs of "outdoor relief" (noninstitutional care). One of particular interest was the giving of subsidies to families to care for a disabled, senile, or mentally ill family member. The notion of such family subsidies currently is considered extremely progressive. Some Scandinavian countries have such programs, and Japan recently began a similar effort (Maeda, 1975).

Other forms of outdoor relief during that period were boarding-out or foster-care programs and the auctioning of paupers to those willing to support them at least cost to the community. Cohen characterizes those programs as an admixture of harshness, charity, economy, responsibility, and stern moralism (1974). Their use declined after the Revolution, with the almshouse becoming the more accepted method of dealing with the problem of dependency.

The almshouse concept was strengthened and persisted during the nineteenth century, given impetus by the Poor Law of England of 1834. Operated as cheaply as possible by local governments (towns and counties), almshouses contained mixtures of poor, elderly, insane, feebleminded, and others. The harshness that was a matter of policy is epitomized by the 1875 report of the New York State Department of Public Charities which stated:

Care has been taken not to diminish the terrors of this last resort of poverty, "the almshouse", because it has been deemed better that a few should test the minimum rate at which existence can be preserved than that many should find the almshouse so comfortable a home that they would brave the shame of pauperism to gain admission to it.

Supervision of institutions by states began in the latter part of the nineteenth century. The same period witnessed developments such as specialization of various types of institutions, segregation of different groups of residents and patients, the rise of private philanthropy, the utilization of hospitals for the well-to-do as well as for the indigent, and the beginnings of homes for aged and nursing homes in their present forms. The use of those types of facilities for those who were not paupers thus came somewhat later than the parallel development in hospital care.

In reviewing the development of long-term care facilities for older people, it must be remembered that large numbers of old people simply did not exist prior to this century and that it is only in the past half-century that the proportion of the total population represented by the elderly increased rapidly. (The 3 million people sixty-five and over were 4 percent of the total population in 1900; currently there are about 22 million of that age, representing 10 percent of the population). Sheer demography, then, was one of the major pressures producing growth of institutional facilities.

By the end of the 1920s, nonprofit homes for aged were the most visible form of care for elderly (Mathiasen, 1960) although older people were accumulating in psychiatric hospitals and county homes. Primarily for the "well aged," nonprofit homes were most often under sectarian auspices. Dramatic increases in long-term care facilities did not occur until after World War II. The growing need for such beds was obscured and inhibited by the Great Depression and by the war.

As the middle of this century approached, significant trends were occurring that ultimately caused a boom in the number of long-term beds. Social Security and Public Assistance decreased the need for institutional beds for the well but indigent aged. As the total aged population grew, there was an extremely rapid growth of those in advanced old age. It is the latter group that is most vulnerable to the age-linked physical and mental impairments (such as chronic brain syndrome or "senility") that often require institutional care.

Another factor at work was that the state psychiatric hospitals were accumulating many people who had been admitted at younger ages and who had grown old in the hospitals. By the early 1960s, older people occupied 30 percent of public mental hospitals beds, while constituting 10 percent of the total population (*Patients in Mental Institutions*, 1964). Cohen's (1961) report for the U.S. Senate Special Committee on Aging stated:

> Any survey of facilities where there are significant numbers of aged persons with psychologic disorders will reveal that this group . . . fares badly. They are given up as hopeless, relegated to back wards euphemistically called "continued treatment" but in actual practice discontinued treatment situations.

During the 1960s many states embarked upon concentrated programs to discharge the elderly to the community. Since community support services were grossly underdeveloped, and since many of the patients required round-the-clock care, large numbers of them went to nursing homes and boarding homes.

Long-term care also was influenced by growing interest in and activity relating to old people in general. Cohen (1974) provides a detailed list of such governmental activities, the highlights of which were: the first National Conference on Aging in 1950; federal participation in cost of care in private institutions (1953); the Hill-Burton Act giving financial aid to sponsors to construct and equip nursing homes; Small Business Act and Small Business Investment Act to provide loans to nursing homes (1958); National Housing Act amended to provide mortgage insurance to facilitate construction or rehabilitation of nursing homes (1959); liberalization of Social Security benefits to disabled (the 1950s); federal financial assistance to states for care of indigent and medically indigent (1940); the first White House Conference on Aging (1961); the Mental Health and Retardation Acts of 1963 and 1965, establishing community mental health centers in order to shift the major locus of care for mentally ill from hospitals to community; Medicare and Medicaid (1965); the Older Americans Act (1965); amendments to the Social Security Act to strengthen enforcement of nursing home standards, to provide for evaluation of patients prior to granting medical assistance for nursing home care, and to require periodic review of care in nursing homes; the second White House Conference on Aging (1971); appointment of a special assistant on nursing homes to the secretary of HEW (1971); and the Nutrition Bill for the elderly (1972).

Thus major factors in the increase of long-term care beds have been the demographic pressures, availability of federal funds to purchase long-term care (OASDI, Kerr-Mills, Medicare, and Medicaid) and federal programs (grants and loans that enabled sponsors to construct, equip, and rehabilitate facilities). Though data are not precise because of different definitions and lack of data collection in earlier decades, the magnitude of the dramatic increase can be seen by the facts that in 1939 the Bureau of the Census estimated 25,000 nursing home beds in the United States; in 1954 there were about 450,000 older people in institutions and by 1970 almost a million. The recent (1973-1974) survey by the National Center for Health Statistics reported almost 1.2 million nursing home beds. (*Montly Vital Statistics*, 1974). As stated in Chapter 1, there are now more long-term beds than acute hospital beds.

During the decade between 1960 and 1970, the proportion of older people in institutions at any one time increased by 25 percent—from 4 to 5 percent. The 5 percent figure so often quoted may be a serious understatement. Kastenbaum and Candy (1973) carried out a study that provides evidence that the chances of an older person entering a long-term care facility at some time are at least one in five. The 4 or 5 percent figure, they point out, was derived from cross-sectional rather than longitudinal data.

In addition to the sheer increase in the number of long-term beds, there have been major shifts that redistributed the beds among facilities of different types. In 1960 the bulk of the institutionalized elderly—92 percent—were distributed in roughly equal proportions among psychiatric hospitals, nursing homes, and "domiciliary" homes (mainly homes for aged). Specifically, 28.9 percent were in psychiatric hospitals, 35 percent in domiciliary homes, and 28.1 percent in nursing homes. Of those in domiciliary homes and nursing homes together (63.1 percent), one-fourth were in non-profit facilities, three-fifths in proprietary facilities, and about 15 percent in county or city facilities (Brotman, 1970). By 1971, 77 percent of the nursing homes, containing 67 percent of the beds, were operated for profit (proprietaries); 15 percent of the homes, accounting for 25 percent of the beds were philanthropic; and 8 percent of the homes and beds were government controlled (*Nursing Home Care in the U.S.*, 1974).

The most recent data available are from the 1973–

1974 National Nursing Home Survey (National Center for Health Statistics, 1975). It indicates that 73.3 percent of all nursing homes (15,033 homes) containing almost 70 percent of the beds are proprietary (11,021 homes), while 26.7 percent of the homes are either government operated or voluntary (4,012 homes) and contain about 30 percent of the beds (slightly less than 20 percent in the nonprofits and about 10.5 percent in government facilities). The 960,260 individuals sixty-five or over constitute almost 90 percent of the total of 1,074,480 people in those facilities (95.5 percent of those in voluntary homes, almost 86 percent of those in proprietaries, and almost 87 percent of those in government facilities).

In short, there has been a large overall increase in beds largely in the profit-making or proprietary sector. The shift in the proportion of older people in various types of facilities was mainly from governmental to profit-making facilities. Though the number of non-profit facilities and beds increased, the proportion of beds they represent has been dropping.

CURRENT STATUS IN DEFINING FACILITIES

During the past few years, long-term care has become a burning social issue. A period of consciousness-raising has occurred. Professionals, the public, and government have become acutely aware of the magnitude of long-term care and the personal, social, and economic consequences. Huge expenditures are involved. Public expenditures for nursing home care rose from 1.4 billion in 1972 to 2.2 billion in 1974 (Worthington, 1975). Abuses such as maltreatment of patients (neglect and in some instances downright cruelty), unsafe conditions, and illegal profiteering have erupted in an unprecedent succession of scandals. Exposés have appeared with increasing frequency in magazines and newspapers and even as books (see Mendelson, 1974; Townsend, 1971). The Sub-Committee on Long-Term Care of the U.S. Senate Special Committee on Aging has issued its *Introductory Report, Nursing Home Care in the United States: Failure in Public Policy* and nine supporting papers. The Senate committee will also issue two final documents: a compendium of statements of national organizations, and a final report by its Sub-Committee on Long-Term Care.

Paralleling activities at all levels of government designed to control abuses and to set and enforce standards are efforts to define long-term care facilities and levels of care provided in them. Regulations have been promulgated for facilities known as extended care facilities (ECFs), skilled nursing facilities (SNFs) and intermediate care facilities (ICFs).

Federal regulations that spell out the definitions and criteria for such institutions place their heaviest emphasis on standards for the physical environment and on medical and nursing requirements and staffing patterns. Little attention is paid to the social needs of those who will live for long periods of time in these facilities.

Public Law 92-603 set the stage for this neglect by reversing the previous federal requirement for social work involvement. It took the regressive position that "the Secretary shall not require as a condition of participation that medical social services be furnished in any institution." The Federal Regulations of April 1975 spelling out the social service conditions of participation are included in this chapter (see Figure 2-1). It should be noted that no facility is required to furnish social services. It is required only to have "satisfactory arrangements for identifying the medically related social and emotional needs of the patient. It is not mandatory that the facility itself provide social services," though it must have "written procedures for referring patients in need of social services to appropriate social agencies." The word "satisfactory" is not defined, nor are there any standards for the qualifications of whoever is to identify the social and emotional needs.

These omissions are in the same vein as the lack of attention to social factors that contribute to the need for admissions. Under Titles 18 and 19, criteria are limited to medical and nursing needs.

This significant area of neglect indicates a lack of recognition of the social needs of long-term care residents that have been so well documented. It epitomizes one of the main issues of institutional care. Specifically, should the overall atmosphere be dominated by hospital-like environments and routines, or by an atmosphere that strives to simulate normal living situations to the fullest possible extent and attends to the social and recreational needs that enrich lives beyond sheer survival?

It is safe to say that at this time there is no general consensus about what the philosophy of care should be. Existing ways of defining or describing long-term care are inadequate. A facility defined "legally" as an SNF, ICF, or ECF may, for example, have as its auspice a nonprofit sectarian "home," a labor union, be part of a private profit-making chain of nursing homes, and so on. Levels of state reimbursement for varying amounts of care and licensing definitions also contribute to the complicated picture. There are regional variations, such as the differences from state to state in the licensing of (or failure to license) boarding homes.

Older people with similar characteristics and needs for long-term care may be found in county homes, state psychiatric facilities, and veterans facilities as well as the types of settings already mentioned. This situation arose because of the ways in which placement decisions were made in the past and still are being made. As described in Chapter 3, those decisions often are made in response to existing fiscal supports controlling bed-availability or the eligibility criteria of various facilities rather than by determination of appropriateness for the individual.

In short, long-term care at present is in a state of chaos and change. Its future form(s) will be determined by the ways in which various issues are resolved and fiscally reinforced. The broad social issues are discussed in Chapter 18 of this book. In turn, those issues have a direct impact on the issues relating to the kind of care and organization of services within facilities that are reviewed in Chapter 17.

Figure 2-1 Federal Regulations Concerning Provision of Social Services in Skilled Nursing Facilities

[19,944] Regulation Sec. 405.1130. Condition of participation—social services.—The skilled nursing facility has satisfactory arrangements for identifying the medically related social and emotional needs of the patients. It is not mandatory that the skilled nursing facility itself provide social services in order to participate in the program. If the facility does not provide social services, it has written procedures for referring patients in need of social services to appropriate social agencies. If social services are offered by the facility, they are provided under a clearly defined plan, by qualified persons, to assist each patient to adjust to the social and emotional aspects of his illness, treatment, and stay in the facility.

(a) *Standard: Social service functions.* The medically related social and emotional needs of the patient are identified and services provided to meet them, either by qualified staff of the facility, or by referral, based on established procedures, to appropriate social agencies. If financial assistance is indicated, arrangements are made promptly for referral to an appropriate agency. The patient and his family or responsible person are fully informed of the patient's personal and property rights.

(b) *Standard: Staffing.* If the facility offers social services, a member of the staff of the facility is designated as responsible for social services. If the designated person is not a qualified social worker, the facility has a written agreement with a qualified social worker or recognized social agency for consultation and assistance on a regularly scheduled basis. (See 405,1121 (i).) The social service also has sufficient supportive personnel to meet patient needs. Facilities are adequate for social service personnel, easily accessible to patients and medical and other staff, and ensure privacy for interviews.

(c) *Standard: Records and confidentiality of social data.* Records of pertinent social data about personal and family problems medically related to the patient's illness and care, and of action taken to meet his needs, are maintained in the patient's medical record. If social services are provided by an outside resource, a record is maintained of each referral to such resource. Policies and procedures are established for ensuring the confidentiality of all patients' social information.

Source: As adopted, 32 F. R. 14930 (Oct. 28, 1967), and amended at 39 F. R. 2238 (Jan. 17, 1974, effective Feb. 19, 1974).

Chapter 3

THE DECISION-MAKING PROCESS, ASSESSMENT, AND RELOCATION

When should an older person in need of care be placed in a long-term care facility and when should that person continue to live in the community?

This question is asked over and over again by families, by professionals, and by governmental bodies that try to establish criteria for the decision. It can never be answered simply because the answer is highly specific to each individual older person, his/her unique personality, capacities and needs, the family situation, and the personal and community resources available to him/her in the particular community at that particular time.

Because of the profound implications for the health and well-being of the older person and his/her family members, the decision merits the most careful consideration. For the past twenty years practitioners and research investigators have been working toward the goal of developing methods of bringing order to the decision-

making process and implementing the decision constructively once it has been made.

This chapter will give some brief information about
the numbers of older people likely to be involved in
decision-making for long-term care now and in the future. Ways in which decisions have been made and implemented in the past will be reviewed. Orderly methods
of assessment of individual and family that are components of the decision-making process will be described.
One essential aspect of that process, the task of assessing
community resources to match individual need is discussed in detail in Chapter 4. Finally, if the decision involves moving the older person to a new living arrangement (whether or not the new environment is a long-
term care facility), techniques for moving that will reduce or avoid negative effects (relocation shock) are
summarized.

It bears repetition that the goal of decision-making is
to determine the best possible plan for the individual
older person concerned. Inappropriate biases can sabotage the formulation of an appropriate plan. Currently
there is an unfortunate tendency to view community
care as a desirable alternative to institutional care. Unquestionably, most older people prefer to remain in the
familiar surroundings of their own homes. All possible
avenues should be explored and services mobilized toward that goal. Chapter 4 summarizes and categorizes
existing support systems. However, the decision cannot
be made on philosophical grounds. There are some elderly people for whom congregate care is necessary socially and from the standpoint of health. The practical
question is which plan will maximize the individual's
well-being and relieve him and his family from excessive
stress.

Number of Older People Who Need Long-Term Care

Estimates of the proportion of older people requiring long-term services vary, depending on the nature of services included in the estimate. Shanas's national studies indicate that one-fourth of all persons sixty-five and over who live in the community require home care services (1974). Adding those who require service because of mental impairments and environmentally imposed disabilities, S. Brody estimates that the target population may be one-third of the elderly (see Chapter 4). Preliminary data from a survey of a section of an urban area place the percentage at 27 percent (Gottesman, Moss and Worts, 1975). Pfeiffer's community study provides evidence of "significant impairment" (moderate to complete) for an overall total of 41 percent of older people when economic, social, and self-care functioning are included (1973). To all of those estimates must be added the 5 percent of all the elderly who reside in institutions at any one time.

Currently, then, it can be estimated roughly that about 8 million individuals need long-term services of one kind or another, including community dwellers and institutional residents. The number of those seventy-five and over is growing much faster, than the sixty-five to seventy-four group. Projections are that by 1990 40 percent of the 28 million older people, or about 11 million people will be seventy-five or over. Impairments and consequently needs for service increase with advancing age. Therefore a conservative estimate is that 10 or 11 million individuals will require some form of long-term service by 1990 and thus will be directly involved in decision-making processes!

Ways in Which Decisions Are Made

Chapter 5 will describe in detail the characteristics of the older people who are found in long-term care facilities—that is, advanced old age, multiple physical and mental impairments, and lack of economic, family, and social supports. However, those characteristics are not the only factors determining admissions to facilities. When an individual's own status indicates that long-term care is needed, other factors determine the decisions that are possible: policy of the three levels of government as reflected in the existence and availability of resources and services, and the perceptions of the providers as to their missions.

"Resources" are created by the various streams of reimbursement for which the individual is eligible. An obvious example is the way in which the development and availability of various types of congregate facilities followed the flow of the federal dollar. The Hill-Burton Program (in 1954), the National Housing Act (in 1959), Medicare (in 1965), Kerr-Mills, and Medicaid fostered the growth of nursing homes and extended care facilities. In the past and at present decisions about placement have been determined not by appropriateness for the individual but in response to fiscal supports provided by the controlling system which in turn governs bed-availability. In the main, the supports have been for medically oriented institutional systems.

In 1965 Dr. William Camp, who at the time was commissioner of mental health in Pennsylvania, described the "dumping syndrome." He referred to a

> phenomenon observed constantly by the admitting officer of every type of facility to which admission of aged persons is sought: the description of the pa-

tient by the referring agency has a miraculous way of adapting itself to coincide with the admission criteria of the receiving facility. Thus the "rather forgetful old man with some preoccupations about food" at the door of a home for the aged becomes "confused and depressed with somatic delusions" on the doorstep of a mental hospital, and has gastrointestinal disorder, other, with relatively intact sensorium on the way to a nursing home.

Dr. Camp might have added that "abdominal distress requiring diagnostic studies would provide entrée to in-patient status in a general hospital." He concluded that "standard diagnostic nomenclature is of little help in the face of odds like these" (Camp, 1965, p. 133).

In many states, when policy dictated reduction of state hospital populations, the locus of institutional care for older people shifted to nursing homes, homes for aged, and boarding homes (often euphemistically called "the community"). Again, the choice of setting was frequently as dependent on the availability of funds to support care as on professional perceptions of an individual's needs (e.g. Bok, 1971).

Currently in areas where Medicaid beds are in short supply, the placement task often is a telephone search for any bed, not the careful assessment of need and selection of a facility or program of community care that can meet individual requirements. Since funding criteria vary (as with Medicaid, Medicare) and are uneven regionally, they may operate as the decisive factor. Thus Pennsylvania's inadequate Medicaid reimbursement rate is only two-thirds that of one neighboring state (New Jersey) and in some instances only one-third the rate in another (New York). The ensuing shortage of Medicaid beds in Pennsylvania keeps many people in the community despite need and a degree of functional and social incapacity comparable to that of their institutionalized peers.

In short, the administrative arrangements, eligibility criteria, and benefits-scope which make up the system at any particular point of decision-making are controlling of disposition.

The most striking feature of the decision-making process as it actually operates has been the absence of order and careful consideration. Most often it occurs in the crucible of an acute crisis or is preceded by long periods of severe strain for individual and family. Attempts to avoid institutional care are marked by a glaring lack of supportive community services. The sequence of events rarely is accompanied by early professional intervention to mobilize the few available resources and aid in a rational decision-making process.

Even at the gateway into congregate facilities intervention is most often absent. Most referrals to long-term care facilities are by the families of the older people themselves. Though some institutions (almost solely the voluntaries) offer evaluation and counseling to determine whether admissions are appropriate, in the main assessment and orderly planning do not occur. Many admissions are direct transfers from hospitals to any available nursing-home bed that can be located. The placements often are precipitated at the eleventh hour when the doctor enters the discharge note on the medical chart, responding to his judgment that acute hospital care is no longer needed, or to pressures from the Utilization Review Committee. Few of the old people receive careful preparation for discharge to a new living situation or even are afforded the opportunity to participate in the decision-making process, though participation is known to be such a critical predictor of their subsequent adjustment and well-being.

Assessment and Appropriate Decision-Making Processes

When and how should decisions be made? and what are the components of a decision-making process?

There is no one moment at which a decision should be made. The "process" should be just that—a continuing process beginning when service needs first become evident. Re-decisions should respond to changes in individual and family conditions and circumstances, to options created by new legislation, and to services that develop. Implied is professional expertise to monitor such changing needs and options and to orchestrate the component services into individualized packages so as to move the individual along the theoretical continuum of care as needed.

Entry into the long-term care system may occur when individuals are at different stages in needing services. Some may be experiencing a mild or recent disability, others may have deficits that have been severe stressors for long periods of time. Determination of the best or most appropriate plan is necessarily highly individualized. It also should be accompanied by relief as much as possible for the immediate and extreme sources of stress that preclude orderly planning. Since the medical, functional, personal, and social factors are interrelated, there must be a sorting-out of the various problems that tend to mask and exacerbate each other. The complexities of these interrelationships that dictate an interdisciplinary approach are well known and accepted by professionals in the field.

While the components of the decision-making process will be discussed separately, it must be kept in mind that the streams of activity may occur concurrently or be ordered in a variety of ways, and that the ultimate goal is assembling the relevant information in a way that makes sense for the particular individual and family.

In recent years there has been growing recognition of the need for assessment as a critical component of the decision-making process. There is general consensus that the assessment should include functional capacities as well as medical evaluation. Functional assessment is "any systematic attempt to measure objectively the level at which a person is functioning, in any of a variety of areas such as physical health, quality of self-maintenance, quality of role activity, intellectual status, social activity, attitude toward the world and toward self, and emotional status" (Lawton, 1971).

The potential utility of complete functional assessment is manifold: objectivity; coverage of all areas of functioning; provision of a more complete picture of the total person; facilitation of communication across professions and disciplines via a common language and terminology; easier assessment of the results of treatment and assistance to the practitioner in monitoring his activities; facilitation of the formulation, implementation, and evaluation of the treatment plan; utilization as a tool in teaching and training; and aggregated data to be used to plan facilities and services (Lawton, 1971; Lawton and Brody, 1969).

As the importance of assessment has been recognized, many systems of assessing medical, cognitive, and self-care functioning have been developed, though no one method has been universally accepted and the battery of instruments is incomplete. One example is contained in the recent document *Patient Classification for Long-Term Care* (Jones, 1973) promulgated by the Health Resources Administration of HEW. Others have been reviewed by Lawton (1971). The instruments developed and used by the Philadelphia Geriatric Center are noted in Chapter 7 and included as Appendix B.

Most of the work to date has focused on medical

status and on physical, mental, and self-care functioning. However, thoughtful investigators are recognizing the need for assessment of behavioral capacities in social, recreational, and occupational spheres.

Development of measures of those aspects of function is as yet in a rudimentary stage. Work is being done at the Philadelphia Geriatric Center to develop such instruments, at Duke (Pfeiffer, 1973), and at the USA (United Services Agency) project in Luzerne County in Pennsylvania and Middlesex General Hospital in New Brunswick, the latter two under the auspice of the University of Pennsylvania (Brody, S., 1975).

Lawton has proposed a classification that provides a theoretical framework for the creation of a rounded assessment system (1972). Approaching assessment from the standpoint of human needs-meeting behaviors, he places those behaviors into a hierarchy of seven behaviors ranging from life-maintenance at one extreme to social role at the other, and including functional health, perception-cognition, physical self-maintenance, instrumental self-maintenance, and effectance. Within those levels of competence are components such as recreation, creative innovation, and personal and social contacts and relationships. The importance of that conceptualization lies in the inclusion of instrumental behaviors and those that reflect the human needs for socialization, recreation, and creativity.

At the present time, limited aspects of individual assessment are receiving so much attention that there is danger that they will dominate and obscure other equally important aspects. In fact, assessment of physical and medical status is being confused with the decision-making process itself.

When carried to the reductio ad absurdum, it is assumed that accurate, thorough medical diagnosis and assessment of physical and mental function can decide, for example, whether an old person is in need of long-term care can remain in the community or requires institutionalization. Such limited assessment is inadequate. First of all, assessment of the current level of such functioning must be accompanied by assessment of potential and the setting of treatment goals which in turn may qualify the ultimate plan of care. Secondly, assessment of limited dimensions of function cannot operate as a sorting machine to assign people to appropriate services and facilities. Detailed information is also necessary about available resources and supports. Individuals with identical functional assessments may require different plans of care. Indicators of different plans are their socioeconomic situations, personalities, physical environments, eligibility for various benefits, and the availability of needed services and social supports, including those that can be provided by families.

Decisions rest on such questions as: What is the person's economic capacity to purchase services? Do those services exist and are they accessible and acceptable? Are there benefits and entitlements that can be mobilized? Are there family members nearby, and what is the state of their health and economic situations? What other responsibilities do adult children have towards their own children, spouses, and other elderly family members? Are they beset by other problems that must take priority? Is their health and well-being affected adversely by the burden of caring for the individual who needs long-term care? Have family relationships historically been sufficiently close so that they can stand the added stress? (Brody, E., 1968; Brody, E., 1971).

Assessment of family and community resources is, of course, a standard clinical tool of the trade for social work practitioners. However, there have been few attempts to develop instruments that afford systematic review of the social support system. To organize such information from the vantage point of the needs-meeting methods, S. Brody identifies five components of health social services that are common to community care, or care in facilities. In Chapter 4 of this book he describes a taxonomy including personal services, supportive or extended medical services, maintenance services, counseling, and linkages and suggests that the individual planning process include checking needs against a matrix of services and entitlements. The OARS program at Duke, which has developed some scales to rate social and economic resources, is one of the few efforts to develop quantititave measures of the need for services of elderly individuals and populations (Pfeiffer, 1973). A project is underway at the Philadelphia Geriatric Center to develop a screening instrument (Gottesman, 1974).

As part of the recent surge of interest in ecology, the importance of the physical environment has been rediscovered as its various aspects operate either as barriers or facilitators of maximum functioning. An excellent theoretical framework and review of the literature by Lawton and Nahemow (1973) is available. In the main environmental assessment (steps, crime in neighborhood, safety and prosthetic devices in the home, and so on) commonly has been neglected as a component of the total assessment process.

Assessment, then, as part, but *only* part of the decision-making process should include all areas of individual need and functioning, and the economic, social, and physical environmental resources that can be mobilized. However, even a complete battery of instruments applied by competent professionals would not have the capability to decide what form long-term care should take. Decision-making relates as well to who makes the decision and the process by which it is made.

People, not instruments, make decisions. And the wishes of the individual and family—what they want and choose and their role in the process—are pivotal factors.

Apart from ethical considerations, the literature in the field of gerontology conveys clear messages regarding: the positive relationships between participation in the decision-making process and subsequent adjustment; the importance to the integrity of the human personality of some sense of control over one's own destiny; the negative effects of the collapse of self-determination; the importance of choice; and the relevance of individual and family personality, sociocultural background, and life-style.

Beyond availability and accessibility of services, what the individual wants—that is, the acceptability of the service—is a major determinant of what plan is practicable. In one study, older people who visited a voluntary home for aged to apply for admission subsequently divided themselves into two groups: those who actually applied and those who did not. The two groups were comparable demographically and in health and socioeconomic status. But the most powerful predictive variable discriminating between them was the more positive attitude towards admission of those who actually applied (Brody and Gummer, 1967; Brody, E., 1969). In a British research study which compared a community based psychiatric service with a traditional hospital service, family preferences were very significantly related to which type of service was utilized for aged patients (Sainsburg and Grad, 1962). Attitude or wish, of course, is a complex response reflecting factors such as personality, family resources and quality of relationships, cultural background, previous life-style, and degree of stress experienced.

The reasons for requiring long-term care have implications for management of the decision-making process. Unlike those who go for hospital care or ambulatory care, long-term care applicants are not seeking care for acute episodic illness, for periodic treatment of chronic illness, or for preventive care. The chain of events leading to admission to congregate facilities or to the need for community care services is very different. Referral to long-term care, the selection of a facility or service, even admission itself is not, in the main, arranged or controlled by the physician. For example, less then one-third of those admitted to institutions come from hospitals; most come from their own or relatives' homes (55 percent) (*Nursing Home Care in the United States*, p. 16). The Medicaid certification of need for care is often completed after the decision has been made in order to comply with reimbursement criteria.

All available evidence emphasizes that for the most part the twin determinents of the need for admissions are social disability and functional disability due to chronic impairments of mind and body. That is, the need for medical and nursing care is not the only reason institutional care is sought. There is a complex interweaving of individual and family, health, social, economic, and environmental factors, with decisions being constrained by current social policy.

Whatever form long-term care takes, whether in the community or in long-term care facilities, it is a social/health solution to social/health problems. By definition, those who require long-term care in any setting will continue to require it for the rest of their lives. They and their families perceive it as a living arrangement. Since medical care is only one component of the service package needed, the strong current trend toward shaping long-term care—in and out of institutions—in the medical model and making the physician the gatekeeper runs counter to all available knowledge.

Since social as well as medical indicators determine

the "appropriate" decision, it follows that social diagnosis and prescription by social practitioners should be included in the decision-making process. Though the physician's medical services are critically needed, the orchestration of all the health/social services needed is not within his province, nor would he want to assume the tasks necessary: awareness of all fiscal entitlements and community services; mobilization and monitoring of the health-social services; making the contacts with meal service, transportation, friendly visitors, homemakers, day-care centers, counseling service, shopping services, telephone reassurance services, home health agencies; acting in the advocacy role to obtain those services initially or to monitor them over time; designing and carrying out careful programs of preplacement orientation and preparation. It is therefore inappropriate, whatever the governance of the health/social service system, to assign the physician the responsibility of making a "total plan of care" as is mandated in current regulations for skilled nursing facilities (Federal Register, 1974).

Emphasizing the role of social factors in decision-making or in the provision of long-term care by no means denigrates the role of physician, nurse, or other medically oriented personnel. Medical evaluation and ongoing care is a sine qua non of long-term care which must be seen in the context of its share and role in providing the total spectrum of social/health service requirements.

One unresolved issue about which discussion is beginning concerns the site at which evaluation and decision-making should occur. Examples are the "paper review," the in-home evaluation, out-patient assessment, and in-patient assessment (as in screening centers). A related problem is the mechanism by which social need should be certified for any form of long-term care. Both issues require flexibility in experimentation and research evaluation of effectiveness.

IMPLEMENTING THE DECISION: RELOCATION

For a certain proportion of older people, the decision-making process results in a decision to move. Some will move to congregate care facilities, others to new apartments in age-integrated or age-segregated apartment buildings, to the homes of their adult children, or to other living arrangements. In recent years there has been much discussion of the "relocation effect" or "transplantation shock" noted by some research investigators. Relocation effect is the apparent negative impact (increased morbidity and mortality) of moving older people from one residence to another.

Following the early studies, other investigators turned their attention to aspects of the relocation phenomenon other than documenting its existence. Studies identified the subgroups of people who are vulnerable to relocation effect and explored techniques of eliminating or softening its impact. The findings have direct implications for how the decision-making process should occur and how moves should be managed. (For detailed reviews of the literature see Lieberman, 1969; Lawton and Nahemow, 1973; Gottesman and Brody, 1975). For it is a fact of life that older people sometimes need to move and that it may be in their best interests to do so. The goal is to use knowledge and techniques to facilitate the move and to avoid detrimental effects.

Among the elderly groups studied have been mental hospital patients, nursing home patients, residents of homes for aged, apartment building tenants, and community residents. The types of moves investigated have been from mental hospitals to other hospitals, to the community, to nursing homes and boarding homes; from one nursing home to another and from one home for aged to another; from the community to a new building; and from one ward to another within a mental hospital, or from one area of a facility to another.

It has become apparent that negative effects by no means can be attributed globally to the moves per se. The characteristics of the people moved and of the receiving facility, the reasons for the move and its meaning to the mover, and the helping techniques used to facilitate the moves—all are qualifying factors. Indeed, positive effects were noted for certain groups in certain situations.

Research has identified the most vulnerable as the physically ill (Aldrich and Mendkoff, 1963), the depressed, the confused and disoriented (Goldfarb, Shaninian and Turner, 1966), and those who are moved involuntarily (Aldrich and Mendkoff, 1963; Miller and Lieberman, 1965). On the other hand, favorable effects have occurred for those who are physically well and those who choose to move. For example, positive effects of moving into senior citizens' housing have been noted (Carp, 1967), and the lack of negative effects in a move to such a setting was attributed by one group of investigators to the voluntary nature of the move (Lawton and Yaffe, 1970). Both Lawton (Lawton and Nahemow, 1975) and Lieberman (Lieberman et al, 1968) report evidence that the expectation of a move may have effects similar to those of an actual move. Disorganization during and immediately after a move increases mortality (Bourestom and Pastalan, 1972).

Factors that mitigate or avoid possible negative effects have been found to be provision of opportunity for choice (Ferrari, 1962; Friedsam and Dick, 1963), careful individualized preparation for moving through counseling and programs of premove orientation to the receiving facility (Jasnau, 1967; *Preparation for Relocation,* 1973), and participation of the older person in the decision-making process. The qualities of the environment to which the older people were moved was the determining factor in a study by Marlowe (1973). Negative impact occurred when the moves were to cold, dehumanized environments. Older people who improved after the moves were found in facilities similar to or better than the previous residence in terms of offering: a higher degree of personal autonomy and independence; respect, concern, and affection; opportunity for constructive activity and social interaction; and access to outside community.

As Liebowtiz (1974) and Brody (1974) point out, accumulated evidence makes it apparent that lack of attention to the psychological and social needs of elderly movers can be lethal, and that provision of such services does a good deal to avoid or mitigate relocation shock.

Many of the procedures in use at the Philadelphia Geriatric Center to handle admissions are described in Chapter 7. When it was necessary to move large groups of people from one place to another within the center, the careful planning process used available knowledge. That particular move has been described in a group of published papers (Liebowitz, 1974; Locker and Rublin, 1974; Brody et al, 1974; and Patnaik et al, 1974).

The clinicians (Locker and Rublin 1974) emphasize the careful preparation of the movers by means of individual and group counseling, site visits to the rooms to which they would be moved, and the participation of the movers in making some decisions in order to give them some sense of control and reduce feelings of helplessness. They also point up the importance of involving families, of educating and preparing staff, and of meticulous attention to the mechanics of moving to minimize upset and disorder. Their emphasis on sustaining services designed to facilitate adjustment after the physical move was accomplished was supported by the research data indicating that it took several months for movers to return to previous levels of adjustment (Brody, Kleban, and Moss, 1974).

In Michigan a group of investigators have been doing careful work to identify techniques to facilitate moves (Bourestom and Pastalan, 1972) from one congregate facility to another. The practitioners responsible for helping older people move into the Philadelphia Geriatric Center's Community Housing also are consciously utilizing methods designed to avoid relocation effects.

The principles that have evolved from practice and research are applicable and can be adapted to helping any older person to move from one living arrangement to another.

Chapter 4

RESOURCES FOR LONG-TERM CARE IN THE COMMUNITY*

Stanley J. Brody

The long-term care system should include a spectrum of medical and health-social services in a variety of settings, available in a multiplicity of arrangements, both in institutions and in the community. Long-term care is a dynamic, changing process reflecting the trajectory of chronic illness. The social worker who counsels an older person and family when long-term care is indicated is responsible for mobilizing the system's resources both to prevent inappropriate institutional admissions and to assure the timely use of institutional services. Of equal im-

*The material in this chapter is subject to continuous modification and additions both by legislative and regulatory action. It is important to check resource availability with the appropriate agency.

portance, the worker uses the long-term care system to support people living in the community who are not into the institutional application procedure. The nature of the population at risk is such that long-term care services are required on a continuing sustained basis, in or out of institutions. Key parts of these services are the identification and facilitation of applications to a wide variety of benefits and services as the changing needs of the older adult dictate. A static determination at any one point in time will not be responsive to the dynamics of the aging process. A continuous review and monitoring of needs and services are fundamental to long-term care.

The long-term care facility itself is a part of a larger interrelated network of services addressed to the individual requiring continuing care. As will be described in Chapters 4, 6, and 7, the social worker in the evaluation or application process can function as one of the main interfaces in the long-term care system as he participates in personal planning with the elderly client. Valid decisions as to the appropriateness of care are based both on individual needs and available and acceptability of resources. Accordingly, the social worker must be aware of community resources so that the client may be helped to avoid unnecessary institutionalization and maximize his optimum level of functioning. The institutions themselves increasingly are becoming involved with the community and the elderly in planning for the entire network of long-term care services. They have potential for serving as the base for a complex of resources which extend out into the community.

The nature of the health-social services needed to support an adequate functioning level in the community is determined both by the goals of care and the characteristics of the target population.

This chapter will therefore begin with a statement of goals and description of the relevant characteristics of the elderly in need of long-term care services in the community. Available resources will be inventoried and described, including medical services and health-social services such as financial supports, personal care and maintenance services, and counseling and linkage services.

Goals

The criteria of need by the elderly in the community are reflected not by the morbidity statistics but rather by a complex of disease, envirnoment, and psychosocial elements which affect their functioning level. The ability of the client to live in the community is intimately related to his capacity to function at a level which assures his coping with the demands of everyday living. Thus the goals of care are the development and use on a long term basis of those health-social services which will enable the elderly to attain maximum independence and well-being.

Target Population

What should concern social workers as they plan, either with the individual in the assessment process or with the community in the development of resources, are the needs/demands of the elderly for services which will enable them to function optimally. The inability of one-third of the aged to be able to live independently without any support services is related to the handicaps to which they may be subject.

These limitations may be grouped into three types: physical, mental, and environmental.

Physical Impairment

While 81 percent of the over-sixty-five suffer some chronic illness, 33 percent have no physical limitations on their activities; 7 percent have some limitations, but not on their major activity; 26 percent have limitations on major activity; and about 16 percent are unable to carry out their major activity. Thus, approximately half of the elderly are somewhat disabled because of a chronic illness.

Of particular importance is the specific level of mobility. Eight percent of the noninstitutionalized elderly are bedfast or housebound. In addition, 6 percent have limited physical ability to move in the community. Overall, more than 30 percent report difficulty in managing stairs. In an environment where those with limited income live in a world of steps—steps within residences, to board buses or streetcars, to descend into subways—the ability to negotiate stairs becomes critical to mobility.

Physical disability as a correlate of aging has been extensively documented.

Mental Impairment

Mental impairment also imposes limitations of function. Estimates of the incidence of mental impairment among the elderly vary from 10 to 25 percent. As with physical disabilities, rates of psychoses, symptoms experienced as physical illness, and organic mental disorders rise with advancing age, often with each condition exacerbating the others.

The average community mental health center catchment area includes approximately 150,000 people. Older people who come to the attention of any long-term care institution may be drawn from one or more of such areas. Included in such an average catchment area are 15,000 people who are sixty-five and over (central city, small town, and rural catchment areas are likely to have more). Of those, there are 130 women to every 100 men, and approximately

14,250 people (95 percent) are living in the community,

750 people (5 percent) are in institutions (including nursing homes and state hospitals),

6,000 people are seventy-five years old or over,

3,700 people are living on poverty level incomes,

1,500 to 3,000 people are living alone, and

2,500 people have some degree of chronic organic brain syndrome.

Environmental Impairment

Social disability and consequent impairment of function arise in part out of environmental hazards. The lower income status of the elderly often results in their occupying inadequate housing located in high-crime residential areas with limited transportation services. Just as mental and physical impairments overlap and mesh, so do environmental limitations.

One aspect of the intermix of personal and environmental factors is posed by the classic question: Should the situation of the seventy-five-year-old lone woman living in an apartment on the second floor of a walk-up be classified as a cardiac or a housing problem? Or, if she is typical of those elderly now subject to the new and widespread phenomenon of fear of assault, is she psychologically able to reach medical service via available public transportation?

A recent Senate Committee report points up the environmental problems of concentrations of the elderly poor isolated in neighborhoods which have experienced radical changes; locked in by what has been euphemistically described as substandard, low-cost housing, frequently among alien ethnic groups; subject to malnutrition; lacking appropriate transportation to the sources of medical care and other services; and often imprisoned in their own homes by an intense fear based on being vulnerable to robbery and attack.

Lack of information can also be characterized as an environmental hazard. Even when services are available, they are often either complexly organized, physically dispersed, inadequately advertised, or encrusted with eligibility requirements all of which deter and discourage their utilization by the elderly and their families for whom they were hopefully designed.

One-third of the Elderly Need Health-Social Services

By any of these measures of physical, mental, and environmental disability, a large proportion of older people in our society are as a group at high risk. The nature and number of their problems are beyond individual and family resources, thus requiring public support through coordinated services and programs. Shanas estimates that the target population of elderly needing services to maintain them at home is one in seven. This may be a conservative estimate. When considerations of mental impairment and environmental hazards are added to those of physical disability, the need for services is possibly one in three.

Of prime consequence is Brotman's report based on the 1970 census that the rate of increase of those seventy-five and over has escalated to three times as great as that of the sixty-five to seventy-four group. "In other words, of the 3.5 million increase in the total older population between 1960 and 1970, only 1.4 million of the increase was in the 65-74 age group with 2.1 million in the 75+ group. The 7.6 million people now aged 75+ make up 38% of the total older population (65+), a significant jump from 33.6% in 1960 and 31.4% in 1950."

The seventy-five-and-over group is substantially more vulnerable to all three classes of insults (mental, physical, and environmental). While 35 percent of those sixty-five to seventy-four with chronic illness were subject to significant impairment of function, 53 percent of those over seventy-five were similarly limited. Riley and Foner's summary of research findings indicate that rates of all types of psychoses rise steadily by age. This reinforces the conclusion that given a functional approach to needs for comprehensive health services, more than a third of the elderly may require health support services.

HEALTH-SOCIAL SERVICES

While the aged need acute medical care, their major requirement is in the continuum of services for the chronically disabled that will enable them to function optimally. These health/social services may be developed through the client's family network or through the provider network, or through a mixture of both. Most elderly have families that do provide support services. A Public Health Service survey reports that 80 percent of home health services are given by families. The critical judgement that social workers and the client and his family must make is to determine when the burden of providing these services becomes socially counterproductive by creating family breakdown.

Health/social services in the community closely conform to parallel functions in the in-patient acute hospital. There are five components of health/social services—maintenance, supportive medical services, personal care, personal planning, and linkages—that are common to both in-patient and community care. Between the extremes of the hospital and independent living are a spectrum of settings where some of these services may be delivered on a semi-institutional basis. Eligibility for these benefits varies by program, by age, geography, income level, physical condition, or previous experience. Social workers in every setting should develop matrices of elibigility for the various benefits that are available in the particular environments most common to their client populations.

Maintenance Services

INCOME MAINTENANCE.   There are a variety of public subsidies and benefits that are available to the elderly as part of a system of income maintenance.

Supplemental Security Income (SSI).   These federal benefits are successor to the Old Age Assistance programs which were State administered and funded through state and federal matching. Like the Public Assistance programs, they are the last and final resource, which theoretically serves as a back-up for all other income support programs.

The SSI program is administered by the Social Security Administration and is funded through federal funds. All persons sixty-five years or older are eligible who are state residents and who are citizens or aliens permanently and legally residing in the United States. They must meet a means test which requires that applicants do not have countable income for the calendar quarter of more than the basic grant. Individual resources may not be more than $1,500—or combined resources of $2,250, if living with a spouse.

The base benefit, as of January, 1976, was $157.70 a month per individual and $236.60 with eligible spouse. This base benefit is subject to "indexing"—it is tied to the Consumer Price Index (CPI) and will vary as the CPI changes. All earned and unearned income is considered countable income, and the benefit is adjusted to subtract the amount of such income. Exemptions include $60 per calendar quarter of earned or unearned income (for example, $20 per month Social Security retirement benefits would be excluded) and $195 of earned income per quarter plus one-half of any remainder. Thus a person earning $50 a week or $650 for the quarter would have $195 plus $227.50 (650−195=455; 455/2+195=422.50) for a total of $422.50 of earned income exempted.

Resources that are not counted in considering eligibility are a home, household goods, personal effects, and an automobile, all of which must be of reasonable value. In addition, life insurance where the cash surrender value, for any individual, is less than $1,500 is not counted as a resource.

States are allowed to supplement the SSI benefit if it is based on need and paid on a regular basis. This benefit is not counted as income. These payments may be made separately from the SSI benefit or included in the monthly SSI check. Cash advances may be made for up to $100 for individuals or $200 per couple where there is a financial emergency and presumptive eligibility.

The SSI is a major improvement over the original Old Age Assistance that it replaced, in that uniform country-wide minimum levels are established for the first time; liens against homes are eliminated; minimum assets including a car are allowed; and significant earnings are permitted.

Social Security. This federal program pays cash benefits to retired workers and their dependents. Its purpose is to replace part of former earnings after retirement.

Social Security benefits include retirement insurance; under which workers who are sixty-five can retire with full cash benefits if they have worked and contributed the required number of years. The worker retiring in 1975 must have six and one-quarter years of credit (based on the requirement of one-quarter of coverage for each calendar year after 1950). Workers can retire at sixty-two with permanently reduced benefits. Certain dependents can receive benefits, too. They include a wife or a dependent husband sixty-two or over; a wife of any age with dependent children in her care if the child is entitled to payment based on the worker's record; unmarried children under eighteen (twenty-two if in school); unmarried children eighteen or over if disabled before eighteen and still disabled. Monthly cash benefits currently (January, 1976) range from $101.40 to $341.70 for retired workers at sixty-five and from $152.10 to $512.60 for maximum family benefits.

Benefits may automatically be increased (indexing) to keep pace with increases in the cost of living (CPI) if laws providing general benefit increases are not passed. Where the CPI monthly coverage rises more than 3 percent, each payment will be raised to reflect the same percentage of increase.

Special payments can be made to certain persons seventy-two and over who are not eligible for regular Social Security benefits. These payments are intended to assure some regular income for older people who had little or no opportunity to earn Social Security protection during their working years. Most of the cost is paid from general resources. Monthly cash benefits range from $64.40 per person to $96.60 per couple. The payments are reduced by the amount of any other governmental pension, retirement benefit, or annuity.

Also under Social Security, the survivors insurance program provides monthly cash benefits to dependents of deceased workers. Monthly cash payments are payable to any widow sixty or older; widow of any age if she is caring for a child under eighteen or disabled and if they get payments; unmarried children eighteen or over if they are severely disabled before eighteen and continue to be disabled; a widow or dependent widower fifty or older who becomes disabled not later than seven years after death of the worker; a dependent widower sixty-two or older; and dependent parents sixty-two or older. Monthly cash benefits range from $57.50 for a sole survivor to $820.80 for maximum family benefits.

The whole program is administered by the United States Social Security Administration through regional and local offices.

Veterans Benefits. This federal program provides more than forty cash or service benefits to veterans and their dependents.

One program of compensation for service-connected deaths for veterans, compensates surviving unremarried widows, children and dependent parents of deceased veterans who died because of a service-connected disability. Monthly compensation ranges from $83.00 for two parents to $121.00 for a widow with one child, plus $29.00 for each additional child. There is an additional allowance of $64.00 if the widow is in need of aid and attendance.

Another program, pensions for nonservice-connected disability for veterans, gives cash benefits to veterans who have had ninety days or more of honorable active wartime service in the armed forces or who were released or discharged from such service because of a service-connected disability. The veteran must have a permanent and total disability preventing a substantially gainful occupation. His income and assets must be limited as prescribed by statute. The annual income of a veteran without a wife or child may not exeed $3,000, or if married or with a child, $4,000. Monthly rates of pension range from $160 for a single veteran to $182 for a veteran with three dependents. Additional allowances of $49 and $123 are available if a veteran is housebound and if he requires aid and attendance.

Pensions to veterans' widows and children provide a partial means of support for needy unremarried widows and children of deceased wartime veterans whose death was not due to active service. Unremarried widows without a child or a child may not have an income in excess of $3,000 annually; with a child, in excess of $4,200 annually. Pension is not payable to those whose estates are so large that it is reasonable they look to the estate for maintenance. Monthly pensions range from $108 for a widow alone to $128 for a widow with one child plus $20 for each additional child; in addition, an allowance of $64 is available to the widow if she is in need of aid and attendance.

Other benefits under veterans' programs include specially adapted housing for disabled veterans; compensation for service-connected disability; dependency and indemnity compensation for service-connected death; guaranteed and insured housing loans; vocational rehabilitation for disabled veterans; war orphans' and widows' education assistance; a burial allowance of $250; automobile grants for disabled veterans; and a variety of other special benefits.

The Veterans Benefits program is administered by the Veterans Administration through regional or local offices. Veterans Assistance Centers providing one-stop service and counseling on benefits are established in selected cities.

Unemployment Compensation. Unemployment compensation is supported by federal grants for administration and provides partial income replacement for a limited period for unemployed workers. The states have the direct responsibility for establishing and operating their own programs. Weekly benefit payments are usually for a period not in excess of thirty-six weeks over a period of a year beginning approximately when the first claim is filed. The federal government and some states provide for additional benefits for a limited time during periods of high unemployment. All workers whose employers contribute to state unemployment insurance programs and federal civilian employees and ex-servicemen are eligible if they are involuntarily unemployed, registered for work, ready for work, and meet the earnings requirements of state law. Where the older adult is forcibly retired, he is eligible for Unemployment Compensation benefits. Benefit amounts vary by state. Usually it is about half the worker's full-time weekly pay within top and bottom limits.

The program is administered by state local employment offices.

Workers' Compensation.   Workers' Compensation is mandatory in two-thirds of the states. It provides income replacement and supplement for disability or death resulting from injury on the job; medical expenses (including hospital care); rehabilitation services; and burial costs. The amount, which is usually based on the worker's wage at the time of the injury, and length of benefits are controlled by state law and regulation.

The program is administered by the State Workmen's Compensation Agency.

Food Stamps.   Food Stamps is a state program supported by federal funds for the improvement of the diets of low-income households. Families buy stamps or coupons worth more than the purchase amount, which varies according to income and family size. The coupons are used for food in retail stores. The coupons may be used to buy any food for human consumption, except for items labeled as imported or luxury items. Almost all grocery stores in food-stamp covered areas are authorized to accept the coupons. Families may participate if they live in an area that has the program, are found by local welfare officials to be in need of food assistance or are receiving some form of welfare assistance, and are unemployed, part-time employed, working for low wages, or living on limited pensions. If families are not receiving some form of welfare assistance, eligibility is based on family size and income, and the level of liquid assets.

The program is administered by the state or local welfare offices in areas that participate in the programs.

PERSONAL MAINTENANCE.   There are many programs which provide environmental supports. Most of these services are under the rubric of homemaker services.

Homemaker Service. The term "homemaker service" has come into use to cover many different kinds of helping activies. The variations arise because of a lack of clear definition of the function, tasks, and qualifications of the provider. The term "homemaker" is used here to describe those functions which deal with environmental support; that is, services which are geared to physical maintenance, such as provision of food and cleanliness of surroundings, as differentiated from personal maintenance.

The basic goal of the personal maintenance service is to restore or sustain functioning and to prevent or reverse individual or family deterioration when the functioning of the person who ordinarily takes care of him/herself or his/her family is impaired.

Qualified persons who are employed, trained, and supervised by local agencies are sent into homes to help the aged, among others, to maintain themselves in their own homes and to enhance the quality of their daily living. Homemakers work under the supervision of a nurse or a social worker or another member of the professional team helping to resolve the problems that make the service necessary.

The homemaker, sometimes for a few hours a day for for a few hours a week, can help an aging person or couple remain in the community. She may do light housekeeping, meal preparation, laundry, or marketing. Although most states now have a homemaker service, few have obtained universal coverage. In many areas the services are nonexistant or limited to particular purposes or groups. Even in larger cities, the service does not significantly approach the need.

Homemaking services do not have a high priority when it comes to the allocation of public or voluntary funds. While there has been a rapid growth of agencies offering these services, including proprietary homemaking businesses, public funding has been fragmentary and inconsistent, resulting in limited and precariously financed agencies.

Some of these services are financed through the following mechanisms:

Public Assistance. Under Title XX of the Social Security Act (Social Services), states are authorized to provide homemaker services as part of social services to the aged.

Older Americans Act. Under Title III of the Older Americans Act, grants are made to states for homemaker programs.

Veterans Administration. Special support is available to handicapped veterans or their disabled widows which can be used to purchase homemaker services.

Availability of homemaker services may be determined through inquiry from local welfare coordinating agencies (welfare councils) or visiting-nurse agencies.

Thorough house cleaning involving heavy work is a common public service in other countries but is only now becoming available here, usually as a profit-making venture.

Home-delivered and congregate meals. "Meals on Wheels" is a community service, offered under voluntary auspices but supported in part by public funds. This service provides at least one hot meal a day to the elderly in their own homes. The expansion of the nutrition part of the Older Americans Act of 1975 (Title VII) and the extension of Title XX (SSA) social services to include home-delivered or congregate meals has stimulated the development of this program. Many institutions have recognized this service as a valid extension of their own feeding resources. With the infusion of $100 million by the federal government under the 1975 legislation, significant opportunities should be available for institutional participation. Inquiry should be made from the state agency administering the aged programs or the local Areawide Agency on Aging.

Congregate meals are increasingly becoming available in a variety of settings, including senior citizen centers, schools, and institutions. They have the advantage over "meals on wheels" because of the socialization and service opportunity presented. The emphasis by the federal administration on aging on integrative programs should result in a continued increase of congregate meals.

Chore Services. A relatively new service to the aged is for the repair of their own homes. The 1976 Older Americans Act (Title III) singled out residential repair and renovation as a priority service. The Title XX Social Services program administered by state welfare departments also includes chore services as being federally reimbursable. Revenue sharing may also be used by local communities to support this and other social services.

ACTION—the volunteer activities acronym summarizing the Retired Senior Volunteer Program (RSVP), Senior Companions and others--is also a resource under the Older Americans Act for chore services.

Personal Care

HOME-HEALTH AIDES.   While there is a clear distinction between personal maintenance and personal care, the service patterns have tended to blur the difference. Personal care describes those services which provide for individual cleanliness and grooming. This would include help in bathing, dressing, and getting about at home. Often these services may be performed by the homemaker as well as the home-health aide. The Medicare administration is currently the clearest arbitrator between the two functions by funding personal care services and denying reimbursements for personal maintenance.

Home-health aides usually are employed and supervised by a home-health agency such as the Visiting Nurse Association. In other instances their services may be purchased from another agency, which may be under a proprietary or non-profit auspice.

Medicare includes personal care as a reimbursable item only when furnished through a home-health agency primarily engaged in providing skilled nursing care; provided on a part-time intermittent basis; and clearly demonstrated that personal care is needed and that the patient is severely limited in function. The physician must regularly certify that his patient is sick enough to need the service and that his condition demands only part-time intermittent care.

In a very few states, medical assistance (Medicaid) programs may provide personal care services as a reimbursable vendor payment.

In a few states, personal care service may be made available through the state welfare program supported by Title XX (Social Service) of the Social Security Act.

Home health care was singled out by the 1975 amendments to the Older Americans Act (Title III) as a priority service to be made available through the local Areawide Agencies on Aging.

A state or local public health department may include personal care as part of their home-health program. Similarly, neighborhood health centers or hospital based home-health care programs may offer the service, although they usually depend on Medicare or Medicaid for reimbursement. The service is rarely covered by any insurance policy, be it Blue Cross or commercial carrier.

Family services agencies, where they exist, often provide personal care on a severely time-limited basis.

Supportive Medical Services

A coordinated home care program is defined as one that is centrally administered and through coordinated planning, evaluation, and follow-up procedures, provides for physician directed medical, nursing, social and related services to selected patients at home. Supportive medical services are here defined as nursing, physical, occupational, or speech therapy aspects of home-health care. Usually they are offered by hospitals, public health departments, visiting nurse agencies and neighborhood health centers.

Medicare reimbursement is available for all these services under conditions specified above (see p. 75). In some states, Medicaid reimburses coordinated home care programs, particularly when they are extensions of hospital service.

State rehabilitation agencies may provide vendor

payments for these services if they are part of a plan to make the client self-sufficient. This is a state-administered federally funded program.

Personal Planning

Counseling services with the client and his family are offered by social workers to help mobilize community and personal resources to help support the client in the community.

Family agencies, both public and voluntary, provide these services, as do community mental health centers and home-health care and vocational rehabilitation agencies. Similar services are sometimes offered by visiting nurses or protective care workers.

The provision of protective services for adults unable to manage their own affairs and unable (or unwilling) to obtain the help they need is a relatively new concept. As the number of aged has increased and their longevity extended, a larger proportion become at risk because of mental impairment. About 7 to 8 percent of noninstitutionalized older people may require protective services.

Most protective legal procedures based on incomptency and guardianship are primarily focused on protection of property. In recent years protective service programs under the auspice of public or voluntary agencies have evolved that are committed to enabling incapacitated adults to live at the maximum level of their functioning in safety and comfort. To ascertain the availability of such services in your community, inquire of the local welfare council or public welfare agency. The National Council on Aging in New York City may be useful if there are no local recources.

Linkages

While all services in fact link the aged to various systems within the community and contribute to their socialization, there are those services whose function is primarily that of linkage. The Areawide Agencies on Aging authorized by the Older Americans Act have been given special responsibility for the planning and establishment of linkage services.

INFORMATION AND REFERRAL.   There are a variety of agencies that perform information and referral services. Most visible are Areawide Agencies on Aging, health and welfare council referral units, Veterans Administration, public assistance agencies, community mental health and senior citizens centers. Family service and the social service departments of health agencies perform the same function. The degree to which follow through takes place—the assurance that the referral process is competed—is fortuitous and depends upon the agency's understanding of its responsbility, the workload the referring caseworker bears, the patterns of cooperation among agencies, and the ability of the referred agency to give service. The availability of funding for the required services is usually a major factor contributing to the success of the referral.

TRANSPORTATION.   Many elderly are handicapped because of the lack of public transportation or their inability to utilize the service where available. There is increasing awareness of the importance in assuring useable transportation for the elderly. However, relatively few special resources have been developed that continue beyond the demonstration phase.

Some communities attempt to reduce the economic barrier by lowering the fare for the aged during non-peak hours. These reductions may be reimbursed through Federal Department of Transportation demonstration grants. More usual is individual reimbursement for public transportation, including taxicabs, through the public assistance system. Caseworkers may authorize special reimbursement for cash or medical assistance recipients.

Special transportation systems may be furnished for specific purposes. Thus there are several Model Cities funded demonstration programs providing special transportation for the elderly to health facilities. Older American Act projects similarly may provide carriers to senior citizen centers. The community mental health and retardation center is another resource.

Escort service may also be available not only to assist the older person physically but give him a sense of safety and security from assault in the street.

OUTREACH SERVICES.   A major contribution of the OEO programs was the revival of outreach as an integral part of the delivery of any service. The immobility and isolation of the aged is particularly responsive to outreach services, preferably offered by workers acceptable to the specific target population. Generally, the more recent pattern is to use indigenous personnel and peers where possible. The role of the police departments should not be overlooked as a readily available resource for case discovery. Neighborhood health centers, mental health and retardation catchment areas, and senior citizens centers are increasingly adding this service. Funding is usually available under the service granting mechanism of the Older Americans Act. Also available are the Service Sections of Title XX of the Social Security Act.

TELEPHONE ALERT.   Many counties and communities are instituting programs of daily or weekly phone calls to homebound elderly. The calling is done under the auspice of police departments, Senior Citizen Centers, family service agencies or voluntary groups such as religious organizations, the Kiwanis, and similar fraternal organizations.

Such a service can readily be performed by volunteers from institutional auxiliaries to persons on the waiting list for admission to long-term care facilities.

FRIENDLY VISITING.   Like the telephone communication, personal, regular scheduled visits can assure the homebound elderly of contact with the community. This is usually a voluntary activity performed under similar auspices to the telephone service.

Medical Services

Medical services for the aged are financed largely under Title XVIII of the Social Security Act (Medicare). Supplementary financing for the medically indigent is available under Title XIX of the Social Security Act (Medicaid). Buttressing the co-pay provisions of Medicare are the "over-sixty-five" programs of Blue Cross.

Forty percent of medical expenditures are currently paid for from individual resources. This is equivalent to the amount spent by the elderly in 1965 prior to the enactment of Medicare.

HOSPITAL INSURANCE.   Part A of Title XVIII provides hospital insurance protection for covered services to any person sixty-five or over who is entitled to Social Security or railroad retirement benefits or to the uninsured who voluntarily enroll and pay a monthly premium. Hospital insurance benefits are paid to participating hospitals, skilled nursing homes (extended care facilities), and related providers of health care to cover the reasonable cost of medically necessary services furnished to individuals entitled under this program.

The hospital insurance program pays a large part of the cost for up to ninety days during each benefit period (a period beginning with the first day of hospitalization and ending sixty days after discharge from a hospital or extended care facility). A deductible of $124 is currently required. Hospital insurance also pays part of the cost of care for up to one hundred days (during the benefit period) in a participating skilled nursing home when admission follows a hospital stay of at least three days within fourteen days of discharge. In addition, the program covers up to one hundred home health visits in the twelve-month period following discharge from a hospital or ECF.

SUPPLEMENTARY MEDICAL INSURANCE. Supplementary medical insurance (SMI) provides payment, after a $60 deductible, for 80 percent of the reasonable charges for the physician's services (including podiatrists and chiropodists), outpatient hospital services, medical supplies and services, home-health services, outpatient physical and speech therapy, and other health care services. This includes one hundred home health visits each year; diagnostic tests, X-rays, radium, and radioactive isotope therapy; ambulance services; prosthetic devices; and rental of durable medical equipment.

It is a voluntary medical program financed by monthly premiums from enrollees and matching payment from federal general revenues. The premium was $3 per month at the beginning of the program. It was increased to $4 in 1968, to $5.30 in 1970, to $5.60 in 1971, to $6.30 in 1974, to $6.70 in 1975, to $7.20 in 1976, and to $7.70 in 1977. The premium may be increased only if there has been a general Social Security benefit increase since the last increase in premium.

The annual $60 deductible must be met before benefits begin. Thereafter, Medicare pays 80 percent of the charge for covered services. The beneficiary is responsible for the $60 deductible and 20 percent of the cost of covered services.

Application for the program requires visiting the local Social Security office within seven months after the sixty-fifth birthday or within any general enrollment period which occurs each year during the first quarter.

MEDICAID.   Medicaid Assistance varies by state both as to eligibility and the scope of benefits. Those aged receiving or eligible for Supplemental Security Income benefits are eligible for the medical program provided under Title XIX. The elderly with marginal income above the SSI eligibility limits are often provided with the same or a reduced amount of benefits. The most usual arrangements for both the medically and categorically needy is for the State buying in on their behalf for the supplemental medical services Title XVIII(B) and supplementary funding for the deductible and co-pay aspects of Parts A & B. Many states offer additional benefits such as prescriptions and dental care.

BLUE CROSS.   Blue Cross offers policies which cover the contributory aspect of the 20 percent of the cost of physician care and the required hospital deductible charge. Often private insurance companies provide similar types of coverage.

THE SOCIAL WORKER'S ROLE

The role of the social worker in long-term care facilities requires knowledge of community resources. The nature of our society and its changing value structure is evidenced by continuously developing programs. The worker, to effectuate his role, needs to constantly replenish his store of information about these dynamic resources. The programs described above reflect those that may be available at any one point in time. It is the responsibility of each individual worker and his department to maintain a current file of resources so that there can be a professional response to the needs of the client.

BIBLIOGRAPHY

Catalogue of Federal Domestic Assistance (Executive Office of the President, Office of Management and Budget). Washington: U.S. GPO., 1975.

Coordinated Home Care Programs, 1964 (Public Health Service, U.S. Department of Health, Education, and Welfare). Washington: U.S. GPO., 1966.

Encyclopedia of Social Work, 16th Issue. Cf. articles on "Aging", "Homemaker Service", "Housing for Special Groups", and "Protective Services for Adults". New York: National Association of Social Workers, 1971.

Social Security Handbook, 5th Edition. U.S. Dept. of Health, Education, and Welfare, Social Security Administration, DHEW Publication No. (SSA) 73-10135. Washington: U.S. GPO, February 1974.

Trager, Brahna. *Home Health Services in the United States* (A report to the Special Committee on Aging, United States Senate, 92nd Congress, 2nd Session). Washington; U.S. GPO, April 1972.

Veterans Administration Fact Sheet, IS-1. Washington: U.S. GPO, 1975.

Chapter 5

THE NATURE OF THE ELDERLY POPULATION IN LONG-TERM CARE FACILITIES

It is by now conventional wisdom that planning of programs and services must be based on knowledge of the characteristics and needs of the particular population for which those programs and services are designed. This chapter therefore will describe the demographic, health, and personal and social characteristics of institutionalized older people. Knowledge about the paths that led them to long-term care facilities will be summarized. Finally, the older people will be discussed in terms of changes in them caused by the very processes of applying, moving into, and living in institutions.

By July, 1974, the number of older Americans (sixty-five and over) had reached 22 million, or slightly more than 10 percent of the total population of 211 million (*Statistical Memo No. 31*). It bears repetition that about 1.2 million of them resided in institutions of various types, and that they represented about 5 percent of the total population of older people in the United States. The number who could be maintained in the community if adquate services were available undoubtedly is offset by the number who need to be in facilities but for whom such care is unavailable because of their economic incapacity, discriminatory practices, and other reasons.

Precise data about the institutionalized elderly is difficult to obtain because data often are collected in the course of surveys of facilities that also care for younger people or of selected samples of facilities. Sometimes the accuracy of the data depends on the accuracy of the records and information provided by the facilities themselves. Further, while there is considerable overlapping in the characteristics of older people in different types of facilities, there are some variations. Nevertheless, it is possible to describe the general characteristics of older people receiving long-term care in institutional facilities.

DEMOGRAPHIC CHARACTERISTICS

Age:

People in institutions are characterized by advanced old age. Almost 90 percent of those in nursing homes are sixty-five and over, and the median age is about 82 (*Long-Term Care Facility Improvement Study*, 1975). Almost 30 percent of the mental hospital population is sixty-five or over (*National Health Survey*, 1973). Since the median age in the United States of all people sixty-five and over is seventy-three, it is obvious that the chance of admission to an institution increases with advancing age. In fact, only 2 percent of the sixty-five to seventy-four group but about 10 percent of those eighty and over are institutionalized. Of the institutionalized elderly, about 17 percent are sixty-five to seventy-four, 40 percent are seventy-five to eighty-four, and 43 percent are eighty-five or over (*National Center for Health Statistics*, 1975). The fact that the seventy-five-and-over group is growing at a much more rapid rate than the sixty-five to seventy-four group (Brotman, 1971) indicates that the proportion of the very old in institutions will increase.

Sex:

Most recent data indicate that women in institutions outnumber men in a ratio of almost three to one (*National Center for Health Statistics*, 1975). Since women outnumber men among the aged in general (about 4:3 in the total sixty-five-and-over population) and particularly among the very old (about 8:5 at eighty-five and over), this is not surprising. Their longer life expectancy also makes them more vulnerable to illness and widowhood.

Race:

Minority groups such as Black Americans, Spanish Americans, and Asian Americans are under-represented in institutions. For example, in 1973–1974 blacks constituted 6.6 percent of those in skilled nursing facilities (*Long-Term Care Facility Improvement Study*) though they were roughly 11 percent of the total population and about 8 percent of the elderly. Probably they have been unable to obtain institutional care due to poor economic status and discriminatory practices (Jackson, H., 1973; Jackson, J., 1973). Their situation in this respect appears to be improving, however, since the 6.6 percent represents an increase compared to the 4 percent in institutions in 1967 (Brotman, 1967). Life-style and the hardiness of those who do survive to advanced old age may be other contributants to under-representation. One study indicates that where facilities are available, blacks are represented in institutions in the same proportion as the general population (Gottesman and Hutchinson, 1974).

Economic Status

Institutionalized older people have significantly less economic resources than older people in general, and most are supported by public funds (Medicaid). This does not mean, however, that they all have been poor all their lives. Since they are in advanced old age, the resources of many have been depleted by long periods of retirement and inflationary trends. Often major and/or prolonged illnesses preceding institutionalization constitute a severe financial drain, and what money is left is exhausted quickly by institutional care itself. A further consideration is that elderly women are poorer than elderly men, and, as we have seen, women outlive men and outnumber them in long-term care facilities.

It must be remembered that these are general statements and that within any averages there are wide variations. For example, while poverty increases the chances of institutionalization, at the same time the poor aged may be kept out of facilities when they cannot afford to pay. Paradoxically, financial considerations sometimes compel institutionalization when more funds are available through government funding for that type of care than for the purchase of services that might enable the older person to stay in his own home. At the other extreme, when money is plentiful, a "one-bed nursing home" can be created in the person's own home, using costly services such as round-the-clock nursing.

HEALTH (MENTAL AND PHYSICAL)

The older people in institutions suffer from many mental and physical disabilities, often in combination with each other. Most of those ailments are chronic in nature. The salient fact about those multiple chronic health problems in relation to reasons for institutional care is that they result in functional disability. In other words, the ailments impair the individual's capacity to care for himself in normal living situations. Gerontologists are in agreement that function rather than diagnosis alone is the key to developing plans for the impaired older person. The services cannot be temporary. The very word "chronic" indicates that services and care must be ongoing.

There are three major types of physical impairment that afflict older people in nursing homes. First are circulatory disorders such as heart disease (36 percent), stroke (11 percent), or speech disorders associated with stroke (14 percent). Next are arthritis (33 percent) and other disorders affecting the skeletal system (42 percent); and digestive disorders such as diabetes (20 percent) (NCHS, 1972).

Mental disorders are extremely prevalent among the institutionalized aged. It is not surprising that those in mental hospitals have serious mental conditions (NIMH, 1972). Roughly one-third are schizophrenic and grew old (often in the hospital itself) as mentally ill people. Many others were admitted in old age as a result of organic disorders such as arteriosclerosis, or the effects of drugs, alcohol, or syphilis (45 percent). It is important to remember that senility is age-related and that many of these people were not disturbed mentally until they were old.

However, old age homes and nursing homes also contain the mentally impaired aged. While no exact data are available, various surveys indicate that at least half of all residents of those facilities have one or more mental conditions. The National Survey (NCHS, 1972) found that 34 percent had advanced senility and 27 percent "less serious" senility; another 17 percent had other mental disorders such as mental illness or retardation. Goldfarb estimated that at least 80 percent of the residents of the facilities he surveyed in New York had seriously impaired mental functioning (Goldfarb 1961, 1962). Many other studies document the large proportions of confused and disoriented old people in institutions of all types (*Psychiatry and the Aged,* 1965; Beattie and Bullock, 1963; Stotsky, 1967; Grintzig, 1970; Gottesman, 1971).

FUNCTIONAL CAPACITIES

How do these multiple mental and physical impairments—most of the old people have at least three or four of them—affect the way older people function and therefore determine the kind of care needed? It must be kept in mind that the description that follows is based on surveys that look at the individuals at any given moment. It is impossible from these descriptions to determine whether or not the person can be treated so that the functioning can be improved. However, in view of the general neglect of health care in many long-term facilities, it is safe to say that many could be helped.

In nursing homes, the most commonly noted disabilities are in the spheres of ambulation and personal self-care. Different estimates of those who can walk unassisted are 80 percent (Grintzig, 1970), 60 percent (Gottesman, 1971) and 22 percent (*National Survey*). The most frequently required aids are wheelchairs, walkers, and crutches, in that order.

Another measure of disability is the amount of help needed in activities of daily living. Here, too, estimates vary depending on which study is being cited. In one survey, about half were reported to get help with activities of daily living, but only 5 to 15 percent were severely disabled (Grintzig, 1970). In another, 55 percent needed some help, but only 20 percent needed extensive help (Gottesman, 1971). Both of those reports stated that about one-fourth of the individuals were incontinent. A more recent survey (*Long-Term Care Improvement Study*) of skilled nursing facilities found almost 58 percent incontinent of feces and more than 43 percent incontinent of urine. The latter study collected information on the patients' ability to cope with basic daily living activities. The vast majority needed help with bathing (93 percent) and dressing (71 percent); about one-third needed help with eating, and two-thirds with toileting.

While these figures are drawn from surveys of nursing homes, they are not too different from descriptions of old people in psychiatric hospitals. As stated in Chapter 2, the major programs to discharge older people from such hospitals to the community have resulted in their placement in homes for aged and nursing homes, blurring population distinctions.

FAMILY STATUS

Thus far we have seen that institutionalized older people in advanced old age are impaired physically and mentally, are in poor economic circumstances, need a great deal of help in their daily activities, are predominantly women, and are under-representative of minority groups. However, more older people with the same characteristics are not in institutions. For example, careful studies have identified 9 to 14 percent of old people living at home as being bedfast or housebound (Shanas and Associates, 1968). As many as 15 to 25 percent of elderly community-dwellers appear to suffer from some degree of mental impairment or illness (*Psychiatry and the Aged*, 1965).

It is therefore apparent that those needing long-term care must differ in other ways from their noninstitutionalized peers. One significant difference lies in the family resources available to help maintain the older person. In general, those in institutions are more likely to lack or to have lost close supportive relatives. One of the major investigators in this area hypothesized that "the likelihood of admission to an institution in old age . . . is partly contingent on family composition, structure, and organization and not only on incapacity, homelessness, and lack of socio-economic resources" (Townsend, 1965). He reported that more widowed older people, more unmarrieds, more childless people, and more with only one adult child lived in institutions. The same study noted that older people with children could live at home to a more advanced stage of infirmity, that geographic distance from relatives was a factor, and that death or sudden illness of close relatives were the most common events precipitating institutional admissions.

Many other studies have strongly confirmed these facts. Only about 10 percent of the institutionalized elderly are married, while 63 percent are widowed, 22 percent have never married, and 5 percent are divorced (*Nursing Home Care in the U.S.*). This contrasts sharply with the fact that 79 percent of all older men and 48 percent of all older women are married (Brotman, 1975).

The institutionalized elderly also have fewer adult children. While more than four out of five of all older people have at least one surviving adult child, this is true for only about half of those in institutions (Townsend, 1965; Gottesman, 1971). That proportion is an average, and is greater in some types of facilities, smaller in others. For example, one report indicated that residents of voluntary homes for aged had more relatives and friends to help them select a facility than residents of other institutions (Beattie and Bullock, 1963).

Where there are adult children, their own characteristics and situations also affect the older person's chances of being institutionalized. For example, people who are in advanced old age, their eighties and nineties, are likely to have children who are themselves approaching or already in the aging phase of life. The capacity of such "children" to care for their parents is qualified by the fact that they may be experiencing some of the age-related problems such as chronic illness, loss through death of spouse, diminished income, and so on. This phenomenon of the different generations of elderly ("old old," "young old," and possibly "middle old") was illustrated by a study which found that 40 percent of elderly applicants to a voluntary home had at least one child sixty years or over, and the "children's" ages ranged as high as seventy-four (Brody, E., 1966). In half the cases, application was precipitated by the death or severe illness of a spouse (25 percent) or adult child or child-in-law (25 percent).

OTHER CHARACTERISTICS OF THE INSTITUTIONALIZED

The literature that has traced the paths of older people to institutions has identified some additional contributory factors. Behavior that is socially unacceptable or that brings the individual to the attention of people in the community may precipitate admission to psychiatric hospitals. At the other extreme, "social invisibility" may keep them out (Lowenthal et al, 1967). The same study indicated that the capacity for "sheer-self-maintenance," and milder impairment enabled some to avoid admission.

My own studies have emphasized multiple causation of applications for admission to an institution (Brody and Gummer, 1967; Brody, 1969). It was pointed out that the reason offered when application is made may be the last of a series of stresses, or the most acceptable socially or psychologically. Or it may be the result of several severe stresses. The studies suggested that other factors at work are the applicant's personality, the quality of family relationships, the coping ability of individual and family, and their socioeconomic circumstances. The availability of resources and services to maintain the older person in the community also relates to the decision.

In short, the accumulated evidence is unequivocal in demonstrating that when older people are institutionalized they have experienced social/health problems to which they have sought a social/health solution (Brody, E., 1975).

A Word About Individuals and Individual Families

Up to this point, the information summarized in this chapter has been about the overall general characteristics of older people in institutions. However it is of utmost importance that they not be regarded as a homogeneous group. On the contrary, they are extremely heterogeneous. They include the "young" old as well as the "old" old and therefore have generational differences. Some are economically well-off, some are indigent. They function at many different levels mentally and physically, ranging from the totally or severely disabled to those who function comparatively well. Some are rich in family ties, others have none. They come from varied cultural racial, religious, educational, and social backgrounds. Some have experienced life-long deprivations or disturbances; for others, problems are age-related. Some have been institutionalized most of their adult lives; others were admitted in old age and will live out their lives as long-term care residents; still others are under care for relatively brief periods of convalescence or for terminal illness.

Particularly significant are individual variations in personality, life-experience, and life-style, and differences in family personality. A few paragraphs about these differences are included here because there is an incorrect but widespread tendency to generalize about institutionalized old people and their families. It is not uncommon to hear sweeping statements about what old people in institutions are like and what they want. Similarly, the families of these people are assumed to behave in identical ways. What, then, can be said about these matters?

It is only in recent years that clinicians and researchers have paid a significant amount of attention to personality in old age. Although there is still much to be learned, in just two decades a sizable body of literature has become available. Review of the literature can lead those interested in studying these matters in detail to many books and articles (Pincus, 1967; Brody, 1974; Neugarten, 1968; Eisdorfer and Lawton, 1973; Neugarten and Associates, 1964).

The view of aging as a developmental phase of life is the most commonly accepted theory of aging. That is, aging has its own tasks (from the standpoint of personality development) that can be successfully mastered, as were tasks of earlier phases of life. Central themes that are reiterated are *individuality, heterogeneity,* and *continuity.*

People carry their own unique personalities into the aging phase of life. The ways in which they deal with events and adapt to stresses in old age are a function of personality and long-standing life styles. Personality does not change sharply with age but becomes even more consistent. That is, personality is continuous over time. Central characteristics become more clearly delineated; values cherished throughout life become more salient.

These findings certainly apply to older people who enter long-term care facilities. They do not change dramatically into "cranky old men" or "sweet little old ladies." Their long-standing personalities determine how they adapt to life in an institution and how they will relate to roommates, other peers, and staff. Their individual patterns will determine how they respond to treatment programs of different types. And their past and current interests and capacities should determine the particular kinds of recreational and social programs they should be offered.

Families, like individuals, have their own unique personalities (Brody, 1974). Though there are shifts in the balance of responsibility as the family moves through various phases in its life cycle, the family personality essentially is continuous over time. Certainly the prospect of placing an elderly family member in an institution is a family crisis. As such, it restimulates family relationship problems (Brody and Spark, 1966; Spark and Brody, 1970). However, at that time the qualitative emotional bonds do not undergo massive radical reversal (Brody, 1974). Where there is a family history of warm, responsible relationships, the old person will not be abandoned or dumped. By the same token, families with long histories of extremely poor relationships do not have the capacity to suddenly mobilize themselves to plan constructively.

Nevertheless, the widespread myth or notion that

families dump old people into institutions persists stubbornly in the face of decisive evidence to the contrary. Gerontological research and clinical evidence are clear in finding that family ties continue to be viable, and adult children continue to behave responsibly (Sussman, 1965; Shanas, 1960, 1961; Rosow, 1965; Reid, 1966; Streib, 1958; Townsend, 1965; Goldfarb, 1965; Psychiatry and the Aged, 1965). Further, studies of the paths leading to institutional care have shown that placing an elderly relative is the last, rather than the first, resort of families. In general, they have exhausted all other alternatives, endured severe personal social and economic stress in the process, and made the final decision with the utmost reluctance (Lowenthal, 1965; Friedsam and Dick, 1963; Goldfarb, 1965).

EFFECTS OF APPLYING TO, MOVING INTO, AND LIVING IN LONG-TERM CARE FACILITIES

Much emphasis has been placed on the fact that many people in institutions are depressed and dependent; have low poor self-image and self-esteem; are lonely; lack privacy and freedom; are unhappy, submissive, and anxious; have little autonomy and self-direction; lack constructive ways to use their time; and are subjected to routinization, infantilization, and desexualization (Brody, 1973). Most professionals and researchers state that it is an oversimplification to attribte the depression, unhappiness, and other negative subjective findings to the fact that the individual is living in an institution. Though all the contributants have not been sorted out, it is now recognized that:

> Differences between the institutionalized and those who are not may have existed before institutionalization.

Differences may be due to the experiences of applying for admission, waiting periods, and actually moving in.

Differences may be due to differences between institutions and the way people in them are treated.

Detailed reviews and descriptions of the many research studies on these subjects are available (Gottesman and Brody, 1975; Lawton and Nahemow, 1973).

It is obvious that the well-being of older people needing long-term care in institutional facilities is influenced by the nature of their care and treatment and by the physical environment itself.

Part III of this guide (Chapters 6 through 15) spells out approaches, procedures, and techniques, based on research and experience, which are designed to minimize the negative effects of all the processes of institutionalization and to maximize the well-being of the older person and his/her family.

Part III

PROVIDING SOCIAL WORK SERVICES IN LONG-TERM CARE FACILITIES

Chapter 6

THE NEED FOR SOCIAL WORK SERVICES

This section of the guide is based on the premise that attention to social needs is an essential element in the care of older people in long-term care facilities from the moment such a plan is first considered until discharge from the facility or death. Certainly, all who are responsible for care and treatment must be aware of social needs and act in such a manner as to support social functioning. Just as many kinds of people other than physicians and nurses provide health services (for example, family members, friends, agencies providing telephone checks or transportation to clinics and doctors, home health aides), so, too, are social needs met by all types of staff, families and friends. However, just as medical care is provided by or under the direction of physicians, social work services should be provided by or under the direction of the professional social worker.

The knowledge, training, skill, and basic value commitment of the profession clearly are required to identify social/emotional needs and implement efforts to meet them.

In Chapters 7 through 15, we detail a possible pattern of specific social work approaches and procedures. They are based largely on social work programs at the Philadelphia Geriatric Center. Obviously this particular model may not be applicable in toto to all other long-term care facilities. For example, assessment also may take place in a variety of settings such as a special unit in a hospital or in free standing evaluation units; and many types of personnel and agencies are involved in decision-making (see Chapter 3).

However, over the years, there have been thousands of requests received by the PGC Department of Social Work for how-to-do-it information. These particular approaches are not offered as definitive. It is hoped that they will be useful. It is also hoped that they will be improved upon by others, just as ways of working constantly change at the PGC when new knowledge and additional experience call for changes.

The conviction underlying these social work programs is that psychological and social factors are of vital importance—to the well-being of applicants and residents, to the determination of appropriate plans, to "adjustment" to the institution, to interpersonal relationships with family, other residents and staff, to the use of medical, nursing, and recreational facilities, and to physical, emotional and mental health. Aged people applying to or residing in institutions are likely to have experienced many of the assaults of aging. The very process of institutionalization is traumatic not only to the aged individual but to his/her family. It is the social worker's task to extend help in support of personal, social, and family functioning, and to enable the older people and family members to use their individual and unique strengths in the furtherance of those goals.

The social component of care is not a luxury to be avoided or eliminated in the interests of economy. It is known from experience and from research that lack of attention to social needs is devastating to all human beings. The older person is particularly vulnerable becuase he/she has fewer resources with which to act on his/her own behalf in obtaining the critically needed social/psychological supplies. The elderly who consider and/or receive institutional care suffer from depletion and deprivation of those resources. If the goal set by a responsible society is to make it possible for them to function at optimal capacity in all spheres (physical, social, and psychological), then efforts must be made to restore and supply the necessary ingredients. The provision of shelter, food and medical care is not enough.

Unquestionably, most older people prefer to remain in the familiar surroundings of their own homes in preference to admission to an institution, and all possible avenues should be explored and services mobilized towards that goal. However, there are some elderly people for whom congregate care is socially and medically indicated and for whom viable alternatives do not exist. The decision is not abstract and cannot be made on philosophical grounds. The practical question, in the light of the older person's and family's current situation and the present status of community resources, is whether admission to an institution will represent a positive change in terms of increased well-being, provision of needed care, and relief from stress.

The personality and unique history of the older person play important roles in determination of the "best" plan. Given similar physical, mental, and environmental situations, a fiercely independent individual may continue to live in the community well beyond the point at which institutional care is sought by his dependent, fearful neighbor. It is often difficult to balance respect for the needs, attitudes, and right to self-determination of the elderly person with the desire of family and professionals to provide care and protection.

Basic to the philosophy of care is recognition that long-term care facilities are the *homes* of older people, whether the stay is relatively short or lasts for the remainder of life. It is for this reason that the Guide throughout does not characterize them as "patients" but refers to them as "applicants" or "residents." Despite their major physical and mental health problems, they should be viewed as whole men and women, not as full-time professional patients.

The institutionalized elderly have experienced multiple assaults and losses. In contrast to crises experienced by younger people, these "insults" tend to cluster. Physical and mental deficits may occur during the same periods in which the old person has suffered interpersonal and economic losses. Gerontologists have emphasized the interrelatedness of deficits in all spheres of the individual's functioning. One of the main difficulties in diagnosis and treatment is sorting out the various problems that tend to mask and exacerbate each other. Thus an interdisciplinary approach is a necessity in the decision-making process and during institutional care.

The prescription for treatment—the plan that can be made—often depends on social factors. When, for example, an older person has a catastrophic physical illness or suffers from severe organic brain damage, the determinants of the ability to maintain him in his own home may be questions such as: Can expert medical care be provided? Is such a plan economically feasible? Are there sufficient resources to finance a housekeeper or practical nurse? Are such personnel available? Are there adult children, and do they live nearby? Have family relations in the past been sufficiently close and warm so that they can now sustain the additional emotional stress and physical effort? Are the adult children beset by personal problems which must take priority? Is their health and general well-being affected adversely by the burden of caring for the older person? Are the adult children also in the aging phase of life?

Psychological and social factors also determine how individuals react and adapt to change in their life situations. One person suffering a stroke may work actively to improve his functioning and cooperate fully with rehabilitative programs; another may become depressed and resistant. Individual differences are illustrated by research evidence that adaptation to an institutional environment depends in part on the fit between the individual's coping style and the demands of the environment. A corollary that might be suggested is that adaptation also depends on the capacity of the environment to be flexible in accommodating to individual differences.

A central theme in work with older people is to identify and capitalize on their strengths or assets rather than to focus on losses and deficits. Existing and latent strengths constitute the foundation on which constructive treatment programs can be built. Thus much emphasis has been placed on a functional approach to assessment and treatment planning. A good deal of work by gerontologists has been directed to developing assessment techniques and measures designed to evaluate functional capacities and thus to facilitate the setting of realistic treatment goals.

Some of the tasks involved, then, in providing the social component of care are individualization, integration of different aspects of the treatment plan, avoidance of fragmentation, capitalizing on individual strengths, mobilization of resources, help to the individual in adapting to his/her changed situation and in utilizing available programs, development of new resources and programs, and modification of the environment.

Social work in relation to long-term care facilities makes the most stringent demands on social work knowledge, values, and skills. The characteristics of the elderly population served, the multiplicity of their problems, the impact on family and society, the comparative lack of knowledge about needed social interventions, and the need for creative institutional and social planning legitimate such facilities as a prime concern of social work in all its traditional forms. Direct services to individuals, families and groups; community organization; education; research; administration; and planning and policy formulation—all are essential ingredients in developing and delivering the required services.

A word about the importance of direct individual and group services: Attention to the overall social and physical environment of long-term care facilities has been long overdue and is a welcome trend. However, the nature of the human condition and of elderly people applying to and living in institutions in particular indicate that services be personalized. There can be no substitute for direct personal help with the trauma of admission to an institution, the loss of a beloved adult child, the anxiety and fear of death occasioned by a catastrophic illness, or many other crushing blows experienced by older people. Important as benevolent staff and supportive physical environment are, additional services are required to help the older people to develop roles, form new peer relationships, channel expressions of feeling and needs, explore possibilities for new interests and activities, or have individual and/or group therapeutic experiences.

It is not appropriate to opt for either individual or

group services to applicants, residents, and families. Those methods are complementary, and both are necessary. Many common problems can be handled more effectively and economically in groups; others dictate individual service.

In long-term care facilities, the same worker(s) often can deliver both individual and groups services. It has been my experience that because caseworkers and groupworkers have a common base of knowledge, skills, and values, they can move easily between the two methods. From a practical standpoint, relatively few facilities can afford to have both, and to choose one or the other leaves a serious void in meeting the needs. In serving applicants and families, for example, individual assessment of social resources, of family functioning, of highly individual personality are a necessity as is individual help in the admission process itself. At the same time groups of applicants or of families can be extremely useful for such matters as interpreting agency policies and procedures or in helping the clients through sharing their feelings and anxieties with each other. The social worker's awareness of the feelings involved that derives from contacts with individuals is a firm foundation for such group services. Similarly, a different dimension of understanding emerges from the group that is invaluable in working with individuals.

The same and additional considerations relate to work with residents and families. It is important for the social worker engaged in serving residents and families to have an office in the area being served, where he/she is part of the total milieu. The intimate knowledge of all the residents, the routines, personnel, physical environment, the texture of the day-to-day life in that area is required for individual services. The same knowledge is the foundation for the kinds of group services that are beneficial for the particular population(s) served.

How Social Work Services Are to Be Provided

The procedural sections that follow are written as though the facility has its own social work staff. Obviously, this condition does not exist universally. In fact, full-time social work service exists only in a minority of facilities, primarily those under voluntary auspices (Kaplan, 1975). Even if we were closer to the desired goal of social work service available at all long-term care facilities, almost all social workers in other agencies at some time will continue to have some responsibility in relation to older people who may need long-term care and to their families. This is true of social workers in hospitals and other health facilities, in family agencies, psychiatric facilities, public welfare agencies, governmental health departments and in many other settings. In some instances, such as that of the hospital social worker helping with a discharge plan, they may carry major responsibility. In other situations, they may make referrals. No matter what the extent or duration of the contact, there should be full awareness of the implications for the clients and the requirements in terms of service.

Many of the principles and procedures described can be adapted for use by such social workers. Almost all of the application procedures and methods, for example, can be used by any social worker involved in the decision-making and placement process: the counseling, assessment, selection of appropriate facility, preparation of older person and family for admission, sustaining help during waiting periods prior to admission. Similarly, the extension of services by family agencies, senior citizen centers and others to residents of long-term care facilities has not been fully explored. Such community agencies often do not view institutions as part of the community nor institutionalized older people as legiti-

mate recipients of their services. The description to follow of social work services in long-term care facilities
might be reviewed by such agencies in order to assess
their capabilities to extend their own services.

I am convinced that the ultimate goal is for every
facility to provide social work service, and that a
minimum of one full time social worker is needed for
each fifty to sixty residents. If the facility also offers services to applicants and families, there should be additional staff for that purpose depending on the volume of
applications and the amount of service given.

As we move toward that goal, there are a variety of
provisional ways of arranging for professional social
work services, depending on the size of the facility, geographic accessibility, and other considerations. For
example, contractual arrangements can be made for the
services of social workers employed by other agencies
(hospitals, family or public welfare agencies, and so on)
on a regular basis. Social work assistants can be utilized
in the facility who work under the supervision of professional social workers.

Currently, there is a good deal of discussion about
using social work consultation in long-term care facilities
in lieu of a social worker who is part of the regular staffing pattern. It is my view that such an arrangement is a
poor compromise and should be regarded at best as a
temporary arrangement until social work service can be
arranged. Social work consultation to the staff of a
long-term care facility is of value in helping them to understand and meet some social needs of residents. When
the consultant meets with other staff and participates in
in-service training, benefits can accrue—such as more
positive attitudes and approaches. However, this is only
one aspect of the social work task. It is a puzzling assumption that consultation can train other personnel to
do social work. No parallel assumption is made that

physicians or nurses should "consult" in nursing homes and that their direct performance of medical and nursing services thereby can be made unnecessary.

Social work consultation and social work service on an occasional or part-time basis share another limitation. Practice and experience indicate that the provision of good social work services requires that the social worker be part of the regular staff of a facility, familiar on an intimate basis with the culture of the facility, with the minute-to-minute routines, and with the personalities and problems of the rest of the staff. Unless that occurs, and the social worker is part of the very fabric of the facility, he/she is an outsider and the value of his/her work is sharply curtailed.

Long-term care facilities have many different organizational patterns, vary in size and personnel, operate under different types of auspices (governmental, voluntary, proprietary), and may emphasize different target populations. The procedures in this section therefore require adaptation to suit the particular populations and unique properties of any particular facility. However, the principles and approach are the same wherever older people are cared for. No matter the nature of the auspice or sponsor, attention to the social components of care and provision of social work services are the mutual responsibility of its administrator and social worker. The administrator should make explicit his commitment by facilitating the social worker's tasks. This involves provision of the "tools of the trade," such as adequate private space for interviewing, secretarial help, recording equipment, and telephone. Most important of all, he/she should communicate to all staff of the facility, by attitude and action, the conviction of the importance of the social services to the well-being of the old people in their charge.

This guide is being written at a time when long-term care facilities are undergoing major changes. Their development currently and in the future will be subject to many influences: population changes, legislation, increased public awareness and the pressure of public opinion, new knowledge developed by practitioners and research investigators, and, it is hoped, more positive attitudes towards the elderly. Therefore, no guide can be definitive and comprehensive. It would be presumptuous to expect that this book could serve all population groups and all auspices. Furthermore, the state of the art is such that much more needs to be known.

Nevertheless, human needs are unlikely to change. Social work principles based on understanding of those needs are applicable. Though widespread popular and professional concern about older people and long-term care facilities is a relatively recent development, some dedicated and skilled professionals have been working in the field for many years. Their efforts provide us with the principles enunciated in the guide, principles intrinsic to human behavior and to the processes of aging. The specific procedures described will be subject to change as the context in which they occur is modified.

Fortunately, the process of modifying that context has begun. The philosophy of care is changing from "custodial" to a more optimistic treatment and service orientation. Concerted efforts are being made to mitigate the negative impact of the "total institution." Research on the characteristics of various types of institutions and their effects on various types of social therapies has already yielded much valuable information.

Certainly social work in long-term care facilities has a much shorter history than social work in other settings. There is a lack of experience regarding the delicate issues of social work practice in proprietary nursing homes. Historically, social work in the main has practiced under voluntary of public auspices. However, it is the proprietary nursing homes that now contain most institutionalized older people. Now and in the future the profession must address itself to working out its relationships to the nursing home industry. Many matters such as responsibility and accountability, ethics, and the nature of the contractual arrangements require clarification.

Whatever the auspice, social work has the foundation on which to build further. There is a good deal of social work experience in long-term care in voluntary homes. Beyond that specific experience, generic social work knowledge and skills are as relevant in long-term facilities as in other settings. From its beginning, the profession has dealt with people, with individual and family problems of all kinds, and with the need for environmental and social change. The challenge is to use existing knowledge and skills creatively while remaining open to new knowledge and participating in its development.

PHASES OF BEING AND BECOMING A RESIDENT OF A LONG-TERM CARE FACILITY

Becoming and being a resident of a long-term facility is a process that has several phases beginning when consideration first is given to the possibility of such a plan:

> Decision-making or application phase
> Waiting period
> Admission
> Residence
> Discharge
> Dying and death

These are, of course, arbitrary and artificial distinctions. The decision-making process may continue throughout even a lengthy waiting period and sometimes well into residency. A waiting period does not always occur. The admission phase begins prior to the physical move and continues afterwards. Discharge may not take place at all, and if it does, like admission, it is a process that includes aspects of decision-making, planning, placement, and post-placement adjustment. The dying process may be concurrent with any or all of the preceding phases.

Whatever the sequence, the total process constitutes major life crises for the old person and family members, with each phase having its own set of stresses. Many losses have already experienced and other are imminent: physical and/or mental decrements; interpersonal losses of family and friends; loss of former occupation and activities, of the familiar environment of home and possessions, of degrees of autonomy or independence, and of economic status. These occur at a time when the individual has fewer resources with which to cope and adapt to the changes.

Therefore, a goal that should permeate every step of institutional care is to help the older person resolve feelings such as grief and anger, set and accept new goals, and maintain and regain mastery to the fullest possible extent. To do so, his/her previous personality pattern and other aspects of functioning should be understood, and his/her strengths emphasized and exploited. The approach is to support maximum functioning—social, psychological, and physical. Case material in Chapter 9 illustrates how help can be offered to individuals and families during application, admission and residence phases of institutional care.

Chapter 7

SERVICES TO APPLICANTS AND FAMILIES

The Application Phase

The prospect of placement of an older person in a long-term care facility and the application process itself are critical psychological experiences for the elderly individual and family members in each generation. If help is to be extended, it is necessary to understand the psychological dynamics involved in the family life-crisis that occurs at that juncture.

Of the many myths and misconceptions about the aged, one of the most persistent is that of alienation of old people from their families. Families often are accused of abandoning their older relatives or "dumping" them into institutions. In reality, there is decisive evidence that family ties continue to be viable and that adult children behave responsibly. Studies of the paths leading to institutional care have shown that placing an elderly relative is the last rather than the first resort of families, and that in general they have exhausted all other alternatives, endured severe personal, social, and economic stress in the process, and made the final decision with the utmost reluctance.

At the aging phase of the family life cycle, emotional bonds continue and are central to the mental health of the old person and all family members. While the historical health or pathology of the interpersonal relations between the generations is a most important component in the complex of psychological reactions, it would be unrealistic to suggest a simplistic model of "healthy" relationship in which there is no residuum of unresolved conflict. When long-term care is being considered the degree or intensity of stress may vary, but feelings are mixed, and family relationship patterns are revealed vividly.

The elderly person may be in a state of intense anxiety and fear. Even if family relations are basically warm and healthy and he/she recognizes the necessity of placement on a reality level, psychologically some feelings of abandonment and rejection are still experienced. For the adult children, spouse, siblings or other relatives, guilt, conflict, and shame may coexist with the conscious or unconscious but very human desire to be relieved of burdens they have carried, often beyond the saturation point. If they themselves are approaching or engaged in the aging phase of life (and this is a common phenomenon today), their own anxieties about aging are reinforced.

The feelings of all family members are communicated to each other, and the distress of each increases that of the others. Even if the older person had not previously lived in the same household, the placement in psychological terms is a separation which stimulates the reactions associated with all separations from those in whom there is an emotional investment. Coming at this phase of life, when the total family is confronted with the fact that this may be the final plan for the old person, it carries overtones of the ultimate separation.

In our culture, another layer is added to the stress experienced even by "normal" families. There still exist strong, deeply internalized, guilt-inducing injunctions against placing an elderly spouse or parent regardless of the most reality-based determinants of that placement. For the children, traditional expectations such as providing financial support and caring for the aged person in one's own home are no longer always appropriate due to social and economic changes. But they still have a strong psychological impact on the elderly parent and adult children. The middle-aged generation may be caught in the bind of multiple emotional and financial obligations to the younger generations, to themselves, and to the increasing numbers of older family members.

Family behavior during the placement process reflects and is part of the natural continuity of past relationships from which it flows. When there is a history of unresolved relationship problems, they are often reactivated, intensified, and acted out at this time. Practitioners often see the flaring of bitter sibling rivalries which may focus on financial planning or opposing attitudes towards what may constitute the best plan for the parent. One adult child may continue to function as the "burden-bearer," while others take no responsibility. Longstanding symbiotic ties between elderly parent and middle-aged child may intensify the suffering at placement, or even sabotage it entirely.

To put the matter in perspective, there is much more evidence of genuine affection and loyalty between institutionalized older people and their children than the reverse. The helping person must not permit negative biases and value judgments to interfere with skilled help focusing on the total family. Such help is a preventive measure in accordance with the broadest meaning of mental health. The future well-being of the applicant as well as the outcome in terms of planning can be affected positively or negatively. The worker, the procedures, the policies, and the physical setting should convey consideration, warmth, and respect. It is particularly important to communicate to the aged person that he/she has value and worth as an adult human being, since so many have lost their feelings of status and self-esteem.

The fullest possible participation should be afforded to the older person and all family members. Practitioners and researchers have shown that favorable adjustment to institutional living depends partly on the extent to which the older person actually takes part in the decision-making process. It is known that many people in institutions have not been given sufficient opportunity to do so. Similarly, the strength of family ties has often been overlooked. Involvement of family members from the very beginning may avoid many future problems for the staff of the facility as well as for the residents.

Because the older person is often physically and/or mentally impaired and in need of care, family members are likely to assume responsibility for planning. This may be expressed by the family's assumption that it should make the decisions and arrangements. It is part of the worker's task to see to it that planning is carried out *with* the older person. The worker should, of course, respond to the family's request for information and discussion of the situation, but the older person should be brought into the decision-making process at the earliest possible time.

The degree to which the elderly person can participate may indeed be constrained by his/her physical or mental impairment. However, the worker's expectations are an important factor. Most of the older people can participate to some extent despite physical and mental impairment. It should not be taken for granted that because of physical handicaps, confusion, or forgetfulness, plans should be made without involving the older person. Ways can be found to permit even severely impaired people to participate.

Goals of the Application Phase

Throughout the application phase, the social work goals are: to counsel; to study and assess; and to screen.

TO COUNSEL.   Theoretically, identification of elderly individuals for whom institutional care is appropriate and the matching of individual to the type of facility which meets his/her needs should occur at the earliest possible point in time. Practically, as a result of the scarcity of preventive resources, the request for admission is often made at a time of crisis and without there having been prior access to evaluative services. It is therefore necessary to assess and counsel as well as to determine eligibility in accordance with the admission criteria of a particular facility.

The restorative process begins with the respect and consideration accorded, examination of the nature of the problem, genuine seeking and testing of alternatives, offering of choices, and the opportunity for the elderly person and his/her family to collaborate in the planning. If the aged person who has suffered multiple personal and social losses is to be "rehabilitated" in mental health terms, he/she needs first to regain some sense of self-esteem, value, and self-direction. If the well-being of his/her family members is to be fostered, recognition of their own problems and efforts on behalf of the elderly person should occur in a context devoid of blame or judgmental attitudes.

Careful exploration of the situation is required to determine whether or not admission to a long-term facility is the best plan for each old person and his/her family. Resources to help maintain impaired older people in the community are badly underdeveloped. However, the worker who sees the old person and family is in a strategic position to prevent unnecessary or premature admissions. Towards this goal, appraisal of the total situation includes the mental and physical health of the applicant, the physical environment, social and economic situation, family relationships, and the family's capacities.

In addition to offering help with the psychological factors, practical matters should be dealt with and the applicants should be informed of services that may be helpful to them: counseling, alternative living arrangements, medical and psychiatric care, financial entitlements, community care services (visiting nurse, homemaker, telephone reassurance, day-care). Chapter 4 details the available supports that should be reviewed.

Apart from the fact that such counseling is in the best interests of the older person him/herself, it is also to the advantage of the facility itself, regardless of auspice. For example, much emphasis is currently being placed by government funding sources on the payment for institutional care being tied to the individual's actual condition and need for care. Thus a facility that accepts inappropriate applicants may find itself without reimbursement.

Many different patterns will obtain in the beginning consideration of institutional care. Some individuals apply directly to the facility and can be seen by the staff social worker. Others may be hospitalized, and the hospital social worker will have the responsibility of helping them plan. Still others are seen by social workers at family agencies or public welfare agencies. In many situations, it is the family doctor whose judgment and advice are decisive.

Whatever the beginning point, social and medical evaluation should determine the suitability of a plan for long-term care, and alternatives should be explored to select the most appropriate facility. Referring social workers should not limit their activities to simply locating a nursing home with an available bed. They should be familiar with the various facilities, keep a file with up-to-date information, and review the situation again with applicant and/or family after the potential receiving facility has been visited or toured.

Thus the initial contact should not begin a process of funneling into a long-term care facility. It can be either the point of entry into a system of community-based services or the gateway to the spectrum of services provided to the aged resident of the institution and to the family.

When institutionalization appears to be the plan of choice, several concurrent processes follow. Continuing social work services should be given in relation to the decision-making process and its psychological and social concomitants. If there is a waiting list for admission, help with interim planning should be offered and available community resources mobilized. Referrals can be made to the public income maintenance programs, to psychiatric and general hospitals and clinics, to family agencies, recreational facilities, nursing homes, and other resources.

The counseling process, then, helps clients and family evaluate the appropriateness of long-term care in general, and specific facilities in particular. Alternatives are explored and referrals made when indicated. The facility's procedures, services, and programs are inter-

preted, and the implications of institutional living discussed. In the process, applicants are helped to begin to
work through their feelings and problems so as to permit the most constructive use of the planning and admission processes.

TO STUDY AND ASSESS.   The second major goal of the
application phase is to study and assess. The importance of an interdisciplinary approach has already been
stressed. Such collaborative efforts must recognize that
determination of the "best" plan is highly individualized.
Although several applicants may be strikingly similar in
their diagnoses and capacities, family and social factors
may indicate different solutions for each. One may be
able to remain in his/her own home with appropriate
supports, another move to the home of an adult child,
and institutional care may be the plan of choice for still
another. A variety of other types of living arrangements
exist and are evolving that may be suitable: high-rise
apartment buildings for the elderly, intermediate housing, and others. The ultimate decision is based on evaluation of the total situation: the older person's resources
(physical, mental, functional, social), the family's resources, and the available community resources.

A vital part of the assessment is the development of
a good social history (Appendix A) to identify the older
person's social needs, his interests, capacities, relationships. Such a history is basic to planning and treatment
both in and out of the long-term care facility. It should
contain relevant information about the individual's
socioeconomic, educational, and cultural background;
previous life-style, life experiences, and adaptive patterns; capacities, interpersonal relationships, occupational and recreational interests, attitudes and responses
to group living; and adjustment to current impairments.

Pertinent information should be elicited from the older person, family members, physician, and social and health agencies to which he/she is known.

TO SCREEN. The third goal is to screen. The admission criteria of different types of facilities determine the nature of the screening procedures. However, they are generally geared to identifying those whose needs for care cannot be met by the admitting facility or those with communicable diseases. An example of the former might be a person whose behavior is dangerous to him/herself or others; he/she may require care in a psychiatric hospital if the voluntary home or proprietary nursing home cannot provide necessary protection.

Formulation of admission policies and eligibility criteria. In many voluntary homes, admission policies and requirements are generally formulated by the board of directors or a board committee that may be called the social service committee. Within the broad policy framework, the department of social work is responsible for social evaluation of each individual request for admission; the departments of medicine and nursing determine physical eligibility. Consultation and decisions may be requested from the administrator in appropriate situations. Unusual cases requiring modification or waivers of policy may be presented to the social service committee (see Chapter 15).

Age and residence. In voluntary homes, applicants are generally required to be sixty-five years old or over. Often they must be residents of the specific geographic area served by the home. However, these policies should not be applied rigidly; they may be waived for special situations. Such waivers should, of course, be approved by those responsible for policy—the administrator, the board, or the social service committee. Waivers are usually based on judgment as to the appropriateness of the placement, and reflect consideration of the applicant's physical and emotional needs. Examples of such exceptions are:

> Persons under sixty-five for whom other facilities are not available may be considered if they require the kind of care available at the facility and if the applicant's (and his/her family's) judgment and that of the social worker agree that he/she would be comfortable in the atmosphere of the particular facility.
>
> Nonresidents of the area may be considered if their children are residents or if they had formerly been residents and their close associations and ties are in this particular area.

Social requirements. The social work process ensures that the applicant has need for the care and services of the facility and that it is the most appropriate plan possible.

Admission to a facility should be voluntary. If able to do so, the applicant expresses willingness to become a resident. If he/she is mentally impaired to a degree which renders him/her incompetent to make such a decision, the responsible relatives may do so. No one, however, can be forcibly "committed" to any facility except a mental hospital.

Health. Health requirements should be consonant with the services the facility is equipped to offer. The details of the evaluation process are described below. It should be noted that many people who formerly were considered "not acceptable," notably the mentally impaired aged, can be successfully maintained in nonpsychiatric facilities through appropriate approaches to care.

Application Procedures.

In the main the specific procedures to be described are those in use at the Philadelphia Geriatric Center. They are administered flexibly in accordance with the unique needs of each situation and are constantly being modified. It is self-evident that they would require adaptation to other settings.

There are three types of cases, designated by the descriptive titles: inquiry; reception case; application case.

INQUIRIES.   An inquiry is the initial contact on each case and may be by means of letter, telephone, or walk-in. A card-form is used by the worker to note identifying data and other brief information (Appendix B) and then kept in a central file for future reference. (If a formal application is made subsequently, the information on the card is incorporated in the case record dictation, and the card itself is destroyed.) The inquiry may be a brief contact during which appropriate referrals are made, general information given, or an appointment for an interview is arranged.

Inquiries and reception cases may or may not eventuate in application. In order to provide continuity, every effort is made to have the same social worker carry the case from initial contact through actual admission. When it is necessary for a case to be transferred, this should be discussed with the applicant and family, and the new worker introduced to facilitate the transition.

RECEPTION CASES.   A reception case is one in which there are several contacts or in which at least one interview takes place. This designation continues until a completed application is returned to the facility. "Reception" may encompass diverse activities such as a home visit, several interviews, referral to other agencies, medical and/or psychiatric consultation, and obtaining medical history and information. When appropriate, the applications forms may be given after the exploratory first interview. Whenever an interview has taken place, it should be recorded by the worker in summary form. A suggested outline for this dictation appears as Appendix C. Of course, not all of the indicated information is always obtained during the first interview; it can be completed subsequently.

APPLICATION CASES.   Application forms include the formal application for admission. Such a form should include identifying information (name, address, birthdate, occupation, names and addresses of responsible relatives). It is useful to require a signed authorization to obtain abstracts of hospital records (Appendix D) so that health information can be obtained. Most facilities also have a medical history form to be completed by the family physician. However the application forms are arranged, they can begin to assemble social and medical information that is needed administratively and that will be useful in developing treatment plans: identifying information about applicant and family, social and medical history, education, occupational and recreational interests, financial situation.

When received, the forms are reviewed for completion, and an application case record is set up (see Chapter 15). Letters are sent to applicant and family acknowledging receipt of application forms, and to hospitals for abstracts of clinic attendance or hospitalizations. A checklist of materials required is a useful aid for the social worker (Appendix E).

THE INTAKE STUDY.   Careful assessment of each applicant from different vantage points is an essential preliminary to appropriate placement and care. The well-rounded assessment provides guidelines for such matters as matching of roommates, placement in accordance with functional capacities, and development of medical, rehabilitative, social, recreational, and occupational treatment plans.

There are four major themes in the intake study that are carried on concurrently:

CASEWORK SERVICES.   Though this guide does not address itself to the dynamics of the casework process, it assumes that skilled help is offered throughout every aspect of the decision-making and the evaluation process. The applicant and family should have an opportunity to tour the facilities; the applicant may be invited to lunch and to participate in some of the activities. Such opportunities provide a realistic concept of life in the institution, serve to prepare the older person for admission, and ease the transition.

FINANCIAL PLANNING.   Financial arrangements vary widely in different facilities. However, it is essential for all concerned to discuss these in detail prior to admission so that they understand their rights and responsibilities. Resources of the applicant him/herself should be reviewed to ensure awareness of available financial entitlements. The fact that family problems often focus on finances underlines the need for sensitivity and skill in dealing with this matter.

SOCIAL EVALUATION.   The applicant may have some characteristics in common with others who reside in long-term care facilities. However, he/she is a unique individual with a particular set of life-experiences, personality, modes of adaptation, wishes, preferences, needs, family relationships and reactions to the new and often painful experiences he/she is undergoing. A good social history is invaluable in understanding him/her as an individual and in developing plans to support social functioning during the application process and after admission. A suggested outline for a social history is given in Appendix A.

HEALTH EVALUATION.   Health includes medical, psychological, and psychiatric aspects of the older person's functioning. While it is extremely important to have accurate and complete medical information, in the elderly *functional* (capacities, rather than diagnosis or pathology) is the most useful measure to determine services required. The different aspects of health are combined here because physical and mental health of the elderly are so closely related. There is a high correlation between physical and mental illness; no sharp line of demarcation can be drawn between them, mental and physical illness affect each other, and the symptoms of impairment in each sphere often mask and exacerbate each other. Therefore, methods that measure functioning capacity are an important part of evaluation.

Information about health of applicants may be obtained from a variety of sources: the family doctor, the older person himself, and the family. Abstracts are obtained from hospitals and out-patient clinics where the applicant has received care. A chest X-ray no more than six months old is required.

If a pre-admission medical examination is part of the procedures, the nurse who has assisted in the examination can evaluate the applicant's capacities in ADL and note on the examination protocol an estimate of the applicant's need for care. The judgment is based on direct observation of the older person's capacity to perform tasks of daily living such as dressing and undressing, responding to instructions, and ambulating.

The social worker administers and completes four forms: PGC Behavior and Adjustment Classification Scale; PGC Physical Self-Maintenance Scale; PGC Instrumental Activities of Daily Living Scale; and the Kahn-Goldfarb Mental Status Questionnaire. Examples of these forms are given in Appendix B.

Some facilities require that all applicants be seen by the staff psychiatrist. When psychiatric time is limited, the psychiatrist may see only applicants whose history includes severe or repeated psychiatric disorder or those for whom the social worker or physician requests an evaluation. Severely disordered behavior or indications that an applicant might present an exceptional management problem are examples of the kinds of persons requiring such evaluation.

When complete, these various histories, protocols, and evaluation forms constitute a portfolio that provides a profile of the physical, mental, emotional, and functional status of the applicant. The social worker by this time will have formed a judgment about the admissability of the applicant and the locale within the facility required. Most often, social worker, physician, and nurse agree.

PLACEMENT CONFERENCE.   On occasion, the professionals involved may disagree on admissability or placement needs, or a particular individual may present exceptional problems that make such judgments difficult. In such instances, a consensus decision can be reached in the course of a conference at which the professionals concerned and the administrator of the facility are present.

APPROVAL.   When the intake study has been completed, the social worker writes a completion summary (Appendix B). The summary includes social information, financial arrangements for admission, classification on the measures noted above, and notation of the area of the facility in which the applicant should live. The case record is then reviewed by the senior social worker in charge of intake (director of the department or supervisor of intake), and the applicant's name is placed on the active waiting list. The social worker advises applicant and family of approval and explains that admission will take place when an appropriate vacancy occurs.

REJECTED APPLICATIONS.   Depending upon the admission criteria and type of services of a particular facility, it may be necessary to refuse admission to some individuals. In such situations, every effort should be made to handle the matter as constructively as possible: to interpret the reasons the facility is not appropriate, to help resolve the feelings engendered, and to help applicant and family obtain needed counseling, services, and care.

The Waiting Period

Many institutions have waiting lists for admission, in some instances necessitating a long interval between application and actual admission. It has been found that many of the negative effects usually attributed to living in an institutional environment actually occur during the waiting period. Observations of hundreds of older people provide some clues to the reasons. The physical, emotional, and economic stresses which contributed to the need for application may be unrelieved. Practical measures to ease this period are to a large extent frustrated by the scarcity of community services (such as day care, homemaker, or temporary care facilities), and by the unavailability of financial aid to enable the family to purchase services for the amelioration of acute pressures. Psychologically the elderly person and family are in an uncertain limbo, and the painful separation process is prolonged and unresolved.

To compound the difficulties, the old person often is subjected to the additional stress of frequent moves. Various studies have noted a preinstitutionalization acceleration of mobility. In one study at the Philadelphia Geriatric Center, 40 percent of applicants to a long-term care facility had moved at least once during the year preceding application. During the first year after application, while on the waiting list, 73 percent moved at least once, and many moved several times. These applicants moved at least five times as often as older people in the general community.

Sustaining the relationship between institution and clients during the waiting period is of value. The social worker should invite and periodically initiate telephone or personal contacts in order to provide reassurance of the institution's continuing awareness of their need for admission, to offer help with new emergencies which arise, to keep abreast of the changing condition and needs of applicant and family, and to give continuing case work support.

Various devices may be employed to organize the waiting list so that information is readily available. An alphabetical card file can be supplemented by a "control board." If the facility is organized by different levels of care, applicants can be listed by appropriate area. Brief information such as name of applicant, age, sex, and date of application can be included. Such a control board provides a graphic picture of the size and composition of the waiting list and the extent of the need for various facilities. It also serves to facilitate selection of an applicant when a vacancy occurs.

Deferred Waiting List

Long-term care facilities often receive applications from individuals who are seeking the security of connection with the agency in the event of future need but who prefer to defer admission as long as possible. It has been found useful to maintain a "deferred" list—that is, to encourage such individuals to remain in the community while assuring them of consideration for admission in accordance with the original date of application if and when their changed circumstances require institutional care and protection. Experience has shown that many deferred applicants either avoid or postpone institutionalization. The access to an interested counselor and the knowledge that protection is available provide the psychological security needed to sustain them. It is, of course, of paramount importance to help this group avail itself of existing services in the community.

Selection for Admission

Long-term care facilities vary widely in their practices regarding admissions. Some adhere strictly to the applicant's place on the waiting list as determined by date of application. In others, the applicant's ability to pay for care is a primary consideration. Applicants whose care will be reimbursed by Medicaid must meet the criteria for skilled or intermediate care. Where there are several different levels of care within the same facility, the level in which the vacancy exists may be a determining factor in the selection of the applicant to fill a particular vacancy.

At the Philadelphia Geriatric Center, where there is a long waiting list, when a vacancy occurs the selection of an applicant from among many in need is a delicate and sometimes painful task.

The primary consideration is the area in which the vacancy occurs, since different levels of care exist within the facility. Obviously if the older person is in need of intensive medical and nursing care, it would not be in his/her best interests to be placed in an area in which only "routine" supervision is available. Conversely it would be inappropriate to use an intensive care bed for a relatively intact individual.

Other factors are:

Date of application. Priority consideration is given to those who have been waiting longest.

Stress on applicant and/or family. The social, emotional, physical, and economic urgency is weighed carefully. Social and emotional factors might be, for example, exacerbated relationship problems due to presence of the older person in an adult child's home; adult children losing time from work or other hardship because of need to care for the parent; lack of supportive relatives. Physical stress might be the older person living under environmental conditions acutely dangerous to health and even survival; the applicant needs nursing/ medical care that the family cannot provide; the family members may be ill or damaging their own health in order to care for the parent.

Advanced old age. Other factors being equal, a ninety-five-year-old might be given priority over younger applicants.

Finally, if the vacancy is not in a private room, the personality and characteristics of the current occupant(s) must be considered in an attempt to "match" roommates.

Though no absolute hierarchy of considerations can be established, all factors should be considered and balanced, and the best judgment of the responsible professionals exercised.

ADMISSION

The actual transition from previous residence to the long-term care facility is a critical time. Although psychological preparation should have begun with the very first contact, the reality of the imminent move has its own impact. The physical disruptions are self-evident. Inevitably, fears and anxieties of applicant and family are restimulated, and there is a psychological recapitulation of the decision-making process.

The duration of the transitional phase varies greatly from one older person to another. In general, a discerning professional can judge when the new resident has really "moved in" to the long-term facility. The manner in which this phase is handled colors the future course of the older person's life. Intensification of services is a necessity in easing this period.

Change is difficult at any age level, and more so when one is old, ill, and views the change as beyond one's control and as moving for the last time. Certainly preventive services applied at an earlier point in time are of prime importance, so that applicants and families do not arrive at the institution's doors exhausted and overwhelmed, having exceeded the saturation point of human endurance for stress. Psychological preparation for admission cannot be separated from the realities of the existence (or nonexistence) and utilization of appropriate services prior to application and during the waiting period.

Relocation effect

There was discussion in Chapter 3 of the various studies that described the phenomenon called "relocation effect" or "transplantation shock," that is, apparent negative effects (including increased death rate) on older people when change of residence takes place. It was noted that despite efforts to avoid moving or institutionalization, it is a fact of life that relocation occurs, and that often it is in the best interests of the older person and the family to make those moves. Research and clinical literature was cited that provides clues to ways of minimizing transplantation shock. To recapitulate briefly, there is positive value in terms of favorable adjustment to institutional living if the older person participates to the fullest degree possible in the decision-making process; if the applicant has been provided with opportunities for choice; and if there has been careful individualized preparation for the move via counseling and orientation. One study in which there were no negative effects of moving attributed the finding to the fact that the older people moved voluntarily.

There is evidence that those who are confused and disoriented, the physically ill, and the involuntarily located, fare poorly when moved as compared to other groups. One explanation advanced for the effect on the confused individual is that while not sufficiently in contact to understand advance explanations of a move, he/she is nevertheless sufficiently aware of familiar environmental cues to become disturbed when the cues are no longer at hand. According to this hypothesis, the mentally impaired individual cannot prepare for a change and when the change occurs, he/she lacks the adaptive capacity to cope with it. It also may be that psychological helping techniques developed in relation to those with intact cognitive thinking are not applicable to this group, and that methods of working with them have not yet been developed fully. Their relative inability to participate in a "willingness choice-making" decision process is compounded too often by negative lay and professional attitudes which deny them the opportunity for participation with the limits of their capacities. Certainly the vulnerability of such older people has implications for setting priorities in service and for additional experimentation with methods of modifying negative effects.

Transplantation shock is usually discussed in relation to the elderly individual. However, the family also experiences the impact of relocation of its older family member. Family anxieties can intensify the difficulties for the older person who, whether intact or impaired mentally, is sensitive to the family's feelings. Therefore admission services should be focused on the family as well as the individual older person.

Pre-admission procedures

When a suitable vacancy occurs, the applicant and family are notified by the social worker that there is the possibility of admission, and an interview is arranged at the institution if possible. The worker should expect that in some situations the actual prospect of admission will restimulate client and family ambivalence about institutionalization and reactivate relationship problems. Plans for admission may be delayed or altered. In some cases the older person and/or family may decide to withdraw the application. The worker's role is to offer skilled casework to enable those concerned to make a decision that is in the best interest of the older person and family, whether or not admission results. If admission is not to occur, the worker should help the family to make an appropriate alternate plan and connect them with all possible supportive community resources.

PREPARING APPLICANT AND FAMILY.   The purposes of the pre-admission interview are:

- To offer casework help to applicant and family in their psychological recapitulation of the decision-making process, and to give them an opportunity to express and receive help with the feelings stimulated.
- To reassess functional capacities and bring health information up to date, since the capacities

of older people may change rapidly. If there is question about the applicant's capacity to function in the area in which he/she is to be placed, nursing staff may be asked to see him/her for evaluation.

- To schedule chest X-ray if one has not been taken within past six months.
- To review financial arrangements.

The worker who will be giving services to the resident after admission is included in the interview and participates in making specific admission arrangements. He/she shows applicant and family the room available, introduces the prospective roommate, and answers any questions about the facilities and services of the particular area.

Other goals of the pre-admission interview(s), with both applicant social worker and resident social worker present are:

> To permit the older person to participate in the admission process, and to forge links from past to future. For example, choices are developed and offered deliberately: what day they wish to arrive, what small articles they wish to bring (family photos, a favorite chair, a radio, TV, plants . . .).

> To review the mechanics of admission. Discussion includes setting time and date of admission and explaining that drugs and instructions for dispensing them should be brought to be given to the nurse. At the PGC, name tapes are ordered at the time of application. They are given to the family when the admission is being arranged to be sewn to clothing, thus minimizing loss through laundering.

The social worker gives the applicant and family a "welcome booklet" that introduces and orients them to the services and programs of the facility. It notes important names (roommate, social worker, nurse, doctor) and describes events that will take place soon after admission (such as medical examination, laboratory studies). The booklet also contains factual information about visiting hours, mealtimes, laundry, canteen, and a host of other matters.

The social worker informs the client that he/she will be present at admission to help him/her get settled and will continue to be available if necessary. However, the client is introduced at this time to the social worker who serves the area in which he/she will live. The resident social worker is available to answer questions, and to give the prospective resident a preliminary introduction to his/her new home. The social worker's presence symbolizes and emphasizes continuity of consideration and care. The resident social worker will work with applicant and family after admission. He/she has an office on the floor and makes daily rounds and thus is in an excellent position to monitor the adjustment period. The application social worker, however, will stop by a few times until the transition has been fully effected.

PREPARING RESIDENTS AND STAFF.   Just as efforts are made to prepare applicant and family for admission, the facility, its residents, and its personnel must be prepared to receive him/her. Whether referrals and evaluations have been made by other agencies or the facility has its own social work staff, relevant social and medical information should be made available to the administrator of the receiving facility to enable him/her to plan for the older person's care and treatment.

A variety of tasks should be carried out prior to admission:

> The occupant(s) of the room should be prepared for their new roommate.

The social worker should write a social summary of the case which subsequently will be incorporated in the social service section of the medical chart. A suggested outline for the summary appears in Appendix B. In order to personalize the new resident and to orient staff to his/her needs, it should include in concise form brief social information that bears on the care, treatment and program planning for the new resident, and present his/her unique needs, capacities, family relationships, interests, and background. Information that is not relevant to care but would violate the principle of confidentiality should not be included. Copies of the summary can be distributed to all department heads (administration, recreation, P.T., volunteers, housekeeping, maintenance, food service) to enable them to prepare to offer personalized help to the new resident.

All health reports and forms should be incorporated in the resident's medical chart.

Notification of admission with appropriate relevant information should be sent to all departments.

Interdisciplinary pre-admission case conference is desirable to review available information about the potential new resident in order to develop a coordinated treatment plan. A post-admission team conference should be scheduled for a prescribed time after admission (two weeks is an appropriate interval) in order to evaluate the resident's adjustment and reformulate the plan if necessary. This should be repeated every ninety days. (The principles underlying interdisciplinary conferences are discussed in Chapter 8.)

A WELCOMING ATMOSPHERE.   Beyond these preparations a variety of other means can be employed to create a welcoming atmosphere. The attitudes and warm concern of all staff are of utmost importance. Some facilities have welcoming committees of other residents. A token gift such as a small bouquet of flowers, a plant, or a toilet kit with comb, powder, toothpaste or other necessities and amenities to greet the new arrival is a warm note of welcome. A handwritten letter extending good wishes from the agency's board of directors is another way of making the new resident feel valued. In appropriate situations, an "orientation volunteer" can be on hand to greet the new resident and to stay with him/her throughout the first day or two. The goal is to provide a friendly, interested person who can help the resident become familiar with the routines, location of facilities, services, and personnel of the institution. The volunteer smooths the way and reports any problems that may arise to the social worker. Such volunteers must, of course, receive special training from the social worker and work under close supervision.

Admission day

On arrival the new resident and family are greeted by the application social worker, the resident social worker, and the orientation volunteer. All except the volunteer are present at the brief admission formalities that take place in the office of the administrator. The nurse is introduced, assures the resident of continuity of medical care, and takes charge of medications. He/she is then accompanied to her room by resident social worker, volunteer, and family members. Family members are encouraged to remain as long as possible to help with the initial tasks of unpacking and getting settled and to be on hand for the first two or three days to provide support. The resident social worker takes an active role in preliminary orientation.

One goal at this stage is to begin the process of

keeping family ties as strong as possible. Even the most devoted family may psychologically equate institutionalization with the relinquishing of all responsibility to the institution. Family members may be unaware of possibilities for their continued activity in sustaining the relationship. One means of doing this is to include the family in planning a program for the resident and for being actively participant in that program. The resident social worker and/or activities therapist should interview the family member(s) immediately after admission for this purpose. The family can be told of the recreational, therapeutic and work-oriented programs that will be tailored to the resident's needs.

At the same time, family members will be asked how they can contribute to the program. Can they set a regular day of the week on which they can take the resident to their homes for dinner? Can they plan regular times to visit so that the resident knows when to expect them? Can they continue previous activities related to keeping the resident's life as connected to family as possible, such as shopping trips, participation in family parties and special events? One way of symbolizing the family's "contract" or commitment is to ask them to complete a form so that institutional personnel can plan accordingly by, for example, having the resident dressed appropriately when the family arrives to take him/her out. An example of such a form is given in the Appendix (p. 347). It is supplemented soon after admission by an activities form (p. 348), which also serves to begin planning for an individualized activities program for the resident.

Intensive social services are offered during the adjustment period. The goals are to provide support and understanding and to help the resident become part of the institutional community and feel comfortable and familiar with the physical facilities, and use the services and programs.

Chapter 8

SERVICES TO RESIDENTS AND FAMILIES

Philosophy of Care

The basic goal of long-term care facilities stems from the meaning of the word "life." Life is defined by Webster as animate existence, as that which imparts or excites spirit or vigor, the exercise of vital activities. Implicit in this definition is a rejection of the notion of custodial care in favor of a positive philosophy of active treatment and rehabilitation. The interrelated and mutually dependent components of "life" in an institution are:

1. Maintenance services, to preserve biological life, such as adequate shelter and environmental safety, food, and sanitation.
2. Health services, to maintain maximum health and functional capacities, such as

medical and nursing care, physical medicine and rehabilitation, and special nutritional programs.

3. Personal services, to provide the care the older people's disabilities prevent them from providing to themselves such as dressing, feeding, toileting, grooming, bathing, and transportation.

4. Psychosocial services: (a) a physical and social environment designed to communicate a view of each elderly person as a unique, dignified, and respected individual, and (b) life-enriching and life-enhancing services to help each individual live with full realization of his/her potential for well-being and enjoyment. In this cluster of services are the social work services, activities (therapeutic and recreational), pastoral counseling, and work-oriented activities.

The importance of meticulous attention to the first three groups of services is self-evident. Although there is a welcome trend to health programs, they are still neglected in many facilities. As important as providing quality health care is the manner in which it is given: the patience, compassion, kindness, and respect, with the caring and hope conveyed.

If only those components of care are attended to, however, the needs of elderly residents are only partially met. Social death may occur though biological life is maintained. The frontiers of long-term care therefore must be pushed beyond survival, subsistence, and the treatment of disease to dignity and enjoyment. To underscore, life must be invigorated as well as supported; mere existence is impoverished and sterile if it is not animate. To give life meaning through dignity, enrichment, and enjoyment, it is essential to emphasize each resident's positive capacities (existing or potential) and to build on the healthy areas: the strengths, function, self-determination, humor, assertiveness, capacity for enjoyment, creativity, gratification of work, and satisfaction of accomplishment. Special efforts should be made to support meaningful personal relationships and to provide opportunities for continuity of social roles and development of new ones—roles such as that of parent, sibling, grandparent, friend, group member, participant in occupational and recreational activities, volunteer service-provider.

The negative effects of institutionalization have received considerable attention in the literature. It has also been pointed out that the poor mental health of many residents is due to the nature of the population as well as to the institutional environment per se, and that various institutions have different characteristics which may affect their elderly residents in different ways. Certainly the constructive approach is to work with both individual and environment. Identification of negative factors offers clues to possible remedies.

A sense of autonomy and control over one's own destiny are overriding factors conducive to mental health; apathy results when they are lost or lacking. The collapse of self-determination, the need to turn to others for care, and the surrender of the direction of one's personal life are among the most profound negative effects of institutionalization. Other detrimental factors noted by practitioners and research investigators are dependency, depersonalization, and low self-esteem; loss of occupation and lack of opportunity to fill one's time fruitfully; geographic and social distance from family and friends; tenuousness of new relationships; inflexibility of institutional routines and menus; loneliness; loss of privacy, identity, own clothing, possessions, and furniture; lack of freedom; desexualization and infantilization; crowded conditions; and the intermixing of the mentally intact with the mentally abnormal.

Attitudes of staff have a direct impact: physical dependency and mental confusion increase when staff have negative, disrespectful, or belittling attitudes. Conversely, more positive mental conditions are related to permissive, friendly staff attitudes and positive expectations. Studies have also shown the favorable effects of freedom and encouragement of competent behavior; of opportunities for choice, social responsibility, and social interaction with other residents and with people outside the institution.

In institutions beginning with a low level of physical and mental care, dramatic improvements have been achieved by attention to basic medical and nursing care. A variety of programs have been developed that aim to improve social functioning. Examples are the therapeutic community, special group activities, occupational and social therapeutic techniques, a highly individualized interdisciplinary program, Reality Orientation, remotivation, and behavior therapy. Activities programs with apathetic elderly resulted in new interest of the residents in personal grooming, conversational interaction, initiation of activity, and desire to work; programs introducing meaningful work effected higher adjustment, better health, feelings of usefulness and contentment, increased self-reliance, and a reduction in the need for excessive care. In an institution providing a high level of care to begin with, even the most regressed older people improved when highly individualized treatment was tailored to their unique life experiences, personalities, and needs. (Chapter 17 summarizes some of the major studies of treatment of institutionalized elderly people.)

In any approach, just as in physical rehabilitation, it is important to gear the goals to the individual's level of impairment. While successful treatment elements are often related to previous occupational and recreational interests, there is also potential for new learning.

Basic to all the clinical and research findings is the clear message that the elderly impaired institutionalized individual retains the "whole person" needs which characterize all human beings. It is paradoxical that increased specialization has often resulted in fragmentation and compartmentalization. While institutionalized old people may share some characteristics, they vary widely in behavior, personality, socioeconomic background, types of mental and physical disabilities, level of functioning, and reactions; and many even represent different generations. Practitioners often tend to view the elderly person in terms of their own specialities, while the interrelationships among the various disabilities—that is, the individual's unique combination of mental, physical, and social problems—require careful study to provide the key to accurate diagnosis and appropriate treatment.

In recognition of the wholeness of the elderly institutionalized individual, he/she should be referred to as a "resident" rather than a "patient." Like his/her peers in the community, and no matter how intensive and extensive the need for medical and nursing services, he/she is only partly a patient. The organization of services and the physical and social environment should reflect an emphasis on the whole individual as a social being and on social as well as physical rehabilitation.

Institutions for the elderly tend to borrow the patterns of the health facilities in which its personnel have been trained. Many of the services offered by general, psychiatric, and rehabilitation hospitals are appropriate to be incorporated in the long-term care facility. However, the atmosphere and service delivery patterns of those other types of facilities are not appropriate. Just as new patterns of delivering medical and mental health services are evolving in the community, so should medical and nursing routines be reshaped as part of social matrix of the long-term care facility.

The aging person's functioning, impaired though he/she may be, cannot be preserved or improved if he/she is assigned the role of full-time professional patient. His/her person and dress, the room in which he/she lives, the opportunity for privacy, the rhythm of his/her daily life, the range of program elements from which he/she can select (or which he/she can ignore) should convey the fact that the institution is his/her home, and should permit expression of his/her personal life-style. Most important, ways should be found to permit as much control as possible over his/her own life. The shape of the programs should serve him/her rather than attempt to mold him/her into firmly frozen routines. To provide a sense of continuity of life-experience, ties with the past should be encouraged through interpersonal relationships (with family and friends), through the physical environment (furnishings and room decorations), and through services and programs.

Admission to an institution need not and does not constitute total separation from family and friends in terms of termination of relationships. Continuity of relationships should be supported and encouraged. As during the pre-admission processes, family members should be included as recipients of the institution's services.

The family patterns of relationship continue to be expressed during the old person's residence in the institution just as they were during the decision-making process prior to admission. Many adult children and other relatives visit regularly, evidence warm interest and concern, and behave responsibly. Other familiar figures on the institutional scene are the relative who has a myriad of complaints about the care of the old person, the daily visitor who attempts to take over institutional routines, and the adult child who refuses to permit rehabilitative and even life-saving medical procedures. When previous interpersonal problems are continued or projected onto the institution and its personnel, help extended to the family members is often the most effective treatment for the elderly resident. Individual counseling and group programs for relatives have been found to be therapeutic in helping them understand their older relative's behavior, resolving their feelings about placement, and understanding institutional programs.

Objectivity is required in evaluating the family relationships of the institutionalized elderly. The latent content of the complaints of many old people is the desire to be young and healthy again—expressions of longings which cannot be fulfilled. When complaints about children are the manifest content of such verbalizations, this should be understood, rather than blaming the adult children for unfeeling rejection.

The success of efforts at stimulating life—animated existence—depends on the climate set by the administrator and the expectations of staff and their willingness to synthesize the life-sustaining functions with the life-enriching activities and to do so with compassion and humor. Long-term facilities must constantly seek new ways of integrating their services to liberate them from dependence on traditional patterns. The new blend should include the exercise of vital activities, the animate life, as a basic ingredient rather than—as occurs too often now—as the seasoning sprinkled, however liberally, on the staple of hospital-like routines.

Staff attitudes and behavior are of prime importance if that goal is to be achieved. Too often, the "good" resident is the one who doesn't assert himself. The regressed, brain-damaged individual, incontinent, confused, and disoriented, may be treated as a child rather than as a dignified adult. It is often easier to "do for" than to encourage the resident to do for himself, simpler to use hospital clothes than the resident's own clothes, easier to keep him quiescent through drug "therapy" than to initiate programs of stimulation and activity, less trouble to overuse geriatric chairs than to have the old people "wandering about" or in "danger of falling."

Decisions regarding the care of all institutionalized older people require the most careful consideration. With the best intentions in the world, an overprotective staff can infantilize and humiliate them through deprivation of the rights and privileges due all adults in exercising choice about their own lives. For example, should a fragile eighty-seven-year-old woman be prohibited from attending a family wedding because it is "bad for her health?" Should residents' diets be controlled rigidly? Should mentally intact people in possession of the facts be prevented from making decisions simply because they are old and in an institution? Or should they have the same right to minor health delinquencies as those living in the community? Do the readers of this guide invariably regulate their lives in accordance with their own best health interests? A delicate balance must be struck between providing quality health care on the one hand and using power vested in staff to control every aspect of existence.

The most sophisticated professional prescriptions for care of the institutionalized often rely for their practical success on those personnel who are in continuous contact with the residents. The professional programs converge at the point of service delivery by nursing aide, orderly, dining room waitress, and maintenance worker. Continuing dialogue at every level of staff development and training are necessary to communicate the goals of "animate life," the importance of personal ties and an appreciation of small gains. The direct-care personnel are the ones with whom the resident is in contact most of the time. They are the implementers of treatment plans, and their intimate observations are necessary in the formulation of those plans. Wherever intensive efforts have been made to foster positive attitudes, not only have there been therapeutic dividends for the residents, but staff morale has improved.

Finally, the goal of animate life must be seen also in the perspective of the long-term care required and realistic expectations of what constitutes therapeutic gain. An acceptance of chronicity with the need for sustained input of services has not been fully realized in relation to the aged in long-term care facilities. Words and phrases like "cure" and "return to community," while appropriate in other contexts, are not always applicable to this group. Physicians have long accepted the need for sustained treatment for chronic medical problems such as diabetes, heart disease, and arthritis. By their very nature, the disabilities of old people in need of long-term care require continuing, sustained treatment.

For the aged, therapeutic gain must be defined in terms of small goals. The more global expectations that are indices of improvement with other groups, such as discharge from institution to community, reemployment, or reconstruction of family relationships, are not always applicable. When the aged person moves from wheelchair to walker, from apathy to a minimal level of social participation, from total disregard of simple grooming tasks to their performance; if decline is forestalled or retarded—these, too, are legitimate therapeutic achievements. For family members, if the pain attendant upon separation or the decline of the parent can be eased to some degree, this can be counted a therapeutic success as well.

All procedures related to care of elderly residents should be suitably molded in accordance with these concepts of maintenance of health, dignity, enjoyment, family relationships, sustained care and treatment, and realistic goals.

GOALS

The overall goals of social work services to residents are:

> To participate in the provision of a comprehensive, integrated and continuous program of care and treatment.
>
> To enable residents (and family members) to use their own personal resources, institutional resources, and community resources in order to function at optimum levels of health and well-being.

Long-term care facilities are essentially living arrangements, indicating approaches geared to consideration of the needs of the "whole" individual with careful attention to psychological and social needs. In accordance with this viewpoint, the social environment should be personalized as much as is feasible within the limits of a congregate living situation. As was true of services to applicants, it is important to provide opportunities for choices and alternatives to the greatest possible extent.

The resident, while a member of the institutional community, has a long personal and social history of connection with family and the outside community. These ties should be supported and encouraged; institutional placement should not represent abrupt and final termination of those relationships.

Finally, it is important to note that the definition of "optimum" functioning and therapeutic goals include arresting or retarding deterioration as well as restoration or improvement. This by no means implies a pessimistic attitude. The objectives are treatment and service, not custodial care.

A question often posed is whether *all* residents of long-term care facilities require social work services on a continuing basis. It is desirable that all residents always have *access* to social service, whether or not services are required at any given moment. The actual need for and utilization of social work by an individual will vary from time to time.

However, there are certain events and situations that by their very nature are stressful to all older people and family members. The preceding chapter described the stresses that occur prior to admission. The initial period of residence is also a critical time requiring special attention. The older person is experiencing new losses: of privacy, familiar places, people, and routines, even of familiar food and furniture. He/she may react to group living by experiencing a sense of loss of identity and individuality. Feelings of helplessness may be engendered by the need to be cared for and be dependent on unknown people. Admission often symbolizes death. Unresolved feelings may be projected onto the institution in the form of complaints about staff, food, roommates, and other aspects of the facility. If disturbed behavior occurs, the social worker should help other staff to understand the new resident's underlying feelings of, for example, anxiety, rejection or fear of loss of control. Other stressful experiences are moves to hospital or infirmary, discharge, major changes in functioning capacity, and interpersonal losses. These will be discussed in more detail below.

The need for services at such times does not imply that all the social work services are crisis- or problem-oriented. On the contrary, social work should consistently aim to effect positive changes in the resident's functioning and in the environment. Residents, like all human beings, need warm personal relationships. They require a sense of belonging and of future, of feeling loved and cared for, and of being worthwhile and productive. The social worker should be sensitive to opportunities to further those positive goals.

STAFFING PATTERN

It is desirable for social workers offering services to residents to be assigned to a floor or section of the facility and to be responsible for social services to all residents in that particular area.

In order to facilitate this kind of service approach, the social work offices for services to residents should be dispersed and located near the living quarters of those residents. In this way, the social worker can become an integral part of the milieu and culture of his/her assigned area. It becomes possible for him/her to establish close working relationships with all other personnel who are in direct intimate contact with the resident and who are responsible for day-to-day care (such as recreation therapist, physician, nurse, orderly, aide, housekeeping and food services personnel). As a member of these floor teams, he/she can convey understanding of the resident's behavior and needs and can also gain insight from the observations made by other personnel from their special vantage points. When a resident is moved to a different floor or facility, the case should be transferred to the social worker in the new area.

Many facilities have infirmaries (and some of the larger ones have their own hospitals) to which residents are admitted for treatment of acute illness. Patterns of social service vary. The social worker from that resident's permanent living area may continue to provide service throughout the period of hospitalization. Such a pattern has the advantage of giving the resident a sense of continuity when so many other changes have occurred in his/her life and environment.

An alternative plan is to have a special social worker assigned to the infirmary or hospital. Such a social worker is able to make daily rounds, is readily available, and is thoroughly familiar with hospital personnel. The hospital staff may find it more efficient and effective to relate to one social worker rather than many coming in from different areas of the facility. This pattern by no means precludes frequent visits from the social worker from the residential area. It is extremely important for the two social workers to be in close communication and to work collaboratively.

At the Philadelphia Geriatric Center, the pattern was changed from the first described above to the latter when a new and enlarged hospital was constructed. One of the factors influencing the decision to change was the size of the facilities. Though located on the same grounds, the geographic distance between some living areas and the hospital is great. Another factor was the availability of the hospital to patients from outside the center complex who live in the community and return there when their hospitalization is over. Such patients all receive social services as a matter of routine, and the presence of a hospital social worker is a necessity.

In order to provide continuity of social work service when the new pattern was instituted, a referral form from resident social worker to hospital social worker and a summary form from hospital worker to resident worker were developed (Appendix M and Appendix N). These are incorporated in the medical chart. They supplement—not substitute for—frequent telephone and personal communication between the workers concerned.

When the facility transfers a resident to an outside hospital, it is of prime importance for the resident social worker to notify that hospital's social work department, to keep in close communication, and to phone and visit the resident. Such continuity is important since it conveys to the older person that he/she has a future: that he/she will be returning "home," and that the facility and its staff still consider him/her parts of its family.

Social Work Methods

The three main methods of accomplishing the social work goals in long-term care facilities, while interrelated, can be grouped as follows:

1. To provide direct individual and group social services to residents and families. Group services will be dealt with separately in Chapter 10.
2. To collaborate with other staff and professionals both in and outside of the facility in developing and implementing coordinated individualized treatment programs and supportive services.
3. To modify the social and physical milieu through participation in effecting positive changes.

Direct Social Services

The social worker represents to the resident and his/her family the interested professional person who is available

(a) for help in relation to the problems attendant on institutional living and the aging process; and (b) to enable the resident to relate him/herself and his/her individual needs to the complex of services and programs. An essential ingredient is the selection and tying-together of the institutional and community services to comprise individualized programs. The social worker, as the advocate of his/her client, provides this liaison.

The social worker offers services to residents with respect to:

1. Orientation to the facility's services and help in enabling him/her to avail him/herself of them on a continuing basis.

2. Maintenance of ties with the community: family, friends, previous group memberships; visits to family, attendance at family social events.

3. Sustaining previous life roles to fullest extent possible, and finding new or substitute roles.

4. Significant changes in resident's life situation, such as preparation for moves within the facility or to the hospital, roommate changes, transfer (permanent or temporary) to other community facilties.

5. Interpersonal and emotional difficulties and problems in social adjustment, such as difficulties in relationships with other residents, family, and staff; emotional problems connected with or exacerbated by changing physical and mental capacities, concerns about bodily functions, and illnesses; problems related to use of the institution's services: refusal to follow prescribed medical regimen, inability or lack of motivation to

participate in appropriate activities and programs, complaints about food, laundry, housekeeping or other services, and so on; behavior which presents problems in management or is disturbing to other residents; difficulties in adjusting to current or new routines; changes in affect, behavior, or personality such as depression, anxiety, withdrawal, uncontrolled aggression.

As during the application phase, family members are legitimate recipients of social services. Not only are family attitudes and relationships important to the overall well-being and adjustment of the resident, but the situation of the elderly family member affects the well-being of his family members. The social worker offers help to the family through the initial separation and adjustment period, supports continuing relationships, and has ongoing contacts with family members with respect to problems concerning the resident. He/she may, for example, interpret the resident's changing physical and mental capacities, treatment procedures, and reasons for moves to different facilities. Other family problems which become apparent but are not related to the resident should be referred to other social agencies for counseling, economic and medical aid, employment, and other services.

Collaboration with Other Staff and Community Agencies

The second social work method is collaboration with other personnel to develop individual and group programs and to mobilize the resources of the facility on behalf of the resident. Though a wide array of services may be available, their existence is no guarantee that they will be used by the resident to his/her best advantage.

Through his/her intimate knowledge of the individual older person and of institutional services, the social worker enables the resident to use them. The resident and the service must be connected through linkages developed and implemented by the social worker in collaboration with other staff. That is, the resident must be made aware of the existence of the services, motivated to use them, and enabled to do so by scheduling and often by way of being transported physically to the site of the service. (In some facilities a special category of personnel called "transporters" are employed; in others, the nursing staff handles this task).

The social worker participates in the development of coordinated treatment programs by sharing with other staff pertinent social information which bears on the understanding and management of each resident. He/she shares in diagnosis and formulation of treatment plans by contributing evaluations of the role of social and personal factors (history, past and present family relationships, previous personality patterns). He/she implements those plans by the direct individual services described above and by the group services described in Chapter 10.

Just as community services were mobilized during the application phase, they should continue to be utilized during the period of residence. The social worker can marshal community resources such as educational services, income maintenance programs, religious activities and many other resources. The facility's own resources are thereby supplemented, the resident's horizons are enlarged, and residents and the facility become more related to the total community rather than separated from it.

The process of communication with other staff of the facility, which began during the admission phase, continues during the period of residence.

Daily rounds and knowledge of each resident means that the social worker is sensitive to problems that arise and is not dependent on other staff for "case-finding." It is important, however, that other staff understand the social worker's role and alert him/her to problems they may note, since they are in frequent contact with the resident. Some criteria for referrals by other staff to social service are:

The resident is experiencing difficulty in adjusting to routines.

The resident is evidencing changes in behavior or personality.

The resident complains of lack of family interest of family difficulties, of conflict with roommate or other residents, or expresses dissatisfaction with services or programs.

Social information and service is needed to assess role of personal and social factors in the resident's reaction to illness, to motivate him/her to more effective use of treatment program, or to formulate a plan for management.

Communication with Other Staff

Communication with other departments is both formal and informal. It is hardly necessary to say that the social worker and other personnel constantly and informally discuss the residents and their welfare. Depending on the needs and size of the particular facility, various more formal methods of communication are possible. Some examples follow.

ENTRIES IN THE MEDICAL CHART.   The medical chart is a most important document for coordinating care of the resident. It is therefore essential that it include pertinent social information, because such information has a direct bearing on the resident's health care. Since health personnel constantly refer to the chart, it is an excellent means of effecting communication. The social service chart summary in the chart separater for that purpose should be followed periodically by a brief narrative summary of the resident's progress and social service activity.

In addition, current information which the social worker wishes to communicate to the medical and nursing personnel is noted on the chart whenever indicated. The social worker should write these notes on the progress notes of the chart. The written comments should always be brief, initialed by the social worker, and dated. A rubber stamp saying "Social Work" is a useful way of making those notes stand out. If more detailed information is required, the progress notes should draw attention to a longer report added to the social service section of the chart.

The format of the medical chart varies in different facilities. The social worker should be thoroughly familiar with the charts, and, if necessary, receive instruction from the physician and/or nurse on how to read and understand them. If the chart does not include a social service separater, the social worker should consult with the medical staff to interpret its purpose and value so that it will be incorporated. Though not all facilities use integrated progress notes, the most progressive health settings are strong advocates of this practice.

CONSULTATION REQUESTS FROM STAFF PHYSICIANS. Staff physicians or other health personnel may send to the social worker a request for consultation on a specific problem. The same consult form used by the physician for consultations from medical specialists may be used for this purpose. The social worker replies promptly in the space provided on the consult form, which becomes a permanent part of the medical chart. The information may, of course, be augmented by other verbal or written communication.

PSYCHIATRIC EVALUATIONS.   If possible, each new resident should have a routine psychiatric evaluation soon after admission. A copy should be sent to the social worker and become part of the case record. The social worker usually confers with the psychiatrist when a special referral has been made, and periodically when a resident is receiving psychotherapy.

INTERDISCIPLINARY CONFERENCES.   The number and focus of interdisciplinary conferences varies widely among different facilities. However, there are several basic underlying principles.

WHO PARTICIPATES.   Participation should not be limited to the traditional professional team of psychiatrist, physician, nurse, psychologist, and social worker. Other staff have major contributions to make and should be involved as the needs of each situation dictate. For example, administration should participate if the treatment plan involves changes in administrative and department routines or modification of policies, changes in staff organization, physical facilities, or the development of new programs. Obviously, in a large institution the administrator may not be able to attend all conferences. There should be regular methods of channeling information to him/her, such as minutes of meetings, special memoranda, and personal communication. Those responsible for recreational and occupational activities view the resident from a special vantage point and are in a position to develop programs that greatly enrich the life of the resident. Direct care personnel such as practical nurses, aides, and orderlies can often provide valuable observations about the resident. Other personnel, such as medical specialty consultants, housekeeping, maintenance, and food service, may be added when indicated in special situations.

Any staff member should have the privilege of requesting a team conference or suggesting that a particular resident or problem be placed on the agenda.

FORM OF CONFERENCE.   While interdisciplinary conferences are a well-established method of evaluating or diagnosing, they are ineffective unless concerted efforts are made to develop specific, concrete plans to implement them. Reevaluation should be scheduled for a specified future time to determine whether goals were achieved and to reformulate the plan. This is in the best interests of the staff as well as the residents. The small improvements that are made gain considerable visibility and thereby counteract the pessimism that plagues facilities where complete "cures" do not take place. Such feedback of the results of their efforts is encouraging to staff and stimulates a dynamic rather than static approach.

In preparation for a conference, each team member should evaluate the resident from the vantage point of his particular expertise. He/she reports his/her evaluation at the meeting. Discussion should result in consensus about treatment approaches and plans. Some methods of spelling out goals and procedures, and evaluating achievement should be employed. Some facilities use variations of the problem-oriented record. A method developed for a research study at the Philadelphia Geriatric Center is a charting form (Appendix O. It compels notation of the particular problem area, prognosis for improvement, specific goal, personnel who are to be active in treatment, and concrete tasks they are to carry out. Finally, it has room to note whether change has taken place by the time of reevaluation. Goals must be specific. For example, a goal should not be "to improve Mrs. A.'s ambulation," but "to help Mrs. A. to learn to use a walker rather than a wheelchair." As the case material shows, many staff people of different disciplines may be involved in that one task.

Social worker's role in team.   A social evaluation should be made by the social worker prior to the team meeting. Additional history may be required of social functioning before, during, and since admission. The report may be oral or written, but always concise and pertinent. It should include aspects of the resident's motivation and capacity to use treatment, as well as social factors that bear on the situation and suggestions for its amelioration.

A recurrent issue about the social worker's role in long-term care facilities concerns the coordination and implementation of the treatment plan developed by the interdisciplinary team. Some insist that this task belongs to the social worker. Certainly, the social worker's role includes helping the resident connect with and utilize all institutional resources and services. However, it is simplistic and unrealistic to expect that the social worker coordinate all team activities.

The pattern in use at the Philadelphia Geriatric Center evolved after years of experience in a setting which serves impaired residents, in which each area is fully staffed with health personnel, and in which there exist many health related departments such as medicine, X-ray, clinical laboratories, physical medicine and rehabilitation (including occupational therapy), and respiratory therapy. The natural and practical coordinator of this particular grouping of services is the senior professional nurse in the particular area of the facility; that nurse is often called the charge nurse or the care coordinator. The natural and practical coordinator of what

may be called the "human services" is the social worker.
The human services include such departments as social
work, activity and/or recreational therapy, diversional activities, pastoral services, and work-oriented activities.

Some facilities are experimenting with a special
category of worker called a "unit coordinator" or other
titles to perform the coordinating role. No perfect solution has been developed or universally adopted. Much
experimentation and evaluation of service-delivery patterns in long-term care facilities should take place.

The PGC pattern requires a strong alliance between
the health team and the human service team. Nurse and
social worker must have open and constant communication, respect each other's viewpoints, values, and skills,
and work together in a spirit of cooperation and mutual
assistance. To the extent that they are able to do so, the
total care of the residents is enhanced immeasurably.
Differences that arise can be mediated and resolved by
administration.

TYPES OF INTERDISCIPLINARY CONFERENCES.   Examples
of interdisciplinary conferences through which coordinated treatment plans are developed are:

> Pre-admission case conference.
>
> Post-admission case conferences to review the
> new resident's adjustment and to reformulate the
> plans made at the pre-admission conference.
>
> Problem-oriented case conferences to deal with
> special difficulties that have arisen with a particular
> resident.
>
> Special program conferences if the facility has
> undertaken a special program, or to facilitate ongo-
> ing programs. Specialists or consultants are often
> added to the basic team for this purpose, depend-
> ing on the nature of the program.

Periodic conferences for each resident to review his/her status in each sphere and revise the program of care if necessary.

"Floor team" or "area team" conferences are an excellent means of coordinating the care of the individuals residing in a particular area of the facility. It is highly desirable for these to take place weekly. They are an excellent vehicle for the development of the care plans required by Medicaid and for collaborative efforts between the "human service" and "health" teams. Problems that have arisen can be discussed, and preventive and therapeutic measures instituted at the earliest possible time. Crises can be averted, and the area personnel have an opportunity to discuss not only individuals, but problems and situations concerning their specific area or floor.

Recording of Consultations and Team Conferences.

Conferences and consultations are invariably noted on the medical chart and in the narrative case record.

RESIDENT MOVES.   On occasion residents are moved from one room to another in the same facility, or, for a variety of reasons, to a different facility. The reasons could be social, such as relationship problems with a current roommate, or need or wish to be closer to dining area, bathroom area, or elevator; health reasons, such as need for hospitalization, infirmary care, or a different level of nursing or personal service. The request or recommendation for such a move may be initiated by the resident him/herself, a family member, or by a staff member of any department. Whether or not the move is voluntary on the part of the resident, it should be discussed thoroughly with him/her and the family by the social worker, and the reasons for the move interpreted.

Moving a resident involves all departments. Clear

communication is an essential component of effecting the moves in an orderly manner for the benefit of the mover, other residents, family members, and institution personnel. The Recommendation for Resident Room Change form (Appendix B) has been developed for this purpose. The form circulates among the following departments: nursing, medicine, social work, and administration. While it may be initiated by any department, it should invariably be returned to the office of the director of the department of social work or to whomever has been designated to centralize moves. In the event that personnel from different departments disagree as to the advisability of a move, the administrator will consult with the staff concerned prior to a decision being made. The form is kept on file until it is possible to accomplish the recommended move. At that time, the social worker prepares the resident, family members, and the roommates involved. The Finalized Room Change form (Appendix B) is then sent to the administrator, who orders the move and notifies appropriate department heads.

TRANSFER SUMMARIES.   If the resident is moving to a facility served by a different social worker, the latter is notified. Transfer of the case takes place at a time selected jointly by both social workers. It is desirable for the social worker to be present at the time of the move to handle any concerns or problems and to minimize disruption.

As at the time of admission, whenever the resident is moved it is important for the personnel who will be caring for him/her to be prepared. In addition to the usual informal verbal exchanges of information, a brief social summary should be written (Appendix B). This summary form can also be used when a new social worker is assigned, even if the resident is not being moved.

Modification of the Institutional Milieu

The third social work method involves modification of the social and physical environment in which the older people live. Any environment has three interrelated aspects: people, programs and services, and physical structures and settings.

THE "PEOPLE" ENVIRONMENT.   This guide has already dealt to some extent with the importance of people to the resident—his/her family, friends, fellow-residents, and staff. Every contact of those in the "people environment" with the resident should communicate attitudes of respect and concern for the resident's dignity. More formally, the social worker interprets personal and social needs and ways in which they should be supported.

Social Work Staff Development.   Another avenue through which social work should contribute is in-service training of both social work staff and other personnel of the facility. Whether the social worker is the only representative of that profession in a facility or is a member of a large social work department, it is important to keep abreast of new knowledge in the field regarding aging, of new resources and facilities, of legislation and governmental regulations, and other matters relevant to improvement of his/her expertise. The social worker's attendance at conferences and institutes, membership in professional organizations, and reading of appropriate journals should be encouraged and supported actively by the administrator.

Where a social work department exists, its weekly staff meetings are an excellent vehicle for staff development. Agendas can include reports on conferences and institutes, summaries and discussion of relationships with other agencies and reports on new resources, presentations and analyses of illustrative cases and groups, examination and improvement of techniques and procedures, and special guests and visitors.

In-service training.   By participating in the in-service training of other personnel, such as nurses, volunteers, and food- and maintenance-service staff, the social worker enhances the overall care of the residents. Several training manuals exist that deal with this subject in detail. In general, the content of training sessions can help other staff to understand the needs and feelings of the residents and their families, the social and psychological concomitants of the losses they have experienced, the meaning and implications of group living, and the relationship between residents' behavior and their past lives. There should be discussion of common problems and ways in which staff can be supportive. It is also advisable to deal with the staff's own reactions to and feelings about the residents and about aging, physical disability, mental impairment, and death.

Volunteers.   In some facilities social work is responsible for direction of volunteer services; in others, this is done by administration or a professional director of volunteers. However, when volunteers give services directly related to the social work department's role they should be trained and supervised by a social worker. Examples are "orientation" volunteers and those assigned as "friendly visitors."

THE PROGRAM AND SERVICE ENVIRONMENT.   The social worker's intimate contact with individual residents and groups of residents enables him/her to observe the impact of the facilities, services, routines, and programs. He/she is therefore in a prime position to initiate and participate in developing new programs and modifying and augmenting those that exist. When such needs are identified, the social worker will collaborate closely with the administrator and other staff to plan for positive change. Interdisciplinary case conferences often reveal the need for changes which can then be planned jointly by the personnel involved.

THE PHYSICAL ENVIRONMENT.   The emphasis on ecology in recent years has restimulated interest in man's relationships to his physical environment. It has been shown that older people as a group are more vulnerable to environmental barriers, stress, and hazards and at the same time have fewer resources with which to cope with them. The elderly in long-term care facilities are even more vulnerable than older people in general. The social worker has a responsibility to observe how the physical environment may impede the social functioning of the older people, and to work with the administrator and staff towards necessary improvements. Examples might be rearrangement of furniture to provide privacy, areas conducive to friendly socializing, pleasant places in which the resident can entertain visitors, redecoration of rooms and social spaces to foster individuality and a homelike atmosphere and to reduce the institutional look.

The social worker should be especially alert to the ways in which the physical environment hinders or fosters the delivery of services and links the older person to the point at which the service is delivered. For instance, a nonambulatory resident is not able to avail him/herself of recreational activities unless there are ways of transporting him/her to the activities or bringing them to him/her. Similarly, he/she cannot utilize casework help if there is no private space in which he/she can talk with the social worker and feel free to verbalize feelings, complaints, and anxieties.

Unfortunately, many long-term facilities in use today are older buildings constructed without information and understanding about how appropriate design can support personal, social, and physical functioning of old people. Nevertheless, many improvements are possible within existing constraints.

Chapter 9

CASE ILLUSTRATIONS

The following case histories illustrate individual services to applicants, residents, and families.

CASE ONE: SUPPORT OF AN ELDERLY PERSON AND FAMILY DURING APPLICATION AND ADMISSION*

Eighty-five year old Mrs. R. had been living with Mr. and Mrs. S., her youngest daughter (age 54) and son-in-law, since the death of her husband eighteen years ago. A six-year-old adopted child was also part of the house-

---

*Case material developed by Mrs. Rose Locker, associate director, Department of Human Services, Philadelphia Geriatric Center.

hold. Mrs. R. had begun to fail physically and became so fearful that she refused to be left alone. If the daughter left the house at any time, Mrs. R. had an anxiety reaction. If the S.'s went out for the evening she waited up for them even if a "sitter" was left with her. Mrs. R. also was having difficulty with the steps in the home, because she had broken her hip one-and-a-half years previously. Her forgetfulness precluded leaving her alone lest she turn the gas on by mistake. She spent most of her time sleeping or clinging to her daughter. The situation caused so much tension in the household that it became detrimental to the daughter's health and marital relationship.

The three other adult children were all in their sixties and could not take responsibility for Mrs. R.'s care. Mrs. S. was angry at her brothers and sister for not sharing the responsibility for their mother and became increasingly resentful of the deprivation of freedom and privacy.

When Mrs. S. began to consider placing her mother in an institutional setting, she suffered intensely from guilt. But she decided that this was the only available and practical solution to the problem. She shared the decision with her mother and siblings. She sought the aid of her older sister and, with the support of the social worker, the siblings shared the planning process.

A social history helped the social worker understand Mrs. R.'s reactions to the proposed plan and the kind of support she would need. The elderly woman's first reaction was an attempt to please her children. Repeating earlier patterns, she feared their displeasure and therefore took a passive role. The pressure was not yet real because of the waiting period. During that time, Mrs. R. and her family received counseling help. Their ambivalence and anxiety resulted in vacillation despite the severe reality pressures.

Finally, admission was imminent. Mrs. R. began to verbalize her fear and anger at the children for wanting to "abandon" her. She had never been "alone" before and feared change. She had experienced abandonment early in life when her own mother died, and the feelings were reactivated.

Plans for her admission were made carefully with full family participation, very frequent visiting, and constant support from the social worker. Prior to admission day Mrs. R. stayed at the Home only for lunch, and it was explained that the daughters would leave for an hour and return. Mrs. R. became very anxious, asked repeatedly for her daughters, and needed a great deal of reassurance from the social worker, whom she had learned to trust. Recognition of her fear that the children would not return was verbalized and reassurance given. In preparation for admission, plans for the move were discussed and meaningful things she could bring with her identified. She was assured of the social worker's presence. She had numerous questions about routines of the Home and how her needs would be met. Concern about her health was paramount: she feared illness, doctors, and hospitals.

On admission day the daughters stayed for several hours to help Mrs. R. get settled and for reassurance. Her familiar pattern of withdrawal under stress was repeated. She slept a major part of the day and clung to the social worker when awake. She now fully verbalized her resentment at her placement.

For the first few weeks she was tearful and angry at the children's "perfidy" and began to annoy other residents with her woeful tale. Mrs. S., too, was deeply upset and wept during her frequent contacts with the social worker. She expressed guilt and fear that her mother would be ill. The social worker reviewed with her Mrs. R.'s previous reactions to stress and her ability to cope with previous losses as long as she had support. It was important that her daughters sustain their visits to help Mrs. R. make the adjustment.

All departments at the Home were supportive. The activities therapy department was successful in involving Mrs. R. in a knitting group in order to extend her range of social interactions. She began to take pride in her work and became friendly with a few of the other residents. Mrs. R. now attends basic English class, goes to all entertainment events on her own, and uses the elevator by herself—though she had previously lacked the security to do so. Her relationships with her children have improved. They continue to phone her every day and visit frequently.

Mrs. S. recently commented that she knows her mother has succeeded in her adjustment to the Home because, when taken out for a visit, Mrs. R. is eager to return "home."

Case Two: Aging Children Have Difficulty Caring for a Very Old Mother

Mrs. N. applied for admission to the Home when she was ninety years old and had been a widow for twenty-two years. She and her sixty-two-year-old daughter, Helen, had never lived in separate households. When the daughter married forty-four years ago, the young couple made their home with the Ns. Despite her fourscore and ten years, Mrs. N. was neat, agile, attractive, and intact mentally. Her vision had been deteriorating for some years, but she continued to function well. The daughter and son-in-law were not as fortunate. The latter suffered from severe angina and had retired from work. The daughter had been working part-time as a salesperson in order to supplement the family's income, but her health, too, was failing. The family physician insisted that their home be sold and that she and her husband move to a small apartment in a different climate. Mrs. N. therefore moved to the home of a younger daughter, the "baby" of the family and only fifty-five years old. Anna welcomed Mrs. N. in her home, although she was working to help her son through college. This arrangement was short-lived, as Anna soon became acutely ill and was hospitalized. There were, in this family, three other adult children. The oldest, Sam, was seventy-one years old and a semi-invalid. He and his sixty-year-old wife were living on their Social Security income. Fifty-nine year old Lou had taken his eighty-two-year-old mother-in-law into his home. And Sarah, a widow of sixty-four, was living in the household of her daughter.

In this situation, the problems of aging experienced by adult children were the factors leading to the request for long-term care of their very old mother.

Case Three: Disturbed Family Relationships Can Prevent Constructive Planning

An adult daughter was locked in a symbiotic relationship with her mother, the latter completely disoriented, incontinent, needing constant supervision to prevent her from wandering away or setting fires. The two women shared the marital bed, while the son-in-law shared his fifteen-year-old son's room. The grandson could not bring his friends home and had difficulty finding a place to study. The daughter was unable to place her mother despite the husband's ineffectual threats of divorce.

CASE FOUR: DISTURBED FAMILY RELATIONSHIPS

An adult daughter agreed with her eighty-two-year-old mother that the latter should enter a Home. The son, who had not spoken to his sister for many years, opposed the plan and for a time sabotaged it successfully by refusing to participate in financial planning. Both siblings were extremely well off economically. Each attempted to obtain recruits for his/her side of the battle, approaching social workers, physicians, nurses, and administrative personnel of the institution. They induced influential community figures to exert pressure, the daughter to force admission and the son to prevent it. Spouses of the adult children and the grandchildren participated fully in the furious accusations. The manifest problem of financial support finally culminated in a bitter court battle. For hours, the principals and their attorneys attacked and counterattacked. The judge openly stated that he feared hearing this vituperative case had caused his ulcers to flare up.

CASE FIVE: A COUPLE IS SEPARATED WHEN ONE SPOUSE REQUIRES INSTITUTIONAL CARE*

Mrs. B. saw her husband, a vital, active man, who had been a respected community figure, deteriorate with severe chronic brain syndrome. She could no longer care for him at home. The decision to institutionalize him was agonizing. She was angry at the fate which had dealt her such a blow. The loss of her husband's companionship when she needed it most was irreconcilable. Their adult son had his own problems and could not

*This case is summarized from a paper by Mrs. Rose Locker, associate director of the Department of Human Services at the Philadelphia Geriatric Center. The paper, Elderly couples and the institution, appears in *Social Work* 21: 2, March, 1976.

provide the emotional support Mrs. B. needed. Added to all this was the threat of dwindling funds and her fear that after a lifetime of saving to provide for her old age she might end up "on relief." She visited Mr. B. at the institution daily, and some of her misery and anger was projected on the staff in the form of complaints about the care he was being given. There was little emotional feedback from her husband or any hope for his recovery. With considerable casework support, Mrs. B. was able to verbalize the feeling of futility of her situation and the fear for her own survival.

Case Six: Facilitating Admission of a Mentally Impaired Applicant*

For much of her life, Mrs. G. lived in the neighborhood of the Home to which she was admitted at age seventy-two. Though relatively intact physically, she evidenced confusion, disorientation, and poor memory. Application to a Home was necessary because she lived alone, neglected to eat, and could no longer take care of herself or her house. The family felt that the death of her husband and brother within the past few years had accelerated her deterioration. Mrs. G. was thoroughly familiar with the Home prior to admission. Several friends were residents and she had visited them daily, walking the few city blocks from her house through a neighborhood she knew well.

Mrs. G. showed somewhat increased confusion on admission, despite careful preparation. The following day she experienced a severe shock when a daughter from whom she had been estranged for several years visited her unexpectedly. Mrs. G. left the Home every day,

*Case material developed by Mrs. Rose Locker, associate director, Department of Human Services, Philadelphia Geriatric Center

walking back to her own house in a reversal of the pre-admission "visiting" pattern. However, she did not complete the cycle by returning to her new "Home." It was not possible to work with her in traditional ways: she had "forgotten" the events and preparation preceding her move; her mental impairment affected the integrative function of her ego, thus hampering her capacity to adjust to environment change.

A two-fold program to help her was developed that did not rely on cognitive functioning. First, the move to the Home was re-enacted. Fortunately, the house had not yet been sold or emptied of furnishings. Her son re-discussed the proposed sale of the house with her. The physical "moving day" was acted out. Mrs. G. was asked to select some possessions to bring with her to the Home (pictures, candlesticks, etc.). A volunteer companion was assigned to walk with her to her house when she started that familiar trip and to bring her safely back again.

Secondly, a concerted effort was made to repattern her days and to really "move in" to the Home. Her lifetime interests were used to develop an active and attractive routine of recreational and occupational therapy.

Gradually the companion's time was reduced. Mrs. G. still occasionally talked of going home to care for her young children but did not wander out and lose her way. With support, she reestablished old friendships and made new friends at the Home.

CASE SEVEN: SERVICE TO A DEFERRED APPLICANT

Miss O. was a tiny birdlike woman who dressed in a stylized and dated manner. She had been living in the same house for forty-one years. After the death of two sisters who had shared the home with her, she continued to live alone. In spite of her many eccentricities, Miss O.

was likeable and appealing. A well-to-do, socially prominent cousin helped financially but took no sustained personal interest in her.

Spry and active all her life, Miss O. became increasingly anxious as she felt herself growing older and more
feeble. She reached out for help by applying for admission to a Home at the age of seventy-three. In her own
words, the problem of planning "baffled" her. The
prospect of dismantling her beloved house with its accumulated possessions of half a century was overwhelming.

She was lonely, had little money, and was undergoing tests for bleeding from the bowel. When the tests
proved to be negative, she decided not to enter the institution but was afraid to withdraw her application lest
she need admission at some future time. The Home's
social worker offered her "deferred status." This meant
that the Home encouraged her to remain in the community as long as possible, that the social worker would
be available to her when needed, and that she could be
admitted if and when her circumstances required.

At intervals during the ensuing years, Miss O.'s situation would flare up and a small flurry of phone calls
and home visits would ensue. Each time, Miss O. went
through the process of conflict, doubt, hesitation, and
indecision. She would review a number of alternatives,
and express her fears about group living. Each time this
was resolved in favor of staying in her own home a while
longer.

Miss O. was sustained by the knowledge that she
could enter the institution if ever it became really necessary. She remained in her own home with supportive
services from the Home's social worker and from a family service agency. The agencies coordinated their services to avoid duplication of effort. During this period
she had surgery twice and spent time in a convalescent

home. Services of a homemaker and domestic were provided.

Gradually, Miss O.'s telephone calls became more frequent. There were many small crises. Finally, twelve years after her initial application, Miss O. was admitted to the Home. Despite the continuous supportive and practical help, she could not longer function alone. With the support of a staff person from the family agency, her cousin, and the institution, transportation and help with closing and selling her house was provided. She made numerous trips back and forth from the Home to her house to wind up the sale of her house and to dispose of her possessions. The social worker, understanding the meaning to Miss O. of this transition, gave consistent support and help to smooth away the numerous little problems she encountered. The security of the deferred list had enabled Miss O. to live in her own surroundings for twelve years after her application.

CASE EIGHT: A ROOMMATE PROBLEM WITH FAMILY INVOLVEMENT*

The bitterness between roommates Mrs. B. and Mrs. L. had reached the point of each demanding that the other be moved. Stormy scenes occurred, with name-calling in several languages, and the adult daughters of both women were drawn into the fray. The battle lines were drawn. Neither resident would move, and the hostilities reached uncomfortable dimensions, consuming staff time as well as causing distress to the two residents and their families.

The social worker met with the daughters. They be-

*Case material developed by Mrs. Sandra Rotenberg, Program Coordinator, Department of Human Services, Philadelphia Geriatric Center

came aware of each other's problems. The sympathy and understanding that replaced the anger led to their active participation in attempts at resolution of the situation. Mrs. B. and Mrs. L. both were present at subsequent meetings of social worker and adult children. Their attacks on each other subsided when each daughter expressed sympathetic concern with her own parent but openly acknowledged the rights of the other older woman. A truce was effected, with the two residents shaking hands.

Minor lapses have occurred since, but on each occasion, intervention by the social worker and the daughters prevented major crises. Mrs. B. and Mrs. L. were helped by the social worker's genuine concern and sympathy and by their daughters, who gave them positive support, encouraging courteous behavior that preserved their dignity and self-respect.

Case Nine: The Interdisciplinary Approach to Social and Physical Rehabilitation

Mrs. C., age seventy-nine, was slightly over five feet tall and weighed over two hundred pounds. She had a fifteen-year history of orthopedic difficulty dating from an automobile accident. A spinal disc had been removed several years ago to prevent complete immobilization. Unable to walk after the surgery, she spent two months in a rehabilitation hospital. After that she was ambulatory with the assistance of two canes but subsequently regressed to the point of being confined to a wheelchair. A brace was fitted, and Mrs. C. received training in the use of a quad cane but complained of the pain and returned again to her wheelchair. While the pain was real, it was aggravated by her obesity and edema of the legs. Despite her apparent resignation to a passive state, confinement to the wheelchair was frustrating to Mrs. C., who had a lifelong pattern of independence. She defended against the anxiety this created by a bitter humor, and an underlying depression was noted. Her real capacity for enjoyment of social contacts was restricted by her inability to ambulate, and she was therefore unable to partake of entertainment and social events to the degree she would have liked.

An interdisciplinary staff conference was held. Medical evaluation indicated that here was no physical reason that Mrs. C. could not walk. However, two physical conditions had to be relieved: a diet was required to reduce her weight in order to lessen the pain in her arthritic knee, and the edematous legs required daily Jobst boot treatments administered by the physical therapist. A complicating factor was the fact that Mrs. C.'s children brought her food when they visited. The social worker conferred with the children to explain the treatment plan for their mother and to elicit their cooperation. The cooperation was given and maintained. The prescribed diet was changed, and nursing supervision over Mrs. C.'s food intake was tightened.

The social worker stoked Mrs. C.'s motivational fires and encouraged her to tolerate the pain that was inevitable in the early stages. On a twice-daily schedule, Mrs. C. was helped to practice her walking. The distance covered each time was noted, and her weight was recorded weekly. All this was put into graphic form so that Mrs. C. could see her progress pictorially. At one point Mrs. C. mentioned that, between the loss of weight and the increasing ability to walk, she looked forward to putting on a corset, a nice dress, and walking to meals like a "person." She achieved her goal through the collaboration of nurse, physician, social worker, physiotherapist, and dietician.

CASE TEN: HELP TO AN ELDERLY FAMILY LIVING IN A HOME FOR AGED*

Eighty-year-old Mrs. K. had always been considered the "pillar of strength" in her family, caring for her two younger siblings, a mentally ill sister (age sixty-five) and a brother (age seventy-two) who was a borderline retardate. The three were admitted to the Home together. Mrs. K., though still sturdy and intact, had gradually been finding the responsibility of the family and a large house too much for her. In the institution she continued her gratifying role of head of the family, supporting her siblings through the adjustment period. She consulted with the social worker about engaging them in occupational and recreational therapy and in other matters pertaining to their care; she herself readily participated in many activities, including the sheltered workshop.

In working with the younger sister, Mrs. L., the social worker emphasized Mrs. L.'s strengths and adequacy. The woman, who had spent many years in a psychiatric hospital, made new friends and showed an increasing capacity to function independently. Though Mrs. K. was somewhat threatened by this loss of control, she readily responded to the social worker's plan to make her an ally in helping Mrs. L. to become more adequate and independent. The sisters were able to sustain a warm relationship while each exercised her own abilities for satisfying activities and friendships. They shared the sense of responsibility for the brother, relieving Mrs. K. and freeing her to some extent to live her own life.

A year later, Mrs. K.'s condition showed a sudden and marked change. Her work deteriorated, and she appeared confused, disorganized, and disoriented. The

*Case material developed by Mrs. Rose Locker, associate director, Department of Human Services, Philadelphia Geriatric Center

physician hospitalized her. Though she improved to some extent, it was subsequently necessary for her to have continuing supervision and care. Both sisters required intensive casework help through this period. Mrs. K., accustomed to being the "pillar of strength," had difficulty in accepting the need to be somewhat dependent. She was encouraged to maintain the maximum functioning in self-care of which she was capable. The younger sister was distressed by Mrs. K.'s physical and mental changes. In addition to the anxiety she felt at the loss of Mrs. K.'s supportive strength, her own fears about aging and deterioration were stimulated. With the social worker's help she was able to weather the emotional crisis and even to be helpful to her sister, visiting often and offering comfort, affection, and emotional support. The brother continued to do well; though dependent, his new reliance on Mrs. L. and on the institution eased the necessary withdrawal of Mrs. K.'s protection.

Though elderly, these three residents had been helped to achieve a new and improved balance of relationships which stood them in good stead through the stress of Mrs. K.'s deterioration.

CASE ELEVEN: THE IMPORTANCE OF RELIGION IN THERAPEUTIC MANAGEMENT*

An eighty-year-old Jewish man recently admitted to the Home refused all food and fluids. The resultant dehydration made it necessary for him to be hospitalized. The social worker asked the rabbi to see him. Gently probing, the rabbi finally elicited the information that when the man's wife had died, he had taken a vow to say "Kaddish" (the mourning prayer) for her each day. He had

*Appreciation is expressed to Rabbi Meir Lasker of the Philadelphia Geriatric Center for use of this material.

kept his vow until his own disability caused admission to the Home and prevented him from leaving his room to go to the synagogue. The rabbi explained what the elderly man had not known: that one could pray in one's own room. Together, the man and the rabbi recited the appropriate prayer. At lunch that day, the man began to eat and drink.

Chapter 10

SOCIAL GROUP WORK SERVICES

Most of the services described in the preceding chapters have been given on an individual or family basis. Social group work services also have a major role and can be utilized appropriately beginning with potential residents and families during the application phase and throughout the entire period of residence in a long-term care facility. The overall goal of individual and group methods is the same: to support maximum functioning (psychological, social, emotional) of the older people and their families. In Louis Lowy's words, "Basic to social work is the use of the group as an instrument for enhancing social functioning of the individual as a social being."

A question often asked is: Should the emphasis in long-term care facilities be on casework services or on group work services? The answer cannot be framed in either/or terms as though one method can substitute for the other. It is obvious that many social services must be given on an individual basis because of the nature of the need, its uniqueness to a given individual, or its immediacy which cannot await the formation or meeting of a group. Among many examples are the confidential discussion of the individual or family situation precipitating an application, the anxiety and stress of the day of admission, the reaction to an illness requiring hospitalization or to the death of a relative, or an acute flare-up of a relationship problem with a roommate or staff member. Similarly, individual service cannot substitute for some of the benefits achieved via the group process, such as socialization, the therapeutic effect of discussing shared problems, the growth and gratification derived from improving interpersonal skills, or the maintenance or development of roles.

There are many areas in which casework and group work methods complement and supplement each other. The adjustment of new residents can be facilitated by a group focused on problems of making the transition from previous living arrangement to living in the facility. Such a group could reduce (though not avoid entirely) the need for individual service. There are many other instances in which a shared experience or problem (past, current, or future) can be handled fruitfully in groups. This applies as well to groups composed of family members. Examples are groups of family members of newly admitted residents or of residents to be moved to a new facility or floor; and groups of family members apparently experiencing major emotional problems in relation to the elderly relative's personal condition or factors relating to institutional procedures and management.

A related question is the identification of differences between social group work on the one hand and therapeutic activities and recreation on the other. Certainly there are areas of overlap. Readers representing the two different professions are likely to be dissatisfied at least to some extent with any attempt to specify the goals, methods, and tasks or to sort them into separate and discrete categories. Other professionals also may work with groups. For example, in addition to the traditional role of the religious leader (in conducting religious services and individual religious counseling) he/she may work with small groups using religious content as the vehicle or medium. Another profession, occupational therapy, may appear similar to activity therapy when crafts and other media are used as the treatment modality.

It is not the purpose of this guide to become involved in spelling out the theoretical or practical differences between social group work and activity therapy. I have a deep conviction that the two approaches complement each other, that both should exist in any long-term care facility that aims to meet its resident's needs fully, and that they must work in close harmony and collaboration. Together with related services, such as work-oriented activities and religious activities, they form a cluster with a common goal. They carry the programming of a facility beyond the meeting of needs for environmental and personal maintenance, survival, subsistence, and medical and nursing care, and speak to the psychological and social needs that make life and health worthwhile (see Chapter 8). Within the framework of that overall goal, each profession has its own identity and its own emphasis in practice. For social group workers in long-term care facilities, like social group workers in any other setting "the distinctive social work constellation (value, purpose, sanction, knowledge and methodology) is the criterion of their orientation" (Lowy, 1962).

Social group workers focus on enhancement of social functioning. The explicit purpose of their groups of residents often is to deal specifically with problems of adjustment, relationships, reactions to the institutional life-style, mastery and roles. They may sometimes utilize specific activities as the means through which their goals can be achieved (arts such as music, painting, and dance; skills in a variety of crafts).

The social group worker often works with groups of family members around problems or issues relating to the institutionalization and care of the elderly relative. Like all professional social workers, he/she also has special training and responsibility with respect to policy that affects residents (both institutional policy and social policy).

There are a variety of different organizational patterns existing in different facilities. In some, the department of social work is responsible for activities and includes both social workers and activity therapists. In others, there are two separate departments. In still others, social group workers are on the staff of the activities therapy department. There are also different patterns with respect to the relationship between activities therapy and occupational therapy; in some facilities crafts are the domain of O.T., while in others they are handled by activities therapy.

At the Philadelphia Geriatric Center, four departments recently were combined into its Department of Human Services (social work, activity therapy, pastoral counseling, and the work activities center). The special skills of the different professionals by no means are "homogenized." The unified department aims to facilitate communication and planning in order to deliver a coordinated and integrated total program.

In the PGC framework, the activities therapists, who are highly skilled in crafts, music and other media, are responsible for using those skills to enrich the residents' lives by stimulating them to constructive use of time. In addition to working with individuals and small groups, the activities therapists plan and implement large group programs of a diversional nature that add pleasure and sheer fun to the lives of the institutionalized (large parties of different types, bus trips, movies, Family Day, trips to theater and concerts). Families are often invited to participate in both small and large group activities.

Whatever pattern obtains in a facility the flow of information among the various professionals, the feedback from one to another, is of prime importance in enhancing the social treatment and care of the residents. The transmission of social history and information about personality, relationships, and background from social worker to activities worker is essential to the development of a therapeutic activity program. The reactions, degree, and mode of participation of a resident in activities is important information for activities worker to transmit to the social worker.

It should be mentioned that there is a welcome trend (small but insistent) for nurses in long-term care facilities to expand their role to participate in groups with social workers and activity workers. In keeping with changing definitions of nursing tasks in long-term care facilities, some also carry out some recreational activities. Since nurses in contemporary facilities far outnumber human service workers and are present round the clock, this development is of prime importance.

In any case, jurisdictional disputes and the exercise of territoriality are not in the best interest of the residents. Depending on the staffing pattern in a given facility and the objective professionalism of those concerned, "turf" problems can be resolved if the focus is firmly on the residents' well-being, and if there is mutual respect on the part of those concerned for each others' professional competence.

Much of the discussion to follow may be relevant to professionals other than social workers who also work with groups in long-term care facilities. The chapter, however, will focus specifically on social group work with older people in long-term care facilities. It will not attempt to summarize the massive literature on social group work. Rather, it assumes knowledge of the general principles and practices of the profession and will deal only with aspects that are relevant to this special population and special setting.

The Populations to be Served

The characteristics of the older people residing in long-term care facilities were detailed in Chapter 5. Those characteristics have important implications as determinants of the nature of social group work services and the manner in which they should be developed and delivered.

Because there is a tendency to think of elderly people in institutions as a homogeneous group, and because they do share many characteristics, the heterogeneity of the population is underlined once again—in age; personality; family relationships; socioeconomic, religious, and cultural backgrounds; functional capacity; and mental and physical health. This heterogeneity should be reflected in the diversity of the group programs.

Even seemingly obvious characteristics such as age and sex require attention. For example, while all old people in institutions are "old," there is wide variability. The sixty-five-year-old and the ninety-five-year-old have lived through very different periods of history and socioeconomic conditions, have had different educational opportunities, and have been exposed to different cultural and political influences.

Women far outnumber men in long-term care facilities, often in a ratio of three to one. In addition, those most prominent in the old person's immediate environment as caregivers also tend to be female—nurses, social workers, food service and housekeeping personnel. Even the family members who visit most often are the females. In this world of women, it is therefore necessary for the group worker to be sensitive to the needs of male residents for association with each other and for groups geared to their particular interests, needs, and problems.

The physical and mental incapacities of the residents are of prime importance in group services. In contrast to group workers in other settings who work with other populations, more attention must be paid, for example, to how the group is to be assembled. Some members must be dressed and transported to the locale of the group session. Attention to their physical needs (such as toileting) during the meeting must be pre-planned. Deficits of memory and orientation dictate different ways of preparing the older people, such as more frequent reminders of the time and place of the meeting and its purpose and composition. The pace and content of the discussions are influenced by these factors.

Sensory deficits such as poor vision and/or hearing are so universal that they are major determinants of such matters as the size of the group itself, the size of the meeting room and the way in which it is lit, the care with which confusing background noises should be avoided, and the speed, pitch, and clarity of the worker's speech. Even the menu for refreshments must relate to the special dietary needs stemming from chronic illnesses such as diabetes and cardiac conditions.

All of these factors combine to emphasize the need for administrative support of group programs, since they have direct implications for the number and nature of staff involved with preparing for and conducting group sessions. Two group workers may be needed on occasion. And certainly the degree of support and involvement of other institutional personnel are critical in the success or failure of the program. Nursing personnel can schedule medical appointments and nursing procedures to accomodate the group meeting, prepare the residents, physically assist in their transportation to and from group sessions, and attend to nursing needs that arise during meetings. Housekeeping, food service, and maintenance departments also contribute their services in such matters as preparing meetings rooms and providing refreshments.

A common denominator among institutionalized older people is the theme of loss. The losses of physical and mental capacities have been accompanied by interpersonal losses and losses of roles. As indicated in Chapter 5, institutionalized older people are particularly disadvantaged with regard to their familial and social networks and supports. Most have lost (or never had) a spouse, almost half are childless, and many have lost siblings and friends. Because so many are in advanced old age, they often have experienced the death or catastrophic illness of the adult child on whom they depended.

The constellation of roles which constitutes a lifestyle has been severely depleted. The institutionalized older person has lost roles such as worker, parent, spouse, friends, member of a particular church or service association, member of a natural circle of friends. Too often, the only role left supported by institutions is that of "patient," and for the institutional resident the sick role becomes dominant. The result is the sharp reduction—even elimination—of the group affiliations and social relationships needed by all human beings, the loss of which leads to isolation, loneliness, and loss of social identity. Role loss is particularly significant in our culture, which is so oriented to work, to future, and to achievement. The old, particularly those in institutions, are acutely aware that they have stopped "doing something" and therefore are devalued by themselves and others. Their psychological discomfort because of this status is exacerbated by the physiological changes that constrain their ability to participate actively.

Major goals of social group work are therefore to offer substitute roles that are meaningful, to relieve anxiety about just "being," to meet as far as is possible the need for participation in groups, and to restore some sense of future. The group offers opportunities for residents to help each other. Restoration of the role of helper to other people is a particularly valuable way of enhancing self-esteem. In short, the group can provide or replace some of the missing social supplies and provide a sense of belonging.

The establishment of a relationship with the social worker is a first step in alleviating the sense of aloneness experienced by the institutionalized elderly. Even when they are physically in the presence of a group of their peers, meaningful interaction with others may be missing. The hopeless feeling that nothing can be done about the older person's loss of mastery of him/herself too often is reinforced by institutional personnel. Through identification and communication with the group leader, the older person can begin to realize that there are some choices, there are some solutions to his/her overwhelming fears and concerns, that someone cares, and that he/she again can be part of a community. He/she is thereby enabled to move toward establishment of relationships with other group members.

Knowledge about the accumulated deficits, weaknesses, and losses of older people in long-term care facilities has operated to present a one-sided picture that obscures their strengths and capacities. Research and practice, however, offer information that justifies therapeutic optimism. It is known that older people, including those in institutions, have a continuing capacity to develop, to learn, and to grow. Despite the massive assaults to which they have been subjected, they retain many strengths and capacities on which group programs can capitalize to their benefit.

The literature on personality theory is particularly relevant in this respect. It tells us first—and this is one of the most consistent findings—that the human personality essentially is continuous throughout life. Secondly, people do not lose their capacity to adapt simply because they grow old. The truth of that fact is reinforced dramatically when one watches the remarkable "adjustment" so many old people are able to make to a life-style as unnatural as institutional living. And third, for the most part the process of disengagement is not desirable, but occurs more often than not as a result of society disengaging from the old rather than the reverse.

Social group work, then, should build on the individual strengths, previous personality, and adaptive capacities to foster continued "engagement" and social relationships. Old people in institutions, like all human beings, must have some sense of mastery and control. The groupwork injunction to do *with* and *for* that is reiterated so often must be built into group programs for this population. If their participation in the planning and implementation of group programs is supported to the fullest possible extent, their feelings of worth, status, of usefulness and of usefulness and of self-esteem will be enhanced. Since the planning itself necessitates communication with others, social relationships will be fostered and isolation reduced.

Finally, the families of the institutionalized are legitimate recipients of group work services for the extension of help with the problems and stresses they experience that relate to their older relatives. The changes which the older person undergoes result in shifts in roles and relationships within the family. Family members must adapt to those changes. Groups in which family members can share their experiences with others help them to gain a reality perspective.

The family members themselves are often in late middle age or early old age and have experienced many of the pressures that accompany those phases of life, such as illness, interpersonal losses, retirement, and poorer economic status. Their reactions to the admission and residence in an institution of the elderly person must be seen in the context of their own past and current lives. Groups focused on common experiences and problems can help them, their relatives, and the institution itself.

The Setting and Preparation for Social Group Work

The manner in which group programs can be planned and implemented always is influenced by the particular setting—its physical environment, staff, and goals.

Long-term care facilities vary widely in size, physical design, auspice, the background and orientation of the administrator, goals, the number and nature of personnel, and many other factors. In any type of facility, the effectiveness of groupwork programs depends on administrative support and understanding and that of other institutional personnel.

In the words of Cohen and Hammerman, "To be effective, group services in the institution must be understood and supported by all significant institutional elements." They point out the complexities of institutional management that require consideration: medical needs and restrictions of residents, schedules of other services and activities, timetables of nursing shifts and schedules, and different perceptions of residents' needs and priorities among staff, families, and residents. In planning and implementing a group program, the task of the group worker therefore begins long before the actual meeting of a group. The conventional wisdom of the social worker who practices community organization is applicable here. A basic principle is to "always involve at the outset all individuals and groups who are needed to implement the solution." If this principle is not observed, a group program is vulnerable to failure not because of malice on the part of other personnel but because a lack of understanding and the accomodations that must be made.

Involvement of other staff includes, but goes beyond, simple clearances such as whether the meeting room will be clean, available, and have appropriate furniture, whether refreshments can be supplied at that time, or whether a change in nursing shifts precludes nursing help in dressing or transporting residents. Sympathetic understanding and support of the goals of the group are needed. The group worker must be aware that other personnel have different orientations and cannot guess what goes on in a group without explanation and interpretation. Indeed, they may fear that the group is a vehicle for airing complaints about them. When the purpose of the group is discussed with other staff, they can relate to the human needs the group aims to meet and often have valuable suggestions to contribute.

The physical structures of many institutions were not designed with group services in mind. Old buildings planned for other purposes often have been converted to nursing homes. Older traditional homes for the aged, constructed with different, more intact populations in mind, did not envision the myriad of services needed, and space is at a premium. Even in many new buildings, with costs high, appropriate special spaces for group programs often do not exist. Of course, there are some facilities fortunate enough to contain rooms planned specifically for groups or other rooms of the right size, location, and design in which to hold group meetings.

The physical comfort and needs of the group participants should be considered to the fullest possible extent. Spaces that are too vast are as undesirable as overly crowded quarters. Other considerations are doorways that permit access by wheelchairs, nonslippery floor surfaces, chairs that do not tend to tip, and appropriate temperatures and lighting. The room should be made comfortable and inviting.

In the main, social group workers must be prepared for the constraints of physical space. Often the group will be a second or even third use of the space. Dining areas, a chapel, a staff or visitors lounge, or a conference room can double as a group meeting room. Careful scheduling and clearances, of course, are critical. In good weather a small outdoor patio or other natural "room" can be used with the added bonus of fresh air and a change of scenery.

Assuming that communication with other staff has taken place regarding the purpose of the group, the nature of staff involvement, and the meeting locale, the social group worker should follow through to ensure smooth implementation. A useful tool is a schedule, preferably on a weekly or monthly basis. It has been found useful to design such a schedule in the form of a calendar which includes the name of the group, the time and date of the meeting, and the name of the group worker(s) who will lead the group. It is desirable for the calendar to include all group services planned for that time, including those planned by social group workers and activities therapists. When participating residents require assistance to prepare for the meeting (in dressing, transporting, reminding, and the like), it is important to provide the staff responsible with a list of the residents' names well in advance of the meeting.

Administration and other staff should have feedback if their continued support is desired. Support can only be expected if information about the course of the group, its benefits, and the outcome is communicated. Finally, like all people everywhere, staff needs recognition of their efforts and cooperation. Genuine expressions of appreciation are facilitators of continued amicable collaboration.

The Members of the Group

Just as the setting (staff and physical environment) must be prepared for group meetings, each group member must be prepared. The group, after all, is comprised of individuals, each with his or her own unique personality, set of circumstances, and interests, and each with different anxieties and expectations with respect to the group meeting. The worker will have identified potential members depending on the purpose of the particular group.

Within the overall framework of purpose, thoughtful consideration must be given to selection of individuals in terms of the level at which the group process can occur. For example, the purpose of a particular group might be to facilitate orientation and adjustment of newly admitted residents. Though all such individuals could benefit from such a group, it would be inappropriate to mix severely brain-damaged residents with those whose cognitive functioning is intact. The nature, pace, and content of the group process is different for different types of residents. However, if residents with differing capacities are required to live in the same area of a facility, a group could provide opportunities for mutual discussion of difficulties in adjustment that relate to shared quarters.

Prior to the first meeting, the group worker will have met with each member individually. For those with whom the worker did not previously have a relationship, this interview serves to establish one. The resident's anxieties about the group meeting will be reduced if he/she is clear about the purpose of the group, knows which other residents will be members, and is aware of when and where the meeting will take place. The interview with each individual also provides the worker with knowledge about personality, background, and other material that can be used during the meetings.

The resident should be encouraged to make suggestions about the nature of the group and other residents who could participate. It is important for the individual at this early stage to see the group as something in which he/she can participate and which will serve his/her needs, rather than as something planned and imposed by others.

KINDS OF GROUPS

Key to successful programming of groupwork services are creativity and variety—governed, of course, by the needs of the residents concerned. Groups may vary in size and duration, depending on purpose. Some groups may have a time-limited existence, such as a committee to plan a special holiday event or an orientation/adjustment group of new residents. For these, it is important that members know at the outset what are the parameters of the group's existence. Other groups may be ongoing indefinitely, such as special interest or socialization groups. Still others may be ongoing but have a built-in turnover of membership, such as a resident's council for which periodic elections take place. All are vehicles through which residents can gain a sense of purpose through interpersonal relationships.

Certain principles of group work in institutions have emerged in the writings of those who pioneered this field and whose work is listed in the references to this chapter (notably Kaplan, Lowy, Cohen and Hammerman, and Shore). Some of the principles enunciated are:

1. The small homogeneous group is important as a counterbalance to an environment in which so many needs are met en masse.
2. Group work activities cannot be isolated from the institutional context and community context.
3. The worker should begin at the level of the group, gearing its activities and goals to the capacities of its members. No matter how impaired the members, they should not be infantilized.
4. Objectives are enhanced feelings of acceptance, status, self-esteem, and self-confidence, stimulation of interests, decrease in passivity, increase in capacity for enjoyment and pleasure, and fostering personal growth and continuing development. Doing with, not for, therefore is emphasized.
5. Groups are effective therapeutic media, not simply means of filling time.
6. Knowledge of the past personal and social histories of group members, their individual interests, patterns, and personalities is basic to identifying commonalities on which the group can be developed. That is, the *purpose* and the *membership* must fit.

7. The heterogeneity of the population must be matched by diversity of the group program.

To inventory all possible groups that can be formed in a long-term care facility is an impossible task. Similarly, any classification of types of groups would be incomplete, and there is considerable overlapping. Nevertheless, for illustrative purposes and with knowledge that others responsible for developing and delivering group services in institutions can add and reclassify, this guide offers an illustrative, but by no means exhaustive taxonomy. Chapter 11 offers some illustrative summaries of groups at the Philadelphia Geriatric Center.

1. Groups Focused on a Common Experience or Problem Related to Institutionalization

GROUPS OF OLDER PEOPLE APPLYING TO OR ON THE WAITING LIST OF A FACILITY.   The anxieties and psychological and physical stress of applicants have been described in detail in Chapter 7. Groups in this instance may serve not only a supportive or therapeutic purpose but can also be a medium through which institutional policies and procedures are interpreted. They can be a means for helping the potential residents make the transition into the facility through establishing relationships based on a shared experience and becoming familiar with the physical setting. The worker's observations of how individuals function in the group can be valuable in subsequently matching roommates. Variation of this group are the group composed of family members of applicants and groups that include applicants and family members simultaneously.

GROUPS OF NEW RESIDENTS.   A new-residents' group enables members to discuss shared experiences attendant upon such a dramatic change in life-style. It also can be the vehicle for building new relationships and for becoming oriented to the facilities, services, and staff of the institution.

GROUPS OF RESIDENTS WHO WILL BE MOVED TO A NEW AREA OF THE FACILITY, TO A NEW BUILDING, OR TO A DIFFERENT FACILITY.   In view of the literature on relocation effect, this type of group is a necessity to preserve life and health when a move is planned. It is an indispensible supplement to individual casework. The sharing of hopes and fears provide mutual support to residents. Orientation to the receiving facility is facilitated, and the transition is eased. The literature contains descriptions of such groups, and a detailed record of how a group move was managed at the Philadelphia Geriatric Center is also available (see references). Families of residents also should have groupwork service to interpret the reasons for the move, to enable them to express their feelings, and to be given concrete information.

GROUPS OF RESIDENTS WITH EMOTIONAL PROBLEMS. Therapeutic gains can be achieved via the group process with groups composed of residents who are depressed, those whose exhibit behavior problems, or those who appear withdrawn and isolated. Such individuals can, of course, be involved in other types of groups as well. Indeed, ultimate involvement in other groups may be one goal of the group focusing on the particular emotional problem.

GROUPS OF FAMILY MEMBERS.   The group leader must always be careful to maintain a focus on the problems and issues that are relevant to the institutionalization of the older family member. Inevitably, personal or family problems emerge that should be referred to other agencies for counseling. Admittedly, this is often a fine line to draw. It depends on the skill of the worker, who must keep in mind the purpose of the group and the mandate of the agency. Examples of such groups are:

1. Families of applicants. (see above)
2. Families of movers. (see above)
3. Families of residents. There are always some family members who experience severe problems centering on the relationship with the institutionalized relative (usually spouses or adult children, but also other relatives such as siblings, nephews or nieces, grandchildren). Though such problems often have their roots, for example, in long-standing relationship problems or in extreme reactions to age, illness, the decline of the elderly relative, and death, they can be extremely distressing and even disruptive. When projected onto staff and the facility in the form of unrealistic complaints, they can impede adjustment of the older person and consume hours of staff time. Groups of such family members can be helpful to them, the elderly residents, and to the institutional staff as well. An example of such a group is given in chapter 11.

4. Non-institutionalized spouses of impaired institutional residents. As more couples survive to advanced old age, situations are increasing in which one spouse requires institutional care while the other does not. The process of separation is painful; the well spouse often experiences a special intensity of guilt. These feelings may be expressed in ways that impede the adjustment of the impaired resident. A group of such spouses can ease their extreme discomfort as well as benefit the resident and facilitate his/her treatment.

Groups to Foster Socialization

There is an infinite variety of groups in this category. Based on common interests that exist or can be developed, they may be built around a specific activity or on discussion and social interchange. Examples are groups focusing on pursuits traditionally male or female for current generations of older people (sports, sewing, cooking); on political, cultural, or religious interests; on hobbies (cards or other games, crafts, plants, music, painting); or on a shared characteristic (a group composed of couples both of whom reside in the institution). Most groups of this type aim to replace the normal social roles and activities that most people have as they go through life and live in the community. They go a long way toward combating anhedonia (loss of capacity for pleasure) and promoting social interchange and close friendships. Chapter 11 contains a summary of a group that illustrates the use of religious content in stimulating memory and social relationships of residents with severe mental impairment.

Groups that Offer Opportunities for Creation of New Roles and Continuity of Previous Roles.

Many of the above-named groups do, of course, provide opportunity for roles that offer status and that foster individuality, self-esteem, and a sense of mastery. In addition there are groups structured around specific roles. Groups formed to plan or implement activities can include the editorial and/or production board of an institution's newsletter and groups to provide service to the institution and other residents (planning special events for holidays, parties, fund-raising). Some groups have as their purpose contributing to the welfare of subgroups of their peers. Among the latter are a hospital visiting committee and a welcoming committee to visit and to offer counsel and hospitality to new residents of the facility. A summary of such a welcoming committee is contained in Chapter 11.

Groups for Self-Actualization and Personal Growth

In this category are groups formed with an emphasis on new learning and new skills. Educational classes on a variety of subjects, painting, sculpture, and music contribute a sense of growth and future. A most successful group of illiterate residents culminated in the members writing letters to distant relatives for the first time in their lives. Its success was due in part to the support and encouragement group members gave to each other.

Resident Councils or Other Means of Self-Government

A common emphasis in the literature on institutionalization is the depression, dependency, and feelings of helplessness engendered. All agree that a major contributant to such detrimental effects is the deprivation of residents' sense of mastery or some control over their own lives. In many institutions there is little or no opportunity for the older people to exercise self-determination or to make decisions or choices even about such matters as bedtimes, bathtimes, menus, room location, medical appointments, and so on. These matters are so basic that most people take them for granted. Constant vigilance and self-examination is required on the part of institutional personnel to avoid unnecessary deprivation of decision-making. Recently there has been a strong thrust to restore such rights where they have been eroded. One expression of this trend has been the Patient's Statement of Rights developed for hospital patients, and the parallel statement required by Medicaid regulations for residents of long-term care facilities.

A residents' council is a vital necessity in long-term care facilities where older people live out their lives. Though it serves many useful purposes, its fundamental purpose is to maximize the degree to which residents can participate in and effect positive change in institutional management. That is, the council is a vehicle through which residents can express their wishes and share in decisions that affect them, thus reducing their powerlessness. The basic philosophy is that residents have a right to express their wishes and opinions, to have a voice in their life-style, and that those who are responsible for running the facility have a responsibility to respond.

If the residents' council is to serve those purposes, it must have the understanding and support of administration and all departments of the facility. There must be mutual understanding and respect. The council should have *real* opportunities to effect some changes. Otherwise, the result would be increased frustration and sense of powerlessness. Even small changes are meaningful, giving the residents dignity and a feeling that they and their needs are respected. At the same time, even when requests cannot be met, the residents gain understanding of the problems of the institution and personnel. Their understanding and their interpretation of these matters to other residents at the least conveys that they are not simply being ignored or treated arbitrarily. The council can be a most useful means of disseminating information about institutional plans, activities, and projected changes.

Special skills on the part of the group leader are required to avoid too much intervention. The aim is to help the group be as self-directed and independent as possible. At the same time, the worker must be sensitive to the fact that representatives of the council often require individual attention to enable them to serve their constituents. Physical disabilities and mental problems such as poor memory or personality difficulties may hamper efforts to carry through their duties effectively. Encouragement, flexibility in expectations, and support are necessary.

Ideally, a representative of administration should attend the meetings routinely. In addition, other staff who are directly involved should be invited as the content of the discussion indicates. For example, the food service manager should be present when menus or meal schedules are on the agenda, or the director of nursing when anything concerning nursing service is to be discussed.

The council should be as democratic and representative as possible. Elections on each unit or floor are desirable to select representatives to the council. Meetings on these units open a channel through which the elected member can be made aware of the concerns of his/her peers and through which they can receive feedback about the activities and accomplishments of the council. New ideas can be generated from the grass-roots which will benefit the institution as well as its residents. In this way, participation can be effected for every resident to the fullest extent.

Groups that Link Institution and Community

Institutional residents generally are deprived of the kinds of activities that keep people in "normal" living situations connected with the community outside their own dwelling (shopping, work, social visiting, vacation trips, volunteer service). All needs are met within the institutional walls, resulting in isolation and a sharply constricted world. No matter how benevolent the administration within the institution, it is essential for residents to feel part of the total community. Groups that take residents out of the institution—psychologically if they are too impaired to be moved physically—and that bring the community into the institution are extremely desirable. Particularly useful for those who live in a world of old people are groups that create involvement with younger adults and children. Benefits accrue to the younger people as well.

As emphasized in Chapters 7 and 8, every effort should be made to keep family ties viable. There are many ways of doing so through social group work activities that involve both resident and family. In addition to those noted above, families can be valuable contributors to interest groups and those using crafts, arts, and new learning as the media. Family members often have special skills and interests. They willingly serve as guest lecturers, discussion leaders, or teachers for scheduled meetings or sessions. Some open their homes for visits or "teas" of the group of which their relative is a member.

Community groups of which the resident has been a member should be invited and encouraged to visit residents and/or make it possible for them to attend their meetings and special events in the community. Veterans organizations, church groups, Y's, service organizations, and schools often are willing to plan special activities in the institution or host them in a community setting. Simply opening the institution to community groups for use as a meeting site or for a particular event is useful in dissolving barriers between institution and the community in which it is located.

Program Evaluation

As with all services, it is necessary to know whether

group programs in the long-term care facility are effective. Do they accomplish what they set out to do? What impact do they have on the people they are designed to serve? on the institution and its staff? on families and community?

The purpose of this guide is not to explicate research methodology for program evaluation. However, social work practitioners, like all professionals involved in clinical work, must be alert to the need for assessing the results of their work systematically. Cohen and Hammerman suggest consideration of the following factors:

> To what extent are the expressed goals of any specific group being met?
>
> How fully are individuals participating in the group activity and with what results?
>
> Has the group experience generated opportunities for self-expression, hope, improved morale or such other dynamics of human functioning that enhance well-being?
>
> Are attitudes and behavior of individual group members being carried over into other spheres of social interaction in the facility?
>
> Does the group enjoy the acceptance and cooperation of other departments in the facility?
>
> Are family and/or community members informed, supportive and involved when this is pertinent to the nature of the group?
>
> Are program goals and results being communicated to the administration of the facility, and are adequate resources, space and time blocs available to the professional worker? (1974)

To this list must be added a fundamental method of evaluation: that of the group itself. Periodic discussion with group members themselves should be built-in to all groups to review the "contract," to assess progress, and to reformulate goals. Apart from such discussion, the behavior of the members is in itself an evaluation. Do they attend regularly? Is there undue attrition in membership?

SOME CONCLUDING THOUGHTS

As described in Chapter 2, in recent years the population in long-term care facilities has increased numerically and its nature has changed dramatically. Change will continue as new cohorts of older people enter—and exit from—institutions. Even a conservative estimate indicates that every three-to-five-year period will witness almost a complete turnover in the resident population of any facility. Just as the institution itself must respond to new needs, so too must the social group worker be alert to the need for change in program content. For example, more native-born old people with more education and higher socioeconomic standards will have very different needs and expectations. The principles and goals of group work will remain the same, but the program content should not be static. It must change to reflect the changing nature of the population.

One of the most striking developments in long-term care has been the influx of mentally impaired older people suffering from chronic brain syndrome ("senility"). There is a scarcity of literature with respect to groupwork with these individuals, who constitute at least half of all those in long-term care. That gap in knowledge should be filled. It probably reflects the general therapeutic pessimism about such people that only recently has begun to dissipate. The structured programs that have been developed and that are described in Chapter 17 are not substitutes for ongoing programs of social group work.

Experience at the Philadelphia Geriatric Center indicates that group work is applicable with these mentally impaired people. The level and content of such groups obviously is very different from that of a group comprised of alert, cognitively intact individuals. Much additional work is needed. As a beginning, several examples of group work with this population are given in Chapter 11.

Finally, as a caveat, the heterogeneity of the population served again is underlined. In addition to variations in all the characteristics noted in this chapter, *individuals vary widely in the extent of their need for groups.* Like all people, some are more "groupy" than others. Group opportunities should be made available to all, and all should be encouraged and enabled to participate to the fullest extent of their need and capacity. But the right and wish of individuals *not* to join must be respected. The skill and diagnostic ability of the social group worker will be called upon to determine when not joining represents pathology and when it is the continuation of a life-long and satisfactory pattern of behavior.

Chapter 11

GROUP ILLUSTRATIONS

The following illustrations show how various types of groups work.

GROUP ONE: NEW RESIDENTS' GROUP

Newly admitted residents to long-term care facilities have major adaptations and adjustments to make. At the Philadelphia Geriatric Center, each new resident is invited to join a new residents' group which has a time-limited existence of three weekly meetings. Experience with dozens of such groups identifies certain common patterns that emerge. The initial session finds the new residents uncertain and awkward. They are helped to overcome this by the worker being active in inviting the members to introduce themselves by name and to tell a little about their previous lives and living arrangements.

The tension relaxes as they get to know each other and feel comfortable with their fellow group members and the worker.

Though the order in which various subjects are discussed varies from group to group, recurrent themes are:

Recapitulation of the events leading to admission and the decision-making process

Difficulties in adjustment (including complaints) such as unaccustomed food, roommate problems, reactions to staff

Problems of adaptation to old age and impairment (particularly sensory deficits such as those of hearing and sight)

Feelings about dependency

Differences between previous living patterns and institutional life

Families and their inability to provide the care the new residents require.

Discussion of these shared concerns and feelings of separation and loss enables the residents to progress to "moving in" to the institution emotionally. Questions are asked about services and activities in the facility, and the worker can begin to link each resident to the appropriate institutional resources. In the course of the series of three meetings, the worker becomes progressively less active. The group becomes cohesive, and individuals relate to each other rather than being a collection of individuals each relating primarily to the worker. Members have been enabled to start relationships and to find their way as knowledgeable residents of their new home.

GROUP TWO: IMPAIRED RESIDENTS FORM A WELCOMING COMMITTEE
TO GIVE VOLUNTEER SERVICES TO THEIR PEERS*

A group of residents who, though impaired, were among the more intact institutional residents, was formed to constitute a welcoming committee for newly admitted residents. Meeting weekly with their social worker, they participated actively in designing the program. Decisions included the timing and frequency of visits to new people, the number of the latter each group member would visit, whether members of one sex should visit members of the other sex (with some initial reluctance, "yes"), the propriety of such visits occurring in bedrooms. As the meetings progressed, group members gradually were enabled to work through feelings concerning the changing population of the institution, in particular the resistance and anxiety about "senile" residents. They discussed the fear of becoming mentally impaired themselves which was stimulated by the increasing number of such older people. Soon they were willing to visit the mentally impaired, giving each other mutual support and reassurance in this effort. The adjustment difficulties experienced by the new residents they visited led to group discussion of their own feelings and reactions on leaving their own homes to move to an institution. They related touching stories of their separations in earlier life from siblings and other family members. Other areas discussed were feelings of rejection, death, and dying, and the limitations of institutional living. The group provided them with a meaningful op-

*This summary is based on a detailed report of the group by its leader, Mrs. Susan Friedman, then a social work student at the Philadelphia Geriatric Center. Mrs. Friedman is now at the Community Service Society in New York. The paper, The resident welcoming committee: institutionalized elderly in volunteer services, was published in *The Gerontologist* 15: 4, 1975. 362-367.

portunity for social interchange, helped its members gain insight and perspective about their own problems, forged interpersonal bonds, and provided them with significant new roles, as well as giving a beneficial service to the new residents. The experience of giving help to others enhanced their own self-esteem and pride.

GROUP THREE: INTACT SPOUSES OF MENTALLY IMPAIRED RESIDENTS*

As more people survive to advanced old age, there is an increase of the number of cases in which one member of a marital pair remains intact while the other becomes impaired to an extent requiring institutionalization. The separation, occurring as it often does after half a century or more of marriage, is particularly poignant. A group of eight intact spouses of long-term care residents, three women and five men, was formed to help them deal with this traumatic experience. It had been the social worker's observation that these spouses were so deeply involved that many spent their entire day visiting their impaired mates, all of whom were severely impaired mentally (chronic brain syndrome). Their depression, anxieties, and guilt were clearly apparent to all staff. Their behavior often disrupted institutional routines, disturbed staff and other residents, and even impeded the impaired residents' adjustment and engagement in therapeutic programs.

In a series of twelve meetings, these spouses formed a cohesive group, forming social realtionships with each other. They obtained some relief from sharing feelings of pain at the deterioration of their mates and the sep-aration from them. One said, "It's like being widowed,

*This group was led by Mr. Steven Rook and Ms. Cheryl Feldman, social workers at the Philadelphia Geriatric Center, and the summary was developed from their minutes of the meetings.

only worse." They told each other the sequence of events that led to the need for placement. Some were able to verbalize their feelings of guilt if they did not spend all their time with the impaired spouse. With encouragement from each other and the worker, some were enabled gradually to take up the threads of a new life with new outside activities and routines while behaving responsibly in continuing their concern for their impaired mates.

GROUP FOUR: ADULT CHILDREN HAVE DIFFICULTY ADJUSTING TO THE INSTITUTIONALIZATION OF THEIR ELDERLY FAMILY MEMBER*

The social worker invited nine relatives to form a group to discuss the problems they were experiencing in relation to institutionalization of their elderly parent or parent-in-law. The selection was based on the worker's observation of the overt and extreme difficulties they were experiencing. The relatives ages ranged from fifty-nine to sixty-seven. The initial sessions witnessed ventilation of complaints about the Home and staff. Soon the group members were able to understand that some of their negative feelings concealed anger at themselves for not being able to care for the parents at home. They began to share experiences about difficulties dealing with a parent's increasing dependency, their guilt at needing to place the older people, and the pain of watching loved ones deteriorate mentally and physically. They talked of fear of the old person's death and their anxieties about their own aging processes and the possi-

*Based on a paper by Mrs. Sandra Rotenberg, a program coordinator at the Philadelphia Geriatric Center, and Dr. Joy Spalding Rabin, then a social work student at the center. The paper, Social group work with families of institutionalized aged, was presented at the twenty-fifth annual meeting of the Gerontological Society, San Juan, Puerto Rico, Dec. 1972.

bility of becoming "senile." Will their own children, they wondered, be as concerned and active in their behalf as they are about their parents?

The group members supported each other through difficult experiences. In one situation, an adult daughter, driven by guilt, insisted on taking her ill mother home for a week's visit. Apart from the physical difficulties of hiring an ambulance and renting a wheelchair, the family was unable to cope with the total care required in feeding, toileting and other activities of daily living. The visit "failed," with the old person and family having been equally uncomfortable. The group was most supportive of the daughter, gained insight into their own guilt as it directed their actions, and were able to increase their appreciation of the difficult tasks performed by nursing staff. Another daughter was helped by the group to make the decision to take a vacation with her own family, the first in the nine years since the ninety-two-year-old parent had been institutionalized. The group also served as a vehicle for making suggestions about care to staff. They reported increased understanding of how the Home functioned, improved communications with staff, and more relaxed relationships with their very old parents.

GROUP FIVE: THE MENTALLY IMPAIRED AGED HAVE A DISCUSSION GROUP*

A discussion group was organized in the area of the institution in which the older people who are severely impaired mentally (chronic brain syndrome) reside. The social worker planned to hold the meetings of the

*This group was led by Mrs. Mary Jeffries, staff social worker at the Philadelphia Geriatric Center, and the summary was derived from her minutes of the meetings.

groups in different settings within the institution, to focus on interaction and socialization, to use topics about the past to stimulate discussion but also to discuss current issues and events, and to use refreshments to create a pleasant sociable atmosphere. Though the worker always came to the meeting prepared with topics and material, the needs of the moment would take priority. In the course of the first few months of weekly meetings, members who previously had few or no social relationships formed real bonds with each other. It was apparent that the opportunity to share their thoughts gave the group a sense of importance, often diminished in an institution.

Discussion focused on many areas. For example:

An imminent move of the group to a different area of the building was related to past moves, and feelings were expressed—such as anger and upset. Mrs. R. said a previous room change had been hard and that she had worried about her possessions. Miss B. recalled being confused by newness and bigness on admission to the Home. The worker responded to these and similar concerns and repeatedly described how the move would be handled. Group members told stories of their big moves from Europe to the United States in the early part of the century and what their experiences had been. One resident, Mr. C., suggested that they should see their new rooms before the move, and this suggestion was followed through.

Clothing was a recurrent topic: the price of men's suits during the Depression as compared to now, dresses versus slacks for women, an accusation from one woman that another had stolen her slips. One man stated he would not go to religious services unless he had a new suit. (This was obtained, and he went happily). The group was encouraged to talk about changes in physical appearance and share their feelings about the changes.

Music emerged as a most important medium. The group missed the "music lady" when the music therapist was on vacation. Mr. B. sang songs and responded to requests from the others for special songs. Mrs. F. pretended to accompany him on the piano. Humor often played an important role in discussions.

The different environments used for the meetings elicited excited reactions. A meeting in the chapel stimulated comments about its beauty, discussion of religious objects, and memories of family get-togethers at the holidays. The chance to be in a quiet, peaceful setting was appreciated.

The individuals benefited from the interaction in the group. One man often took responsibility for introducing people to each other. Another translated for his friend. A woman was enabled to have a few minutes respite from tending her sick husband. Efforts were made by the worker to develop choices: which of three beverages to select, what the temperature in the room should be, whether the door should be open or shut, who would take charge of refreshments.

Individual needs required sensitive handling. One person with a short attention span became fidgety after fifteen minutes and would be returned to his room. Another, who usually screamed constantly, was perfectly contained during the meetings. The group members were encouraged to express feelings about each other's behavior and statements. As a result, disturbed residents became more aware of their effect on others.

Experience with this group illustrates some principles of working with the mentally impaired:

> Small groups are indicated (no more than eight people).
>
> Short meetings are best, usually no longer than a half hour.
>
> Identification and reintroduction of members at the beginning of each meeting are necessary, as is a review of previous meeting.
>
> Name tags support memory.
>
> Simple topics are best, as the group must be worked with at its own level.
>
> Refreshments greatly enhance the meeting and promote social behavior (passing cookies, offering to pour juice, etc.).
>
> A lengthy period of time spent in gathering the group together is to be avoided. The first arrivals get impatient.
>
> Worker must expect and respond to variability in mood, behavior, and orientation of residents from one meeting to another.

Group Six: A Religious Leader Evokes Response
from
Residents with Severe Chronic Brain Syndrome*

A small group of five residents suffering from chronic brain syndrome was convened by the rabbi of the Home. It was the rabbi's intention to stimulate recall in these residents by using the religious holiday of Succoth with its concrete religious symbols as the medium. He began by speaking for a few moments about the significance of

---

*Appreciation is expressed to Dr. Meir Lasker, rabbi at the Philadelphia Geriatric Center, for this material.

the holiday, its historical background and its current significance. The religious objects—the Lulov, and the Ethrog—were shown, and their meaning explained. The rabbi called the group's attention to the custom in the little towns of Russia and Poland in which the *shamus* of the synagogue would knock on doors each morning of the festival, calling out, "Come and bless the Lulov and the Ethrog." The rabbi then asked the group, "Who remembers the blessing over these symbols?"

The rabbi described the group members reactions as follows:

> Mr. B. recited the blessing quite clearly. Mr. C. added that in the Sukah it was the custom to break bread and drink a cup of wine. At my request, he recited the blessing over the bread and wine. Mrs. D. then told of her experiences in the Sukah as a child. She remembered that her father always invited poor guests to join the ceremony and that they ate their meals in the Sukah. Mr. B. interrupted to point out that the night of the Day of Atonement after the closing service and dinner, he and the other children would bring the necessary wood needed to build the Sukah. Mr. T., who till then had remained silent, remarked, "I remember that I, too, helped." The only one unable to recall anything about this festival was Mrs. M., who said that her parents were not religious and, having been born in the United States, she was never in a Sukah.
>
> Mrs. D then asked, "What is that light over the Ark?" When I explained that this was the perpetual light, several raised the question: "Why are these two lions on the Ark around the Ten Commandments?" It seems that through visual representation their curiosity was aroused; their memory of past events was coming to the fore.

In a subsequent meeting of the group, the rabbi introduced the American flag and Israeli flag, explaining the meaning of the colors. He then asked who remembered the hymn sung when the American flag is raised. Mrs. C. hummed a bit of "My Country Tis of Thee." In response to a similar question about the Israeli flag, the silent member, Mr. T., cried out the response and sang the first stanza. The other members of the group joined in repeating it, then began to tell each other stories of their early life.

Chapter 12

DISCHARGE AND AFTER-CARE

Much of the material in this guide is about older people in need of permanent care in a long-term care facility. However, such facilities also may serve those who require temporary care for convalescence, diagnosis, and evaluation, or rehabilitative services. In addition, the changing condition of some of those who were admitted for long-term care may subsequently indicate that other kinds of institutional service are needed, such as those provided by a psychiatric hospital or acute general hospital.

In recent years there has been much attention paid to the fact that some people who reside in long-term care facilities could live in the community with appropriate supports. There has been a corresponding thrust to develop what have been called alternatives, such as day care, transportation services, meals-on-wheels, and living arrangements with less comprehensive services. As stated in Chapter 1, the word "alternative" is unfortunate, since one or more of the named services cannot really substitute when comprehensive institutional care is needed. Nevertheless, it is certainly true that some older people have been placed in long-term facilities inappropriately, though the percentage suggested varies and has not been established firmly.

As community care facilities and services develop, and as the trend continues that ties reimbursement to the individual's need for care, it is likely that efforts will continue to discharge appropriate residents. It is a sad fact that to date programs to do so have too often been characterized by a lack of thought, planning, exploration, resources, or careful preparation of the older person. A case in point was the wholesale discharge of elderly state psychiatric hospital patients in many areas.

It is emphasized that discharge from a facility for any reason whatsoever should occur with the same careful assessment and counseling of individual and family that was described in Chapters 3 and 7.

SHORT-TERM PLACEMENT

When it is known at the outset that the placement in the facility will be temporary, the social worker should see the older person and family as quickly as possible after admission to begin discharge planning. Family members and professionals who will have a continuing responsibility for the care of the older person should be involved at once. The same principles described in the guide sections on services to applicants and residents are relevant here; that is, an interdisciplinary approach, careful assessment, psychological preparation of older person and family members, and options and freedom of choice to the fullest possible extent. Just as it is important to prepare the long-term care facility to receive the client (see Chapter 1), when discharge is planned it is necessary to prepare the appropriate people, organizations, agencies, and physical surroundings. Services that will be required must be mobilized (see Chapter 4) and necessary equipment secured in addition to preparing those people who will be responsible for giving the care.

The older person and family often view discharge with mixed feelings. The older person may experience anxiety and fear about leaving the security and protection of the institution; he/she may doubt his/her capacity to manage, and/or feel guilty about "being a burden" to his family. Family members may feel uncertain about their capacity to provide needed services, worried about disruption of their normal routines, and reluctant to assume additional responsibilities. Social work support during the transition and for a time afterwards is an important ingredient if the plan is to be carried through constructively.

Discharge of Long-Term Care Residents to Other Institutions

Most modern homes for aged and nursing homes extend themselves to contain residents who evidence disturbed behavior and/or mental illness. With careful exploration of the problem and expert management and treatment, the resident often may be enabled to remain in the facility. Occasionally the need for a different type of care requires transfer to a psychiatric hospital or other resource. The older person and family members may react with anger to what they view as "being thrown out." Such reactions should be understood in terms of their underlying anxiety, fear, and sense of helplessness. Here, too, skilled casework is needed to ease the transition, and the same careful planning is necessary as in admission and other types of discharges. The long-term care facility should not foreclose the possibility of re-admission, since after a period of treatment the older person may improve to the point where he/she can again be offered residence in the facility.

PERIODIC REVIEW AND DISCHARGE OF LONG-TERM RESIDENTS

Admission for permanent residence in a facility ideally should have taken place after other options were thoroughly explored. Nevertheless, it is advisable to review each situation at periodic intervals. Events may occur that make it possible for the resident to return to community living. For example, a family situation may have changed, the resident's functional capacities may have improved with care and treatment, or new resources for care and service may have developed in the community.

The utmost sensitivity is required in such situations. The resident, who thought of admission as a permanent plan, has often given up his/her own home and possessions. He/she has had to make major adaptations in adjusting to institutional life and has come to think of the facility as home. He/she should be involved at every step, his/her wishes consulted, and his/her choices respected. Certainly, efforts should be made to encourage more independent life-style. For some individuals, a trial period of the new plan may be suggested, with assurances of return to the facility if indicated. This may enable an uncertain or ambivalent older person (or family) to try his/her wings without feeling that the door irrevocably has shut behind him/her. When a resident has been in a facility for a long period of time and really does not wish to leave, it is a cruelty (and a risk to life and health) to uproot him/her forcibly.

Finally, it is emphasized that discharge of a resident has an impact on two other groups. Families who will need to provide supportive services should be assessed for their capacity to do so and should receive skilled help. Discharge of the resident may be counterproductive if it places too much stress on family members. And other residents of the facility, those who are not being discharged, will have a complex of feelings; envy, loss of a friend or roommate, anxiety about who will replace him/her, hope or fear that he/she will be next to be discharged. Those who remain behind need social work attention to deal with their reactions.

Chapter 13

DYING AND DEATH

In recent years, there has been an upsurge of intense interest by practitioners and research investigators in the dying phase of life. Previously it had been a neglected area of concern. A major contributant to this interest has been recognition that more than 80 percent of persons of all ages die in an institution of some type—a hospital, a facility for the chronically disabled, a nursing home, a home for aged, or another long-term care facility. Major controversies have erupted and eventuated in court cases about when artificial life-sustaining machinery can be disconnected, and even whether medical personnel who do so are guilty of murder.

Crucial issues are being raised and discussed all over the country by professional groups and government bodies. For example, the United States Senate has held a series of hearings called "Death with Dignity." Discussions focus variously on understanding and managing the dying person; the reactions of the family during that process and when they are bereaved; special groups of "dyers" such as children and those suffering from specific diseases; attitudes and reactions of professionals and other caretaking personnel as they affect the dying person; ethical, moral, financial, and legal aspects of prolonging life by heroic measures; determining when death can actually be said to have occurred (brain death, cardiac death, etc.); the role of spiritual counseling; the desirability of terminal care in one's own home when possible. A major concern relates to the machinery of the modern hospital and other institutions as they infringe upon the dignity and comfort of the dying person.

Though one in ten of all people in the United States are sixty-five or over, more than six in ten of those who die each year are in that age group. For those in long-term care facilities, the very old, the proportion is even higher: the death rate is 30.6 per 1,000 for those between sixty-five and sixty-nine and rises progressively to 190.8 for those eighty-five and over.* Data produced by Robert Kastenbaum and Sandra Candy indicate that about one-fourth of all deaths of older people occur in long-term care facilities. Most people who live in such facilities also die there. It is obvious that the subject is an important and legitimate one, not only because of the weight of statistics, but because of the profound meaning of the dying process to those who experience it, to families, staff, and the other residents in the institution.

There is general agreement that there is much to be learned, that the education of professionals must include content on this subject, and that there is a great need for modification of attitudes and behavior. Though knowledge is incomplete and there are still many unanswered

---

*Data provided by Herman B. Brotman, Administration on Aging, based on PHS Vital Statistics Report for 1969, issued July, 1972.

questions, some valuable information regarding the social aspects of giving care to dying people and their families is available.

Experts point out that currently the dying phase of life is primarily managed as a medical problem and that there has been general neglect of the psychological and social aspects. Personal, social, cultural, and religious considerations play important roles in reactions to and management of the dying.

If skilled help is to be extended, there must be awareness of these factors and of the complex emotions and reactions being experienced by the dying individual—among them intense fear, anxiety, anger, depression, defeat, helplessness, and hopelessness. Elizabeth Kübler-Ross suggests several phases through which a dying person passes: denial, anger, bargaining for time, depression, and, finally, acceptance. Whatever the sequence, such feelings are almost invariably present. However, those who work with very old people have seen evidence that some approach the end with relative equanimity.

Certainly there is individuality in the way one copes with and adapts to the possibility of death, as there is individuality in the way people live out their lives. Erik Erikson's eighth stage of personality development, "late adulthood," is the development of a sense of ego identity versus despair (fear of death). It involves in part "acceptance of one's one and only life cycle" and comes only to the person "who in some way has taken care of things and people." In his words, "The lack or loss of this accrued ego integration is signified by fear of death." The implication is that in old age acceptance of death may relate to the extent of one's satisfaction with the way one's life has been lived.

Most contributors to the thinking in the field have found that those who are dying are often isolated and deceived. In particular, the many who die in institutions may experience a sense of loneliness and emotional abandonment. There frequently is a conspiracy of silence and denial on the part of others. The dying person is almost totally dependent on institutional staff.

There is currently much professional discussion about whether or not to tell the individual that he/she is dying. The preponderance of evidence suggest that most are aware of their status despite the efforts made to deceive them, and that most want opportunities to talk about their emotions and fears.

The literature contains suggestions, based on experience and research, about how to help the dying. Such advice bears striking similarities to the principles of good social work practice with the elderly in general:

> Attention is required to social as well as medical needs. Though dying, the individual is *still alive*.
>
> Hope should be maintained. The dying person should not feel that those who are responsible for his care have given him/her up.
>
> The fact that he/she is dying should not mean that the individual's wishes need not be considered. He/she should have as much autonomy and choice as is possible.
>
> Communication with staff, peers, and family should be maintained. Interpersonal relationships should be preserved to the fullest extent possible.
>
> Status as a dying person should not mean that other roles are obliterated—e.g. as a family member or friend.
>
> Attention should be paid to the need for privacy and meaningful possessions.
>
> Competent behavior should be encouraged to the fullest possible extent.
>
> Individualization is essential. It is important to

listen to the dying patient carefully, to provide him/her with opportunities for discussion, to make it apparent that he/she is cared about, to treat and address him/her with attitudes of respect, and to help him/her sustain a dignified self-image.

The physical milieu should reflect attention to social as well as physical needs.

It should not be assumed that the patient is unaware of his/her surroundings and does not hear or understand discussion of his/her condition.

Most dying individuals wish and should be given the opportunity to make material preparations for death. Some want to express their preferences about funeral arrangements. Many want to straighten out their affairs. No matter how few or seemingly insignificant their possessions, they may wish to designate who is to receive the things which for them have real or emotional value.

Family members require help during this phase. Their reactions and behavior have a direct impact on the dying person. They themselves may be suffering from painful feelings such as guilt and loss, or from feelings of relief that they feel others may find unacceptable.

All staff should have an awareness of their own feelings, for they influence their reactions to and treatment of the dying individual. These matters should be included in in-service training programs. Staff should have an opportunity to develop understanding of the reactions and behavior of family as well as those of the dying person.

In short, just as social services in long-term care facilities have as their goal helping residents to live with dignity, they also should be directed towards helping the older person to die with dignity.

Chapter 14

PLANNING AND SOCIAL ACTION; TRAINING AND EDUCATION; RESEARCH

PLANNING AND SOCIAL ACTION

Social workers in long-term care facilities and those in other settings who deal with older people currently or potentially in need of long-term care should be concerned with factors in the broad social and physical environment such as legislation, governmental policy and action, service resources, housing, income maintenance, and health programs. All of these have a direct impact on the well-being of older people and their families, and all are determinants of the plans the clients can be helped to make. The social worker, because of his/her intimate case-knowledge of how such matters affect clients, is in a prime position to identify gaps in resources or restrictive or confusing regulations. He/she therefore has a professional responsibility to take steps designed to transmit his/her information and to participate in action to translate that knowledge into policy and program.

The current situation of older people is one of the major contemporary social issues. Within the total group of aged, those in need of long-term care and those receiving it are a particularly disadvantaged subgroup. This guide cannot review all the inequities and service-gaps, nor detail methods to remedy them. The literature in the field and the background and concluding chapters of the guide delineate some of the issues and proposed solutions. What is emphasized is that by the very nature of the profession of social work, the task is incomplete and ineffective if it includes the modalities of direct services, modification of institutional milieu, research, education, and training but omits attention to the broader social context.

TRAINING AND EDUCATION

The shortage of personnel interested in aging makes training and education a special responsibility. Those facilities with professional social work staff therefore should serve as sites to train social work students from graduate and undergraduate schools of social work. Social work in a long-term care facility can provide a wide variety of experience. It combines family-focused social work, medical and psychiatric social work, social work with the chronically disabled, and other specialties, and utilizes all social work modalities.

For a long time social work, like other professions, had difficulty attracting people to work with older people. There has been a significant change in this negative climate. More and more schools are seeking long-term care facilities as field placement sites for their students. Even high schools are developing programs to give volunteer services in facilities and to expose the young people to the human services field in long-term care. It is desirable to take students if at all possible. The number who can be supervised, however, must be evaluated in terms of the staff time available and required.

Some large institutions also train physicians, nurses, mental health workers and others. Social work should participate in those training programs in order to integrate the social aspects of care in the students' approaches and experience as early as possible.

RESEARCH

Chapter 15 of this guide details some of the data that should be assembled as a matter of routine. Those data, when analyzed and interpreted, constitute a form of research that should be carried out on a continuing basis. Not infrequently, they suggest areas that should be examined in more detail. For example, a number of facilities in the past found it important to document the changing characteristics of applicants (health, socioeconomic, and cultural) in order to plan their policies and programs appropriately. Other examples of findings that should be explored further might be significant increases or decreases in the number of applicants or the geographic area from which they come. Of particular interest for additional study are the applicants an agency has not been able to serve. Such studies can often be designed and carried out as part of the regular work of the social work staff, but it is desirable to obtain research consultation if possible.

On a broader scale, social work has a responsibility to utilize research findings in the field of aging that have implications for practice and to participate in the development of new knowledge. The social worker in a long-term care facility occupies a vantage point to identify issues that should be researched and to facilitate studies being carried out by research investigators from other disciplines and professions.

Designing, funding, and implementing formal research studies are complex matters. Research is a highly specialized technique, and formal studies must have the benefits of expert consultation and/or direction by a trained investigator. Some large facilities have such specialists on the staff full- or part-time (such as a research social worker, psychologist, or sociologist). Research should be viewed by social work as an important modality that, properly used, is in the best interests of the clients. To be useful for policy and program planning, knowledge must be retrieved, organized, and tested. One of the most important skills of the social work practitioner is careful, sensitive listening to the client or groups of clients. Research is an extension of the listening role. It can be another way of listening to clients so that data are produced to document the need for change and to point to the directions it should take.

It is essential to protect the rights of individuals who are the subjects of any research study. No one should be unaware that he/she is part of a project or should be compelled to participate against his/her will. Informed consent invariably must be obtained.

Chapter 15

ADMINISTRATIVE CONSIDERATIONS

The structural relationships of social work to long-term care facilities have been shown to vary widely. Among the determinants of administrative patterns are the size of the facility, the amount of social work time available, the nature of the auspice or sponsoring body, and whether the social worker is a part-time worker or there is a large or small social work department. There are, however, some factors and goals that are applicable in most settings.

Relationship to Administration and other Departments

The department of social work should be a major functional unit of a long-term facility. As such it should maintain close liaison with administration and with all other departments. There should be social work representation at administrative staff meetings and on all important committees, such as the utilization review committee, research review committee, and education committee.

It is the administrator's responsibility to provide social work offices that are accessible to clients and family, adequately furnished, equipped with appropriate supplies, and that afford privacy for interviews. There should be provision in space and budget for clerical support and for assembling a library of relevant books, journals, and reprints.

Relationship to Activity Therapy

Because of the mutuality of concern of social work and recreational or activity therapy, special mention is made of their relationship. Different patterns exist in different facilities. In some, there are separate departments. In others recreational therapy services are supervised by or part of the social work department. In still others, there are separate departments, but there is a social group worker on the staff of the activities department. Whatever the pattern, each group of specialists is in a position to note needs that can be met by the others. Close cooperation and coordination is essential if the common goal of enhancement of the well-being of clients and families is to be met.

THE SOCIAL CASE RECORD

Purpose

The purpose of the social case record is to provide a concise, orderly, permanent, and transferable record of personal and social information about the client and his/her family. Information is noted which is germane to the provision of social work services, assessment of eligibility and appropriate placement, social diagnosis, formulation of treatment plan, and reformulation of treatment goals in accordance with the client's changing needs. The record should be organized in such a way as to facilitate communication among staff who use it.

Confidentiality

The case record is a confidential document. Selected information may be made available to other personnel and/or to recognized community health and welfare agencies requiring that information in order to render appropriate service to meet the client's needs. Except for such instances, the records are considered to be privileged communications available only to social work staff and to authorized professional personnel directly involved in the administration of matters related to the client's care.

Application Case Records

The application case record can be organized into three categories of materials:

CASE RECORDING OF SOCIAL INFORMATION. This section, consisting of the social worker's dictation, is fastened at the top of the lefthand side of the opened case folder. Recording is filed in reverse chronological order, the most recent recording on top. In general, the recording includes:

> 1. An account of the social worker's contacts with the client, family members, and other life-figures, and social and health agencies.

2. Professional evaluation of the needs, attitudes, feelings, problems, and relationships of the client and family.
3. Assessment of the applicant's personality, physical, mental, and emotional status, and functional capacities.
4. Social history and background information.
5. Financial information about family and adult children relevant to assisting with financial planning.
6. Evaluation of current situation and recommendations for social treatment.
7. Brief description of casework approach and its utilization by the client(s).
8. Re-evaluation and reformulation of diagnosis and treatment goals as the needs and condition of the client and family change.

While these areas are always covered, there is no rigid order for obtaining the information. Summary dictation with subject headings is preferred. This by no means precludes brief notation of the client's utilization of casework help. Detailed process recording, however, is usually the practice only for students and new social workers. All entries are dated and the name of the social worker appears after each entry. A guide for dictation of the initial interview(s) appears in this manual in Appendix B. This may be modified in any way as dictated by the nature and content of the interviews. Subsequent entries are usually in narrative form, but with subject headings whenever possible.

When a case has been fully studied, the worker prepares the completion summary, organizing the material in accordance with the form outlined (see Appendix B). This summary is always filed at the top of this section of the case record. Subsequent contacts and information are entered chronologically with the previous recording, and the completion summary is kept up to date.

APPLICATION FORMS AND CORRESPONDENCE.   These materials are fastened at the top to the right-hand side of the open application folder. On top is the completed application form and the medical authorization form (Appendix B). Correspondence is filed behind these items, in reverse chronological order.

MEDICAL AND PSYCHIATRIC INFORMATION, AND EVALUATION FORMS.   These materials, fastened together as a unit, form a free-floating packet within the case record folder. When the applicant becomes a resident, this packet, with the social service chart summary added, is sent to the medical records librarian to be included in the resident's medical chart. The packet contains the following materials: the Kahn-Goldfarb mental status questionnaire; PGC Physical self-maintenance scale; and the PGC instrumental activities of daily living scale. All these forms are shown in Appendix B. The social worker completes the forms, and they are stapled together as a unit. An X-ray report taken within the previous six months is filed directly behind this unit when it has been reviewed and initialed by the physician. The medical history form required by the particular facility follows this material, which in turn is followed by all abstracts from general and/or psychiatric hospitals and clinics.

Resident Records

When the older person is admitted to the long-term care facility, his/her medical chart becomes a central document for information relevant to his/her care. The medical and functional assessment materials which have been assembled by the social worker are transferred to the medical chart. The chart should include a separator for social work entries as it does for medical specialties. As described on p. 346, the social service chart summary is placed in the chart just prior to admission. Thereafter, the social worker should make brief entries on the progress notes of the medical chart (always signed and dated) of all information relevant to the overall care of the resident. Longer notes are inserted in the social work section of the chart, and attention is drawn to them by a brief progress note.

Depending on the needs and wishes of the administrator, some of the materials sent to him/her for his/her file are a copy of the application form (with data identifying resident and family), and a summary of the financial arrangements.

The social worker continues to maintain the social case record. If there are different intake and resident workers, the record is transferred to the resident worker. The case record follows the resident if he/she is moved to a different area served by a different worker. It includes the detailed narrative and summaries accumulated during the intake study. It also notes continuing contacts and services during the period of residence. At periodic intervals (preferably every three months), a brief summary of this social information is written and placed on the medical chart.

Social Service Statistics and Reports

Goals

Statistics of the department of social work are a vital administrative tool, an integral part of the program, and should be organized in an orderly and concise manner. The purposes are:

1. To report to the administrator and the board of directors on the volume and type of activities carried out by social work.
2. To reflect changing community needs for the services of the facility.
3. To enable the agency to budget and to plan needed services, programs, and facilities.
4. To maximize the use of staff. That is, to indicate the need for changes in or additions to staffing pattern and to facilitate assignment of cases and other responsibilities so that the workload is distributed equitably and effectively.
5. To record data in such form as to be retrievable for internal departmental studies and formal research projects.

A monthly statistical report and a comprehensive annual report should be prepared for administrator and board.

The wide variety of types of facilities precludes suggesting forms and procedures that can be universally adopted. However, one way of helping agencies relate to changing community needs is to record and analyze requests for service. Knowledge about the number of such requests, their nature, the demographic and health characteristics of the population, the geographic areas from which they come, and the services that they have utilized in the community and those that were unavailable, provides the agency with the data it requires to modify or expand its services.

Forms should record, at the minimum, information about inquiries, reception cases, applications, admissions, rejections, withdrawals, deaths among applicants, and the type of care required. One possible way of developing such information is suggested here.

Monthly Statistics Kept by Social Workers Serving Applicants

Each social worker offering services to applicants makes entries on two separate forms.

The Social Worker's Worksheet (Appendix B) aids in organizing work and keeping records. This form is retained by the social worker.

The social worker's monthly report (Appendix B) records the name and disposition of each new inquiry, reception case, and application handled by the worker during the month, as well as admissions, rejections, deaths, and withdrawals. It notes the volume of cases handled each month in each category. This form is given to the director of the department on the last day of the month, and is used to develop the composite department monthly statistics.

Department Director's Monthly Statistics on Applicants

The director of the department maintains the monthly report of status of applications (Appendix B). This notes for the month the names of every new applicant, every applicant whose application is closed and the reason for closure (withdrawal, rejection, admission, death), transfers between active and deferred status, and the placement needs of each person listed. It is the responsibility of the social worker to notify the department director when any of these activities occurs.

The monthly social service statistics report form (Appendix B) is derived from the monthly report of status of applications, from the control board and from the social workers' monthly report. This form includes data with regard to the active waiting list, deferred waiting list, inquiries, and placement needs of the applicant group. One copy is kept on file in the department, and one is sent to the administrator, who in turn uses the information in his/her reports to the board of directors. Where a social service committee exists, a copy should be sent to the chairperson.

Annual Statistical Report

The director of the department develops an annual statistical report which is incorporated in the annual report of the department.

If the statistics described above have been maintained regularly, the data can be aggregated readily, and annual statistics can be developled and compared with those of previous years to detect changes and trends. Examples of information that can be tabulated annually are:

> Gross figures re: numbers of inquiries, applications, admissions, withdrawals, rejections, deaths, number of applicants on active and deferred lists.
> > Placement needs of applicants on waiting list
> > Admissions by sex and facility
> > Reasons for withdrawals and rejections
> > Geographic location of applicants
> > Living arrangements of applicants
> > Family composition of applicants.

Annual Social Work Report

The annual report of the department to administration and board should include:

> Interpretation of annual statistics, particularly as they indicate trends requiring modification of or additions to services and programs.
> Review of various regular activities of the de-

partment (services to applicants, residents, and families)

Summary of activities of social service committee

Review of staffing and projections of future staffing needs

Summary of staff development program

Summary of activities in education, training, and research

Summary of other professional activities (conferences, papers, publication, organizational work)

Evaluation of the work of the department and statement of immediate and long-range needs and goals.

Social Work Job Specifications

General Considerations

The suggested specifications for social work positions are intended to delineate in broad terms the education, professional training, capacities, level of performance, potential, and major responsibilities of each position. There may be overlapping—some of the same tasks may be performed by social workers in every category. Further, new career lines and training programs are being developed. Therefore, flexibility is called for in applying this section of the guide, as with other sections.

It is assumed that after the initial period of in-service training and experience every worker in each category will be able to perform with maximum independence, though his/her supervisor will be readily accessible.

For all job titles including the phrase "social worker," some knowledge, abilities, and personal characteristics are basic. In brief, the social worker should have some understanding of human behavior and relationships, some knowledge of social problems and welfare programs, and some knowledge about older people in general. He/she should be able to interview, to speak and write clearly, to work cooperatively with other people, and to use supervision and consultation. In all categories, it is of utmost importance that the worker respect the individual human being and be able to relate to older people with warmth and sympathetic understanding. He/she should be physically and emotionally stable to the extent that his/her personal problems do not impede services to the clients.

Though desirable, it is not necessary for the social worker to have had previous experience in a setting serving older people. Social work skills are transferable. Work with the elderly has elements of medical, psychiatric, family, and other types of social work. Specific content can be learned while working.

It is intended that the "social worker" positions offer an alternative career line for those who have not had full professional training leading to a graduate degree. Given the current and projected shortages in professional social work personnel, it is unrealistic to assume that there will ever be enough graduate (professional) social workers to fill the increasing number of social work positions. In addition, many social work tasks can be carried out by appropriately trained workers who do not hold graduate degrees.

Definition of the Professional Social Worker

A professional social worker shall have graduated from a master's degree program in social work from an accredited school, or have graduated from an approved doctoral program in social work, or have graduated from a master's or doctoral program in a related field as long as he/she has subsequently completed two years of full-time experience in a social work position. In states that have licensing laws he/she must meet the criteria and hold a license. He/she may function as the director, associate director, or assistant director of a department of social work, as a consultant, as provider of direct services, as a specialist in research or education, or as administrator or supervisor of one of the social work programs.

Director

Where departments of social work exist, the department director heads one of the major functional units of the facility. The director plans, develops, and administers all social work programs and services and employs and supervises professional and secretarial staff of the department. In order to implement the goal of providing integrated programs of care, he/she coordinates social work activities with those of the other major departments (administration, research, medicine, nursing, psychology, recreation, housekeeping, food service, volunteer). He/she consults with the administrative head of the facility and keeps him/her advised of all aspects of the department's work.

It is the director's responsibility to prepare statistics reflecting volume and nature of department activities and community and institutional needs, and to communicate to administration trends which may indicate a need for new or modified policies, facilities, or programs by the director. He/she hires social workers for such research projects and supervises that portion of their work concerning delivery of social services to applicants and residents.

The director prepares annual social service reports which summarize department activities, staffing, changes in procedures and policies. The report includes an evaluation of the department, suggests goals for modification or addition of services and programs, and outlines plans for their implementation.

If there is a social service committee, the director works with it in order to maintain liaison with the board, to review broad admissions policies, to inform them of social work activities, and to advise them of legislation and other community or agency affairs that are germane to operation of the agency and the department of social work.

The director represents the agency in the community by participating actively in related professional and community organizations, committee membership, and presenting papers and publications. He/she should have several years postgraduate experience and be a member of the Academy of Certified Social Workers.

Senior Professional Social Worker

A senior professional social worker, under the general direction of the director of social work, may supervise an assigned unit of graduate social workers, social workers, and social work students (graduate and undergraduate), or carry responsibility for administration of one of the programs of the department (such as intake or resident services or research programs) These responsibilities may also include carrying a partial case load. He/she may be associate or assistant director of the department and/or act as the director's delegate to share some administrative and community responsibilities. He/she participates in staff development, internal research, and policy development. A senior professional social worker has a sophisticated level of understanding and skill. He/she carries out his/her job responsibilities with consultation from the director but does not require frequent or close supervision. He/she has the capacity to evaluate the performance of personnel he/she supervises and to interpret agency policy and practice. Through review of groups of cases, he/she is able to identify client and agency needs which are guidelines for development or modification of programs and policies. His/her language skills are such that his/her reports are clear, logical, and well written. He/she should have at least two years of postgraduate experience.

Duties of the Professional Social Worker

Under the supervision of a senior professional social worker or the director of the department, the graduate social worker provides an assigned case load of clients with skilled individual and group services. He/she works with client, family members, and other professional and nonprofessional personnel around personal, emotional, interpersonal, and health problems. He/she undertakes diagnostic studies to identify the nature, cause, and extent of the client's difficulties and participates with other disciplines in planning and implementing treatment programs. He/she enables client and family to marshal their inner resources and coordinates institutional and community resources to effect maximum functioning and social adjustment. He/she calls the attention of his/her supervisor to the effect of agency policies on his/her clients, to the need for policy modification, and to gaps in institutional or community resources. The graduate social worker is able to organize his/her work and relate to agency policies and procedures in orderly fashion. He/she may require consultation but has sufficient understanding and self-awareness to select the areas to be discussed and to initiate the discussion. He/she exercises full professional responsibility in covering a case load, record keeping, and in producing reports, statistics, and so on at the appropriate time.

Consultants and Specialists

A consultant may be a professional social worker with special expertise who advises the department and/or administrator on particular areas of interest and concern. Examples are specialists in research or training. They may be involved for brief or extended time-limited basis periods or be permanent staff members.

Where he/she is the only professional social work staff at a particular facility, he/she may provide:

> Consultation to the administrator on policy, program, and development of an overall plan for social work services
> Supervision of bachelor's level social worker(s)
> In-service training of the facility's personnel with respect to social needs of residents
> Direct individual or group services to selected clients and/or case consultation
> Information about the liaison with community resources.

Bachelor's Level Social Worker

The bachelor's level social worker should have a bachelor's degree, preferably from an undergraduate social work program or with a major in the social sciences. Under the supervision of a senior professional social worker, the social worker carries an assigned case load of clients and provides them with individual and group services. He/she enables the clients to maintain or achieve improvement in their personal, health, and social situations through provision of supportive and environmental services that are preventive and rehabilitative in nature. He/she is able to recognize and identify to his/her supervisor case situations in which emotional or psychiatric problems are such that referral for intensive service by a graduate social worker or psychiatrist is indicated. He/she undertakes the social study of clients and family members within the framework of department and agency established practice. He/she has sufficient professional understanding and self-discipline to relate sensitively to the client's needs and feelings without interjecting his/her own needs and feelings. The social worker organizes his/her work, covers a case load responsibly, and relates to agency policies and procedures in orderly fashion.

Case Aide

There are no specific educational or experimental requirements for case aides. Eligibility for this position is determined by assessment of the individual's personal attributes.

The case aide performs specific tasks that worker, the case aide performs specific tasks that have been designated as part of the overall study or treatment plan of the client and family members. Examples of such tasks are instrumental assistance such as driving the client to medical appointments or to visit relations; helping the client to shop or to avail him/herself of institutional or community services such as recreational activities; and friendly telephoning or visiting. In relation to the department of social work as a whole, the case aide may perform services to facilitate and enhance its overall operation. He/she may, for example, collect and collate statistics, reorganize files and case records, and catalogue publications for the department library.

SOCIAL SERVICE COMMITTEE

Many voluntary homes for aged have a board committee that concerns itself with social service activities. Historically, many such committees were known as "admission committees." Such committees still exist in some facilities. Their tasks were implied in the old name: they interviewed and evaluated applicants and made the decisions about admission. Gradually, it was recognized that the need for admission is a complex of medical, psychological, and social factors, and that the care of the older people in those facilities required skilled professionals. This has been paralleled in progressive institutions by professionalization of the intake evaluations and decisions.

Those admissions committees which relinquished their original function freed themselves to participate in broader, more appropriate ways. The designation of "social service committee" more accurately reflects their new expanded role. While the specific activities may vary widely, one possible pattern is suggested here.

Meetings

The committee should meet at regular intervals with the director of the department of social work. The administrator, other social service staff, personnel from other departments, or speakers from other agencies and organizations may be guests on specific occasions for special purposes.

Minutes

Minutes are prepared by the director of the department and mailed to the chairperson after each meeting. Copies are also sent to the administrator and are kept on file in the department.

Functions of the Committee are:

1. To provide liaison between the board of directors and the department of social work. The chairperson of the committee attends board meetings and makes reports to that body on the work of the department of social work. The committee represents and interprets the department to the board. It transmits social service statistics regarding trends and shifts in the volume and characteristics of persons needing service and the kinds of facilities and services required. Such reporting enables the committee to serve the planning function of the board. Other reports may be concerned with special programs and activities of the department, illustrative case material indicating problems in the community, and so on.

2. To make, review, and modify broad admission policies. Case material may be presented by the director of the department or a social service staff member to illustrate a need for modification or extension of admissions policies. Other material may be presented which demonstrates how current policies are being administered—for example, rejected applications, discharged residents.

3. To be conversant with all activities of the department of social work. The agenda of the meeting may include reports and presentations designed to familiarize the committee members with the diverse activities of the department or other departments of the facility and the relationships among them. Such reports might relate to research projects; residents services; operation of other departments; use of psychological, psychiatric, medical, nursing, recreation, and volunteer services; role of the agency and social service in the total community; and legislation germane to the operation of the institution and the welfare of its applicants and residents. The committee is thus enabled to fulfill its function of interpreting the facility to the general community.

4. To provide liaison between the board and residents. As part of the meeting, the members of the committee may visit those residents who have been admitted since the last meeting date. This serves the dual purpose of a personal welcome from board to resident and permits the committee to see the various facilities and services in actual operation.

Agenda

In addition to the material outlined above, the director of the department of social work prepares and presents statistics regarding inquiries, applications, admissions, and transfers. The agenda, then, includes statistics, special case presentations, visits to new residents, guest presentations, and descriptions and discussions of new or projected facilities and services.

Part IV

ISSUES

Chapter 16

ISSUES OF CARE AND TREATMENT

Various aspects of long-term care, whether in institutional facilities or in the community, are among the burning contemporary social issues here and in many other countries as well. There are many broad social issues, such as the share of the national dollar that should be allocated to institutional care, the nature of auspices, regulation and quality control, and legislation. Another set of issues relates to the direct care and treatment of those who reside in such facilities: the kinds of old people who should be grouped together in their living areas (integration or segregation), optimal size of facilities, types of facilities, kinds of personnel required and their training, the roles that can be played by institutions vis-à-vis the community, physical design and furnishing, and the variety and types of treatment programs.

It is obvious that the two kinds of issues are interrelated. For example, the number and types of personnel and the nature of the treatment programs that are required and can be utilized are related to funds available and governmental requirements as to staffing patterns. Similarly, the physical design of a facility must conform to the Life-Safety code and other criteria set by the three levels of government.

Separating the two sets of issues is to some extent artificial, but they are dealt with in separate chapters here for the sake of organizing the material. This chapter will discuss issues specifically focused on the direct care and treatment of older people who are in long-term care facilities. Chapter 17 will describe various types of experimental psychosocial treatments that have been tried. The broad social issues are elaborated in Chapter 18.

As indicated in Chapter 2, there is no clear, generally accepted value system about what long-term care is, what life should be like in long-term care facilities, how the different services needed should be organized and blended, or about appropriate treatment programs. It was indicated in that chapter that the historical development of long-term care has resulted in current versions being a patchwork of pieces borrowed from other types of institutions from which they evolved. In short, long-term care facilities often are hazy about their goals, and goals vary considerably in different institutions. In general, long-term care has not as yet developed its own clearly delineated personality as have hospitals and various other types of institutions.

The lack of consensus about long-term care is underlined here because it is basic to all other issues of care and treatment. The goals of the institution determine the nature of care and treatment in environmental matters such as the location of the facility, its architectural design, and furnishings as well as in matters such as the organization of services, the staffing pattern, and treatment programs.

As yet there has been no real experimental attempt to design the new "something" that is a long-term care facility. The something new would aim to approximate normal living as far as possible and be flexible in accommodating various life-styles of residents. Such an attempt would begin with the needs and characteristics of the older people who require congregate institutional care. From analysis of those needs and characteristics all else would flow. The design of such a model would meet constraints such as existing governmental regulations, union job descriptions, and professional investment in roles and "turf."

The lack of total freedom to resolve some issues does not mean that we need to be pessimistic about the potential for experimentation and improvement. The state of the art in long-term care is such that there is plenty of room to make significant gains. The constantly changing population requires flexibility to respond to changing expectations and needs.

WHO SHOULD BE IN INSTITUTIONS

This issue has been discussed in earlier chapters of the guide. To summarize, it is inappropriate to frame the question in either/or terms—that is "alternatives" versus long-term institutional care. No one should be in an institution if he/she can be maintained outside of an institution at a decent level of health and well-being, if the plan does not place severe stress on the family, and if he/she wants to remain in the community. There will always be a need for institutional care for those who need round-the-clock services of a type that cannot be provided elsewhere. And there is no firm set of criteria to identify people in need of such care. The condition of the elderly person and his/her need for services must be evaluated on an individual basis in the context of the social and health supports available at the time and in the particular community and with consideration of his/her wishes and those of the family. The assessment and decision-making processes are spelled out in Chapter 3.

THE MIX OF SERVICES

There is general agreement among progressive practitioners and research investigators that the institutionalized elderly require a broad spectrum of services including maintenance services (shelter, food, and so on), personal services, health services, (medical, nursing, rehabilitative), and psychosocial services (social work, recreational, therapeutic and work-oriented activities, pastoral counseling; see Chapter 8).

Agreement is not as general among those who fund, administer, and practice in institutions about the mix of services in terms of emphasis and the balance among them. In some circles, this issue is debated in terms of the medical versus the social model. It is unfortunate that it is framed as an either/or question.

As was spelled out in Chapters 4, 7, and 8, the characteristics of the older people in long-term care, their needs for service, the nature of the decision-making process, and the permanence of the institution as their living arrangement indicate that a *social-health* model is most appropriate. Both experience and research offer firm documentation of this view. When it is so clear that both are needed, it is a rather odd assumption that health services and social services are in competition.

The issue sometimes is symbolized by discussion as

to whether the older people should be referred to as "patients" or as "residents." It it logical and legitimate that health personnel see the older people as their patients. All people, no matter what their age or living arrangement, are patients at times. But for most people, designation as "patient" is reserved for their visit to the physician's office or a short-term hospital stay. Those who reside in long-term care facilities have no other home; they do have other aspects of their personalities that must be supported if the sick role is not to be the only one left to them.

Designation as patients or as residents is not a matter of semantics. Apart from the fact that an emphasis on the whole person is in the best interests of the older people themselves, there are practical reasons. A prime example is the fact that funding mechanisms are often tied to service needs, and the current pattern emphasizes funding for medical and nursing services. Funding for social and recreational services is either grossly inadequate or nonexistent.

The real issues are how to fund and deliver all needed services and to experiment with blending them in new ways to maximize the social and health functioning of the institutionalized elderly.

THE MIX OF PEOPLE: INTEGRATION VERSUS SEGREGATION

In the past, there was a strong trend toward assigning people to different types of institutions on the basis of diagnosis and function. Thus, the "well aged" went to home for aged, the physically ill to nursing homes, and the mentally impaired to state and private psychiatric hospitals. More recently this trend has been reversed because of the large number of old people, the coexistence of mental and physical impairment, the increase in the number who reach advanced old age and the parallel increase in those who suffer from chronic brain syndrome, programs in many state to discharge elderly patients from psychiatric facilities, the gradual relaxation of admission criteria in homes for aged, and the realization that as the population of "well aged" ages, they become physically and/or mentally impaired.

Currently, most institutional facilities for aged contain the mentally and physically impaired. There is variation from facility to facility. Some refuse admission to or discharge the "difficult to care for" person. Some attempt to screen out those who have chronic brain syndrome. Others try to avoid caring for those with functional psychoses or severe behavior disorders. Such selectivity is due to the policy of a particular institution rather than to any generally accepted principle.

The reality is that most institutions find themselves caring for a mixed population and are confronted with the problem of grouping them in different living areas. How should this be done? The views expressed here are based on experience at the Philadelphia Geriatric Center and discussion with other providers.

There is general agreement that there are some subgroups of older people who should be in highly specialized facilities. Those who are so acutely ill physically that they require hospital care are an obvious example. In another group are those whose functional mental disorders are so severe that they are dangerous to themselves or others, or whose behavior is so disordered that they cannot be managed despite skilled efforts to do so. This latter group really requires a psychiatric facility and should not be in a long-term care institution unless it has a separate unit with specially trained staff and appropriate physical space and equipment.

The two groups mentioned constitute a minority of

those requiring long-term care. Grouping the remainder still is a complex problem to which there is no simple answer. A multiplicity of physical and mental health problems and different levels of functioning coexist in an endless number of combinations, making categorization of individuals difficult. Most professionals agree that the relatively intact (that is, those whose impairments do not require round-the-clock supervision and who are capable of self-care) should not be mixed with the severely impaired. Those who are mildly forgetful can often live with the more intact, depending on their level of functioning. When such individuals are in contact with relatively "normal" people, their maximal functioning is supported. On the other hand, residents with marked confusion and severely disordered behavior definitely should be segregated. They require more intensive staffing patterns and create anxiety on the part of the more intact older people. Their behavior is often disruptive and distressing (rummaging in bureaus and closets of other people, smearing of feces, sleep disturbances, removal of clothing).

While the physically competent should not be integrated with extremely disabled residents, mental functioning and the accompanying behavior is the prime discriminator.

Some practitioners feel that even those with relatively mild functional mental disorders make poor adjustments, are dissatisfied and disturbing, and should be segregated. However, experience indicates that these individuals need not be separated invariably. Good results can be achieved at times by placing them selectively based on careful evaluation of behavior, functioning, and degree of potential disturbance to others.

A major reason for "segregating" along the lines suggested is that different groups require different treatment programs. Apart from the need for differing staffing patterns in terms of physical care, psychosocial treatment programs (such as those described in the next chapter) must be geared to the needs and levels of functioning of the particular older people for whom they are designed.

THE PHYSICAL ENVIRONMENT: DESIGN, SIZE, AND LOCATION

The kind of physical environment which is most desirable for institutionalized older people is a question that is in the beginning stages of exploration. A recent report issued by the United States Senate Special Committee on Aging on nursing home care notes that the physical structure of a nursing home has far-reaching effects on the quality of care provided, and that an institutional appearance is best avoided. Many facilities are buildings that were originally designed for other purposes such as homes for well-aged, large family homes converted to small nursing homes, or short-term convalescent homes that became long-stay institutions. A good many of the new facilities were constructed along similar lines without much thought given to innovative design focusing on the need of the potential residents.

An increasing number of providers and architects are becoming interested in the design of physical facilities for older people. That interest, of course, spans individual residences, retirement villages, high-rise apartment buildings, small-unit group housing (such as the Philadelphia Geriatirc Center's Community Housing program) and other arrangements as well as long-term care facilities.

In 1974, the Philadelphia Geriatric Center opened the Weiss Institute, a new building for mentally impaired people, after a concentrated ten-year program of exploration and research to determine what such a facility should be like. The preconstruction investigations included conferences of experts from all over the world (professionals and researchers representing all disciplines), research in physical design and treatment programs, and consultation from all departments of the center. Detailed descriptions of the planning process and the building itself are available elsewhere (see reference list).

In brief, the goal was to design a building that would be prosthetic and therapeutic. Its design aimed to eliminate architectural barriers to functioning, to provide all known possible aids to functioning, and to facilitate a wide range of existing and experimental treatment programs. It also aimed to create space that could be rearranged flexibly to facilitate experimentation with using space in different ways.

The basic design of the institute's three long-term care floors is rectangular. The building also contains a geriatric hospital, outpatient diagnostic unit, classrooms, physical medicine department and other programs. The private and double rooms for forty residents on each floor—each with private bathroom—are arranged around the periphery of a very large open space, approximately 40 feet wide by 120 feet long. The semicircular free-standing nursing station permits uninterrupted visual access to the rooms. A dining area and a lounge are at one end. There is a free-standing gazebo with interior benches, and each floor has a therapeutic kitchen for the use of the residents themselves. There are also offices for a physician and for a social worker and activities therapist.

The large central space of the Weiss Institute is a dramatic departure from the long, narrow corridors of traditional nursing homes. It fosters social groupings rather than isolation and permits residents to see what is going on at all times. Bright primary colors are used on doors and in furnishings to color code each room for easy identification. Textures of floor coverings, prosthetic supports such as handrails and grab-bars in toilets and on sinks, easily visible clocks, dividers to demarcate space, specially designed furniture, lighting, and many other features combine to maximize resident functioning. The inviting living room encourages family visiting, and the large open space facilitates group recreational programs.

The Weiss Institute is, of course, only one of many possible innovative designs. Its effectiveness is being tested by research. To date it can be said that those who use it and visit it (residents, staff, and families) agree that it is a decided improvement over more traditional designs.

Some administrators and professionals feel that a fifty to seventy-five bed institution is best for purposes of coordinating services and facilitating communication among staff. Others point out that the larger institution permits a wider range of services and employment of full-time professional staff and makes it economically feasible to provide and utilize equipment such as that necessary for X-ray, clinical laboratories, physiotherapy, and a heart station. The larger facility also permits economies by means of centralized maintenance, food, and housekeeping services.

Some large facilities, such as the long-term care buildings at the Philadelphia Geriatric Center deal with problems of size by organizing functionally into smaller units. For example, each unit or floor has an assigned physician, social worker, and activities therapist as well as a nursing care-coordinator and staff. The floor develops its own "culture" and can become a cohesive unit—a small facility operating within a larger one.

As for location of a facility, the day is gone when it was deemed desirable to locate the old people as far out in the country as possible so they could enjoy the trees and birds; or when the facility was placed so that it did not "spoil" residential neighborhoods. It is generally agreed that facilities should be part of the community—for the benefit of the community as well as the older people. Location should facilitate family visiting. Older people are diverse. Some like the country or suburbs, others are most at home in busy urban areas. In this instance, as in all planning for older people, the diversity of facilities should match the variety of tastes and wishes of their occupants.

New Role of the Institution

Progressive administrators, researchers, and professionals of all types are in agreement that the institution, by virtue of the fact that it is a "total" mini-community, can foster an undesirable situation in which its residents become isolated from the world around them. At the same time, the larger community is in need of a variety of services that some institutions are in a position to provide. Ways therefore are being tried to dissolve the barriers between institution and community to their mutual benefit.

There are many methods of bringing the outer community into the long-term care facility. Encouragement of visiting from family and friends of the residents is basic. Other community ties of the residents that existed prior to admission can also be fostered. Many residents had group associations such as church or synagogue, veterans' organizations, Golden Age Clubs, fraternal orders, and charitable or service organizations. Identifying those links to the community can lead to invitations for them to visit or to arrange for the resident to attend their meetings. Many such organizations, whether or not a resident had been a member, are most willing to plan programs of entertainment. Schools are receptive to programs in facilities at holiday times or visits to socialize with the older people. Educational institutions can offer courses given at the facility. Many other possibilities emerge when imagination is exercised.

The trend toward the institution playing an expanded role in the community developed in recognition that many contain concentrations of equipment and personnel that can be utilized more fully. It often is more economical to use an institution's facilities than to start a new free-standing service. For example, the Philadelphia Geriatric Center prepares thousands of meals daily for its own community of 1,000 older people and more than 700 staff. Its kitchens now also prepare meals that are sent to a community center's hot lunch program for the elderly and that are delivered to older people at home in the center's community housing project. As part of an experimental program, the Logan program of Services to the Elderly, a variety of services are delivered to older people residing in the vicinity of the center: meal service, housekeeping service, minor home repairs (or chore service), a telephone network, and information and referral service. The center also allows its facilities to be used as a meeting site for groups such as a Golden Age Club.

Another recently instituted program at the PGC that serves the community is its Baer Consultation and Diagnostic Center. This program offers a thorough interdisciplinary evaluation to older people, no matter what their place of residence. The basic work-up includes medical, psychiatric, social, psychological, and nursing evaluation. X-ray and laboratory studies are routine, and special studies are ordered as needed. The procedures occupy a minimum of two days. They conclude after the team conference is followed by a conference with patient and family to communicate findings and make recommendations. In this way the professional staff of the center, highly skilled in care of older people, extends its expertise to the larger community of the elderly.

Other programs that have been developing in a variety of facilities in the United States are day care for the impaired elderly and temporary care to permit family vacations or to tide families over emergencies.

TYPES OF CONGREGATE CARE FACILITIES

The word "institution" conveys a facility characterized by concentrations of aged in the upper brackets of the aging phase of life, who are mentally and/or physically impaired to an extent requiring round-the-clock supervision, and for whom such placement is most often permanent. Between such total-care facilities and totally independent community living, a wide range of intermediate arrangements exist and are evolving. While called by many other names, in reality many of them are congregate care facilities, and their wide acceptance may provide some clues to shape the new look of the institutions of the future. In 1965, writing about the PGC's apartment buildings, the York Houses, Waldman stated, "It would appear that we have somewhat restructured and made palatable a service that dates back to the 12th century"—a home for the aged.

The most visible of the newer forms of congregate living for the elderly are apartment buildings, hotels, and retirement villages for the elderly which have increased rapidly in the past ten years. Apartment buildings range from those which provide only shelter to those with one or more additional services such as medical care, meals, housekeeping, and recreation. Many of the tenants could not live independently of these services. Nevertheless, they do not consider themselves to be institutionalized. Lawton's broad research indicates that the decision to include services may affect the characteristics of the population which applies. That is, the offering of services appears to attract older, sicker, and less active people.

"Boarding" homes and "foster" homes for the elderly are increasing. They vary widely in quality of service but obviously are providing some personal care services. There are also some efforts being made to create new types of dwelling arrangements. For example, the Philadelphia Geriatric Center has experimented with "intermediate" housing by purchasing small one family dwellings on an adjacent street and renovating them to accommodate three elderly people in each in efficiency apartments. A number of services are included (building maintenance, a "hot line" telephone for medical emergencies, and social services), and others (main meal, housekeeping) are provided at the tenant's option. A specially designed medically oriented, federally sponsored apartment building for the physically handicapped is in operation in Fall River, Massachusetts, and its impact has been evaluated by a research group headed by Sherwood.

The heterogeneity of the aging population is such that only a broad spectrum of congregate care facilities can meet its needs. Undoubtedly, those which are short of institutions in terms of saturation services should and will increase. Research is needed to establish criteria for their selective use and to determine the differential impact of these facilities on the health and general wellbeing of the residents.

Personnel and Training

One of the major tasks confronting the long-term care field is the need to upgrade and professionalize personnel at all levels.

Professional schools still have much to accomplish in

recruiting and educating administrators, recreation therapists, physicians, nurses, social workers, psychologists, and others to work in long-term care facilities. However, there has been progress in recent years. A process of consciousness-raising has been underway, with the result that more and more young people are being attracted. Many professional schools are establishing relationships with institutions that are serving as training sites.

A parallel deficit exists in the recruitment and training of those who provide the minute-to-minute care and services. Most of the direct contact of the residents is with nurse's aides, orderlies, LPNs, food service, and housekeeping personnel. Their attitudes and approach to their jobs and the residents are of prime importance. But an attitude of tender loving care must still be accompanied by knowledge and skill.

The direct-care staff are often poorly paid and have had little or no training prior to being employed in an institution. They need the feeling that their work is important and that they are regarded as dignified and valuable employees. Training programs should be geared not only to the specific skills required but also to sensitizing the workers to problems that should be reported or referred to professional staff. When programs of training are carried out, the direct-care staff are primary therapeutic agents. The work becomes less routine and more interesting, the job is more attractive, and there is likely to be less turnover in staff.

There are many ways to approach the training tasks. Every institution should have an ongoing program of in-service training. It is desirable to supplement this basic program with special programs such as sensitivity training or attendance at appropriate courses given outside the institution. Some large institutions offer a varied program of courses attended by staff of long-term care facilities in their geographic area. (Examples are the Frederick D. Zeman Center for Instruction at the Jewish Home and Hospital for the Aged in New York City, and the Regional Training Center at the Philadelphia Geriatric Center).

One direction for the future is exploration of ways in which existing job definitions can be reorganized. Strict delineation of roles that have been carried over from other settings such as hospitals are not always appropriate to long-term care. A few facilities are experimenting with new constellations of tasks. One such idea is the creation of a "geriatric aide" who combines some aspects of the jobs of nurse's aide, housekeeper, and food service personnel. The idea is for the nature of the job to evolve from the needs of the residents and the facility in order to provide care that is less fragmented. Obviously certain tasks would have to remain with the specialist, but many employees could expand and redefine their roles. Many people feel that long-term care is so different from hospital care that separate training programs should be developed. The personnel would be educated to appropriate approaches from the outset, rather than needing to unlearn and relearn subsequent to training in other types of settings.

The importance of training cannot be overstated. The most benign intent in the administration of a facility, the most advanced physical plant, and the most sophisticated and humanistic programs can be negated by inadequate numbers of personnel or by personnel who do not have the necessary training and attitudes.

Chapter 17

EXPERIMENTAL TREATMENT PROGRAMS

When used in its broadest sense, the word "treatment" applies to every aspect of institutional care. Institutions in themselves should be a method of treatment in the dictionary meaning of "to provide care for" or "to seek cure or relief." They have value only if they offer their residents a situation that improves upon their previous situations and that is the best one possible for each individual at that particular time. Further, it is not enough for the institution simply to be better than any existing alternative. In every aspect, it must strive to provide care in such a manner that each resident's potential for health and well-being is maximized. "Cure" and "improvement" are not always possible with the population being discussed; retarding or arresting decline are also legitimate treatment goals.

There are many aspects of institutions as treatment facilities. Many types of treatment should be provided by many professions: medical, psychiatric, social, nursing, recreational, psychological, and other therapies are all forms of treatment. Chapters 6 through 15 describe the social work treatment. It has been emphasized throughout that these various treatments must be integrated if they are to be effective and that the treatment begins with the first contact between institution and the older person and family and ends only with discharge or death. Chapter 16 discussed the issue of the creative blending or mixing of these professional treatment services so that institutional living can approximate a normal lifestyle as closely as possible.

An increasing number of experimental treatment programs are being designed, applied, and in some instances tested via research. These treatment programs aim to go beyond good custodial care and to effect additional improvement in the residents' behavior, wellbeing, and functioning. One aspect of their significance lies in the fact that they are therapeutically optimistic. That is, they assume that something can be done and do not view insitutionalized old people as at the end of the road, without potential for improvement.

Some of the better known of these treatment programs will be summarized briefly in this chapter. The programs described will be limited to those focused on psychosocial interventions. Other forms of treatment are not included, such as medical care, individual and group psychotherapy, social work, activities therapy (such as art, music, work), drug therapy, electro-shock treatment, hyperbaric chambers, surgical treatment, and so on.

In reviewing some of the treatment programs for possible application, the reader should keep the following considerations in mind:

1. The summaries presented below are not sufficiently detailed to be used as a basis for replicating the programs. Those who wish to do so should read complete descriptions of the appropriate program (most are listed in the references of this guide) and obtain expert consultation when indicated.

2. The programs described in some instances were tried in facilities that began with relatively low levels of care. It is therefore difficult to sort out the effects of the specific treatment and the effects of improvements made in other aspects of care.

3. No one program is a panacea. Some programs catch on because they seem simple to apply, or because they have an attractive title, or simply because they seem to make sense. At times a given program may become so popular that it reaches fad proportions. Any given program should be used selectively keeping in mind its specific applicability to a particular subgroup of institutionalized people. The elderly in long-term care are heterogeneous and certain kinds of people respond better to certain kinds of programs. For example, a treatment for those with chronic brain syndrome may not be appropriate for those with a functional psychosis or those with a reactive depression. Further, as was emphasized in Chapter 10, it must be geared to the level of the group to which it is to be applied.

4. The use of one particular treatment program does not mean that no other treatment is necessary. Often, elements of several treatments can be combined effectively.

These treatment programs do not substitute for the skilled professional services which themselves are therapeutic. The interdisciplinary approach is a necessity to integrate the different aspects of treatment.

5. The fact that improvements achieved as a result of any of the treatments dissipate when the treatment is withdrawn (particularly for individuals with chronic brain syndrome) does not mean the treatment was unsuccessful. The conditions toward which such treatments are directed are *chronic*. Chronic psychosocial conditions require continued treatment just as chronic medical conditions require continued treatment. In beginning a treatment program, therefore, the expectation should be that, if successful, it will be continued.

6. Expectations and goals should be spelled out at the outset and should be in keeping with the potential of the people to be treated. As has been emphasized throughout the guide, goals for institutionalized older people must be more limited than those for other populations. Some methods of evaluating whether or not the treatment is effective should be built into the overall plan.

7. To be successful, any program instituted must have the strong backing of those responsible for administering the facility and all personnel who will be involved in any way. Most programs require changed behavior, attitudes, and routines of all institutional staff. Their understanding and support are therefore essential.

8. Finally, treatment technology for in-

stitutionalized older people is at a very early
stage of development. Many new ideas undoubtedly will emerge. It is important to
keep in touch with the professional and research communities, to evaluate new programs critically for their applicability to any
given facility and its population, and to be
receptive to trying those that may be appropriate.

The following summaries by no means constitute an
exhaustive survey. They are simply examples of some of
the major programs that have evolved in recent years.

INDIVIDUALIZED TREATMENT OF EXCESS DISABILITIES

This treatment was developed and tested via research at
the Philadelphia Geriatric Center. It was designed for
residents with moderate to severe chronic brain syndrome. The key concept of this highly individualized interdisciplinary program was to identify and treat each
resident's "excess disabilities" (EDs). The phrase excess
disability was defined as the discrepancy or gap between
the resident's actual functioning in any sphere (social,
physical, psychological) and his/her potential functioning. Thus, if a resident was wheelchair bound, but evaluation indicated potential for walking with a walker,
he/she would have an ED which could be treated. Or if a
resident sat alone sadly all day without any social contacts but was presumed to have the capacity and need
for socialization, that would be an ED.

Basic principles of the program were individualization, the interdisciplinary approach (psychologist, nurse,
social worker, physician, and psychiatrist plus other
specialists as needed), and the setting of realistic goals.

Each resident received a thorough evaluation by each of the professional team members. At the meeting of the team, all EDs were identified, the treatments were decided upon, and assignments for carrying out the treatment were made to various staff members. The treatments decided upon relied heavily on the individual's history, past interests and skills, personality, and experience. One year later, the same complete evaluation took place again to see if each specific ED had responded to the treatment.

The research evaluation indicated that the treatment had been successful since the EDs of the residents treated improved significantly as compared to a control group which had the same evaluations but had simply continued to receive the usual treatment programs at the institution. Most EDs fell into one of seven categories: locomotion, personal self-care, social relations, family relationships, organized activities, individual activities, and emotional discomfort (depression, anxiety, and so on). Although improvements were made in all categories, it is interesting that the greatest gains were made in the areas of activities and family relationships.

Some other findings of the project were:

Treatment of a specific ED did not spill over to other EDs. That is, if a resident was treated to improve an ED in the area of socialization, he/she did not improve in other areas unless they too were being treated.

People with a particular kind of personality, notably "aggressive," mangerial types, responded best to treatment.

When the experimental treatment ended, the gains made gradually dissipated.

Families (contrary to popular notions) had not abandoned their institutionalized family members but continued to visit and to be very much involved with the old people. Relationships with families were extremely important to the older people.

The researchers emphasize that the success of the interdisciplinary approach was due to insistence on the setting of very specific goals (such as focusing on EDs) and to follow-through of treatment with the reevaluation time specified. They point out that in contrast to many experimental programs the residents studied already had been receiving a high level of care. The success of the treatment therefore cannot be attributed to improvements made in the general level of care. The individuals receiving the treatment were those about whom there is too often the pessimistic attitude that they are beyond treatment.

This kind of an individualized approach should, in one form of another, go on in all facilities for all residents. It is not a substitute for various group approaches nor are they substitutes for individualization. Though it was tested in relation to a specific mentally impaired population, its methods are applicable to any institutionalized people, and it can be combined with other treatment programs.

Milieu Approaches

Milieu therapy was one of the first attempts at a positive treatment approach for institutionalized people. Since the earliest efforts by people like Maxwell Jones, Harry Stack Sullivan, and the Menningers, many variations of this type of program have been developed and tested. Most reports describe programs that began in psychiatric hospitals, and many were aimed at patients of all ages. Among studies that examined the effects of milieu treatment on older people, are those that are listed in the references as articles by A. Rechtschaffen, S. Atkinson, and W. Pappas; those by E. J. Burdock, J. Sklar, and F. J. O'Neill; those by Richard Sanders and his colleagues at Philadelphia State Hospital; and a major series by Wilma Donahue and her colleagues (in particular Leonard Gottesman) at Ypsilanti State Hospital in Michigan and other facilities.

The underlying concept of milieu therapy is that the social environment itself can constitute the treatment. The form of milieu therapy called the Therapeutic Community involves every aspect of the treatment environment including all relationships with staff and peers and all activities.

The theoretical base of milieu treatment is ego theory. It aims to strengthen ego functions by capitalizing on those that are still intact. The environment is structured in such a way that the individual is encouraged to try new skills in dealing with the social environment and in assuming social and vocational roles. The staff and environment provide opportunities that set up an expectation of appropriate responses on the part of the patient. Those expectations are geared to the level of functioning so that they do not over-tax the patient.

Participation of the patient in the organizing and running of the "community" is maximized. A variety of activities have been used in conjunction with milieu therapy: crafts, occupational therapy, and social groups. Some programs involved other modalities such as redecoration of the physical environment, aspects of self-government, time-place orientation, structured groups, sheltered workshop, and roles and activities out of the hospital.

Milieu therapy, like some other treatments, requires the cooperative efforts of all staff members. Often, the traditional roles of staff are modified to fit the demands of the program. Retraining and in-service training are therefore necessary on an ongoing basis.

Most of the research programs that have tested various forms of milieu therapy report success in improving behavior and in increasing the discharge rate for those treated, though some proportion of those discharged eventually were readmitted. Many of the programs included patients of varying ages and diagnoses. More investigation therefore is required to identify the particular kinds of people who respond best to this therapy. Other limitations of milieu therapy are the risk of individual needs being lost through the focus on the group and the fact that it is difficult to sort out which of the many treatment factors accounts for changes that occur. There is no question however, that milieu therapy has been a major and positive influence in reshaping treatment approaches, particularly in relation to mental hospital patients.

REALITY ORIENTATION AND ATTITUDE THERAPY

Reality orientation (RO) had its beginnings at the Veterans Administration Hospital in Topeka, Kansas in 1959, and it was elaborated under the direction of Dr. Folsom at the V.A. Hospital in Tuscaloosa, Alabama. The Guide for Reality Orientation at the latter facility describes RO "as basic technique in the rehabilitation of persons having a moderate to severe degree of memory loss, confusion, and time-place-person disorientation."

Reality orientation has two phases: "24-Hour Reality Orientation" for any confused person and "classroom RO" for any who need intensive sessions for gross confusion. The latter was developed at the Tuscaloosa Hospital in 1965 to supplement the basic program. Attitude Therapy is often employed together with RO.

A prominent feature of 24-hour RO is that it is to be used by every staff person who has any contact with the elderly resident. It therefore relies heavily on the training of direct care staff (aides, nursing assistants, housekeepers, and so on) and on their adherence to its principles and practices. Classroom RO can be conducted largely by nursing assistants. All individuals who exhibit the symptoms of confusion or disorientation are included in the program, regardless of the etiology of those symptoms. The goal is to reverse the downhill process.

The basic technique is to constantly repeat to the patient concrete information such as his/her name, his/her location, the time, day, and date, daily events that occur such as which meal it is and the names of the foods served. He/she invariably is told where he/she is going (to the doctor, to the bathroom), what will happen, and what is expected of him/her. Staff are instructed to be patient, to address the older people by their correct titles (not by first names), to repeat direction often, to reward the patient for correct responses and to gradually decrease direct assistance when he/she is able to be more self-directing. As the name of the program suggests, all conversation and activities must be reality oriented. The atmosphere should be quiet and friendly.

RO uses environmental aids to reinforce staff approaches. One of the main aids is the RO Board which spells out the name of the facility, the year, date, and day, and other information such as the weather, a special activity that will take place that day, and the names of staff. Other environmental aids are large calendars and clocks, and color coding of key places and doors.

When Attitude Therapy is to be used in conjunction with RO, a specific attitude toward each patient is decided upon by the staff team. The *Guide to Attitude*

Therapy published at the VA Hospital in Tuscaloosa states:

> Consistent expression of a positive and expectant attitude by staff is also necessary with Reality Orientation. Usually, Active Friendliness is used in approaching the geriatric patient. This is a supportive ego-building attitude that helps the patient to feel that he is worth something after all, that someone cares, that life has not passed him by. Often a Matter-of-Fact approach is needed in conjunction with Active Friendliness according to the behavior the patient is exhibiting. The rationale is that he should learn to accept some responsibility for his own behaviors. The Matter-of-Fact attitude prevents staff from doing for the patient those things he can do for himself and influences him toward more positive self-care. Other attitudes may be necessary in dealing with the person depending on the behavior he is exhibiting.

Classroom RO, as its name conveys, takes place in special classrooms and is aimed at those who require more intensive work in a structured environment. Small groups (four to six people) are the rule and participants are selected by the treatment team. There are two levels—the basic class and the advanced class. The same instructor conducts the intensive daily half-hour session for a minimum of ten weeks. Detailed instructions for conducting these classes are available from the VA Hospital at Tuscaloosa. Successful completion of the "course" is marked by a graduation exercise. The patients may then be moved into programs such as remotivation, resocialization, and other therapeutic groups.

RO has become extremely popular in recent years, stimulating much interest in the community of those caring for institutionalized older people. One report from Tuscaloosa indicated that as of July, 1969, about 20 percent of those in an RO program had improved to the point where discharge from the hospital was possible. Another report of a study of 125 men in the program found that 68 percent of them remained at their initial level of functioning while 32 percent improved. The investigators felt that this is encouraging in view of the fact that older institutionalized people generally decline. Their experience indicated that the decline was arrested for most and some actually improved. To date, however, there have been no reports of controlled research studies to evaluate RO. That is, the groups studied in various reports were not compared with groups that did not receive RO therapy.

Caution must be exercised in application of RO. In particular, the prescription of a single "attitude" towards a given individual seems overly simplistic. It may obscure the need to explore the reasons for certain kinds of behaviors. RO also requires much judgment on the part of staff. Most facilities inevitably contain people of varying levels of functioning in the same areas. Universal application of the repetition of names, places, and so on has the potential of infantilizing, even insulting those whose cognitive capacities do not require it. Like any other specialized program, RO does not substitute for other types of programs that should be ongoing.

Many aspects of RO are useful. As with any new treatment technique aimed at confused and disoriented people, it assumes that improvement can occur. This in itself is encouraging. In RO, that attitude is conveyed to all levels of staff who work as a team. It certainly adds a dimension to the roles of direct care personnel, involving them in a therapeutic rather than custodial approach. Many aspects of RO staff training are those that should be incorporated in any training program such as respectful attitudes, the creation of a calm and friendly atmosphere, and giving people information as to what is happening to them. The "props" such as the RO board are useful for all institutions, where even residents who are cognitively intact can lose track of days and dates.

REMOTIVATION

Remotivation, like milieu treatment, began in psychiatric hospitals. Its goals are to stimulate people to become involved in thinking about the real world and to help them relate to others. The staff person responsible is often a specially trained nursing aide or attendant who meets weekly for a period of about three months with a small group of five to twelve patients.

In preparation for each meeting, the remotivator gathers materials on a particular topic—visual aids such as pictures, articles, movies, or props that are used in the particular activity to be discussed. The subject matter always relates to the world from which the group members come and they are encouraged to participate in discussion about it.

Each meeting follows a pattern of five successive stages: creating a climate of acceptance; building the bridge to reality through introduction of the topic; detailed discussion of the topic and use of the previously prepared visual aids; discussion of work, particularly work the group members used to perform; and finally, summary of the session by the motivator; his/her expression of appreciation; and reminder of the time and place of the next meeting.

Remotivation is often used after an individual has successfully completed Reality Orientation. It has been used in many different settings with people of different ages and in some instances with confused elderly patients. We are not aware of any research evaluation of this technique. Professionals in the field feel that it has reached many people, but that others do not respond because of the abstract thinking it requires.

Behavior Modification

One of the more recent of the new therapies, behavior modification aims to effect changes in specific behaviors rather than to change personality through deep therapy. There are many techniques that come under the overall rubric of behavior modification. L. Krasner states that there are four major types of behavior modification techniques: positive reinforcement (in which desirable behaviors are systematically rewarded); desensitization (in which the individual is taught to overcome his/her fear of a particular behavior through relaxation); aversive procedures (in which the individual is punished for undesirable behaviors); and modeling (in which the individual's behavior changes when he/she observes the behavior of appropriate models).

Of the four techniques, reinforcement techniques are the most widely used in institutions. Originally, they were an outgrowth of the famous experiments of Pavlov in which he substituted a new stimulus to cause a response previously elicited by another stimulus. In practical terms, a person changes his/her behavior if the desired behavior is followed by feelings of pleasure or a token reward.

In "token economies" that have developed in institutional settings, the token earned by desirable behaviors can be used to purchase things. In one such program in a psychiatric hospital the tokens purchased daily needs such as food, bed, and privileges. In another experiment, an attempt was made to stop undesirable behavior by withholding desired rewards. In still another that at-

tracted wide attention, wine was the most effective pur-
chasable item in stimulating desirable behavior, while
cigarettes were second in popularity. As might be expected, the attractiveness of the product depended on
the individual patient's previous attitude toward it.

An article by Eleanor K. Barns and her colleagues
(listed in the references) states that reinforcement
therapies can be used in homes for aged to help residents establish more independent roles. That is, it can
foster self-care, unit work, and social behavior such as
helping others or starting an activity. Reinforcement
therapy can be used on an individual basis as well as
with groups.

Like some other therapies, these techniques require
special training and commitment of staff. Special skill
and judgment is necessary in the selection of behaviors
to be treated and in implementing the rather complex
program. Many attempts have successfully improved behavior, but it usually is not sustained if the program is
not continued. It has been suggested that success relies
more heavily on relationships with staff than on the particular reward used. The personality of the individual is
thought to be predictive of his response to such a program.

OTHER PROGRAMS

Among other formal programs of treatment are Resocialization, Sensory Retraining, Self-Image Therapy,
and a wide variety of activity therapies (dance therapy,
art therapy, movement therapy, and crafts). Those who
are interested in finding out more about them can do so
by reading articles listed in the references to this chapter. Reviews and additional references also appear in the
article by Eleanor K. Barns and colleagues, and in book

chapters by Leonard Gottesman and Elaine Brody and by Ruth Bennett and Carl Eisdorfer (also listed in the references).

It is underlined that any and all of these programs should be used with caution and under professional guidance. Most are in the experimental stage. Some work for certain types of people and not for others. While most have demonstrated some success, none is an unqualified success. All require sensitivity and judgment in application. And, as stated in the beginning of the chapter, none substitutes for basic professional services of experienced physicians, social workers, psychologists, nurses, and others.

Chapter 18

SOCIAL POLICY ISSUES

by Stanley J. Brody

The American community is now aware that the economic cornucopia has finite limitations. On a variety of levels, it is perceived that our resources are limited and that choices must be made from among many purposes as to how they are to be allocated. Currently, over $134 billion are being spent for health services. This represents 8.6 percent of the gross national product. Since long-term care is part of the national health expenditure, decisions as to how much money is to be designated for health will influence what resources are available for long-term care.

Similar value judgments must be made as to the division of the health dollar among the various priorities that are presented. Ambulatory care, home health service, acute-care hospitals, rehabilitation centers, housing with services, intermediate care, and skilled nursing care are some of the many services that crowd individual and legislative agendas of need. Resolution of which service needs will be funded will depend on both individual and community values. Choices will be expressed through individual direct payment for these services or commitment to them by private insurance arrangements. Collective individual assessment of priorities may be evidenced by the benefits pursued through group arrangements such as union contracts. Thus, a concern for the well-being of retired workers may evoke provision of third-party payment for nursing home care or other forms of long-term care.

On a broader nationwide and state level, legislators are deciding how much of the public dollar should be allocated to long-term care. To a large degree, the decisions will reflect community values placed on longevity and upon the well-being of the elderly. The decision will also be determined by the effectiveness of interest groups who express their interest in the aged and, in particular, those elderly at risk.

The debate on national health insurance is a forum for the expression of those concerns. Initially, this discussion was for the most part narrowly focused on acute care needs and the services anticipated were restricted to ambulatory physician visits and acute hospital care. While Medicare has made provisions for the long-term care services of home health and skilled nursing homes (originally termed extended care facilities), the administration of the program was such as to virtually abort these services. Medicaid is a clearer recognition of the need for long-term care services, both in the community and in institutions, without the time limitations of Medicare, but only for the indigent.

Currently, the debate is being expanded. The Administration and Congress are initiating proposals which seem to recognize the value of increased public support for long-term care through community agencies and in institutions. At the same time, the high cost of acute care is acknowledged and various regulatory devices sought to control the high expenditure for acute care hospitalization. For example, long-term skilled nursing home care was proposed as a part of a national health insurance proposal by the Kennedy-Mills bill. Senator Moss and others have introduced legislative proposals for extensive provision of home health services.

Among the issues facing consideration of public reimbursement of long-term care are the problems of defining the need for care, what these services should be, how they should be assured both quantitatively and qualitatively, and what the method of financing should be.

Need/Demand for Long-Term Care

Needs for services are usually perceived as being defined by providers. Most often these decisions are expressed in the course of delivery of care. Thus, the need for skilled nursing homes is operationally decided by physicians or social workers as part of the disposition process on discharge from an acute care hospital. Similar decisions are made for home health care or for housing arrangements. Because of the nature of current payment arrangements for these services, the physician is almost invariably a central figure to these decisions. Even if the family and the individual are making long-term plans they will inevitably become involved with the physician because of the requirements of third-party payment systems or of the admitting agency. In turn, these determinations are conditioned by the existence of resources and their geographical placement.

Needs, too, are determined by the provider agency.

Adequacy of fiscal reimbursement and the convenience of the provider are controlling considerations. If the state reimbursement formula is deemed inadequate by the nursing home operator, the applicant too often will be denied admission. Such denial extends to applicants for skilled nursing home care even under adequate Medicare reimbursement, if the proprietor anticipates that at the end of the Medicare funded stay the applicant may then be dependent upon inadequate Medicaid payment for support. Providers are known to pick and choose from among applicants even when funding is not an issue. Severely brain-damaged, incontinent, or bedfast potential residents, or those who are members of minority groups, may be turned away for reasons of convenience of the provider. Staff may either not be available in suitable numbers or express a preference not to be confronted with residents perceived to be unpleasant or difficult. In short, needs determination for long-term care by providers does not present a totally objective evaluation of what optimum service arrangement is required.

Demand for services is characterized in terms of consumers' perception of need. Not only does such a demand statement suffer the same constraints as the provider determination of need, that is, the availability and location of resources, but more controlling is the mechanism to pay for the services. Appropriateness of services is often less a determinant than fiscal accessibility. For example, the placement of a relative may be based on whether the service is eligible for reimbursement by a public payment system.

There is no clear statement yet available of what is the need/demand for long-term care. Such an assessment will require establishment of criteria which may be applied to the trajectory of chronic illness that, if met, will create the need/demand for services. On the basis of such criteria the changing dimensions of the problem may be defined and evaluated. This information, made available to policy-makers, will enable them to anticipate the size and scope of the problem and to consider appropriate solutions.

Given the changing demography of older people, both in numbers and in health status, current population predictions combined with these criteria may be extrapolated to anticipate the course of future needs. Many of the resources necessary for rendering long-term care require lead time for their development. Not only do residential institutions require a gestation period of planning, financing, and implementation, but so does the provision of suitable personnel. The training process similarly involves planning of curricula, recruitment of students, financing the learning, and the time of the educational experience.

The lack of clarity as to needs/demands will remain a major obstacle to the resolution of the long-term care issue. Funding research through the new National Institute on Aging, the Administration on Aging and other public and foundation resources is the first step to acquiring knowledge. Perhaps an even more difficult task is the development of the methodology to furnish the information.

Long-Term Care Services

Just as there is a problem in defining need/demand, so is there in the spelling out of the specific dimensions of the responsive services. The kind, quality, and auspice under which they are to be rendered are three dimensions of this issue.

The pervasive problem of definition continues on through the description of appropriate services (see Chapter 2 for discussion of this issue). Long-term care is seen as a spectrum of services responding to different needs/demands along the trajectory of chronic illness and chronic disability. At different points in time, framed by varying conditions, services should be availabe to improve, modify, and support the changing problems of adaptation of the chronically ill.

Each particular type of existing service is subject to multiple definitions either by law, regulation, or practice. Home health service can be seen as providing all or part of personal care, homemaker, escort, chore, counseling, extended medical, or meal preparation services. They may be rendered by home health aides, homemakers, volunteers, social workers, occupational, physical or recreational therapists, licensed practical nurses, registered nurses, nurses' aides, physicians' assistants, nurse clinicians, or physicians.

Varying kinds of residential facilities present the same problem. To some extent many of these resources are in developmental stages, and there is as yet no clear prescription of which services are appropriate to which condition. Some of the confusion is evident by the different appellations which may be used for a chronically ill individual. Client, inmate, patient, recipient, beneficiary or resident are some of the terms which may be used simultaneously by different providers coming from different disciplines but treating the same person (see Chapter 3). The use of these terms reflects different perceptions of need and may create different demands on the part of the individual and his/her family and determine what system of funding may be available to meet these demands.

The funding sources also contribute to the confusion of descriptive terminology. A skilled nursing home. with an extensive rehabilitation facility, in-depth social work, a full activities program and a complete high quality nursing program may be characterized identically and funded equally with a facility which is virtually a custodial institution. The only similarity between the two institutions may be their accommodation to minimum physical and staffing requirements.

The range of quality of care within broad classifications of services is so diverse as to defeat the usefulness of the categorization of the facility. Under such circumstances the task of matching the need/demand becomes even more difficult and implementation of the plan of treatment improbable if not impossible.

The recent evolution of homes for the aged from a role designated for the care of the well aged to that of nursing home care for the seriously handicapped elderly has not afforded the field time to establish adequate criteria for quality of care. A similar observation may be made with respect to other forms of long-term care in the community. Thus, senior citizen centers have been developing from a response to the well aged for socialization and recreation to more complex programs which may include congregate feeding, medical care, rehabilitation therapy, and counseling. New models are emerging such as day hospitals which may parallel or overlap the function of some more advanced senior citizen centers. Legislative perception of priorities from among the needs of the elderly swing wildly from the well to the frail elderly. While on the one hand Congress will enact in the Older Americans Act a call for primary concern for the poor and severely handicapped elderly, they nevertheless will express equal concern when confronted by application of a means test for senior citizen center services.

Essentially the problem of developing criteria of quality of care is clouded by the lack of clarity as to the target population and kind of services to be afforded. This in turn reflects the confusion as to the purpose of the programs. The issue of the nature of the long-term care institution is a residual of this absence of defined purpose. The current focus on physical criteria is a expression of governmental myopia. Staffing considerations are limited, in the most stringent of public regulatory efforts, to formulas of medical personnel (nursing) to number of residents. The same focus on physical facilities is evident in senior citizen centers. The medical focus is likewise present in home health care programs.

The basic question that must be confronted is care of whom for what: what goals are the programs designed to serve? The objectives remain to be defined in terms of target population and services. Thus, if the service population of a skilled nursing home was seen as the severely handicapped elderly and the services in terms of maintaining the highest level of functioning, then criteria of quality of care would emphasize social work, rehabilitation therapies, and activity programs.

The issue of auspice is important because of expressions of concern about the motivation and capability of profit-making institutions in providing a quality service, while about 70 percent of the beds are under such auspices (see Chapter 2).

The dichotomy between profit-making and not profit-making auspice is not confined to the long-term care issue. It runs through the entire gamut of the provision of health care. The physician, pharmacist, and other fee-for-service individual providers share this problem with health care institutions such as acute care general hospitals. In the long-term care field, home health care is increasingly the domain of profit-making enterprises. The development of the proprietary nursing home in recent years was in large part a response to generous public financing of their construction. The admittedly inadequate funding under Medicaid in most states has contributed to the low level of care in both private and voluntary nursing homes.

In New York State, financing of care has been virtually on cost of care as asserted by the provider. The Moreland Commission, in the most recent of a long series of New York State investigatory groups, concluded that many proprietary homes give good care but that the industry was riddled "with real estate operators seeking the fast buck" (Hess). In the few attempts to research the significance of proprietary or nonprofit auspice no clear determination of level of care has emerged. The voluntary sector, confronted with inadequate funding, has not demonstrated a clear superiority of performance. It can be said, however, that advances in improving the quality of care in nursing homes have emerged primarily from the voluntary agency. In the main, voluntary homes do provide a larger budget for social work and recreational activities. Many proprietaries who have access to upper income consumers are able to deliver a level of care which, in the absence of any clear criteria, seems adequate. Indeed, many voluntary agencies find that when the fee structure is increased to cover an adequate level of care, the consumer demand expresses a preference for non-voluntary agencies. To some extent this is conditioned by the reaction to a "charitable" auspice, and to a sense of class distinction by the applicant and his family.

Certainly, where the nonprofit agency is governmental there is no clear superiority of performance. The unending public challenges of care given in state mental hospitals and schools for the retarded give witness that public auspice is no guarantee of adequate care. The county home is a history emerging out of a gothic past. Many local public homes give excellent care, but many equally are burdened by politically dominated admissions and staffing, inadequate funding, and ancient physical facilities.

Regulation and Reimbursement

The two approaches used by the government to control behavior are those of the carrot and the stick. Often the two mechanisms are used together. In recent years, this has been the pattern for skilled nursing facilities. Thus, in order to receive public reimbursement, the nursing home director must be licensed. Of course, such a program will only be effective if the facility is dependent on public financing either through Medicare or Medicaid.

Regulation is a form of quality control. It is responsive to those problems in addition to constitutional issues. The question of the purpose of regulations parallels the previous discussion of the goals of long-term care. If the purpose is to answer a shortage of beds, then regulations may serve to enable that there be a maximum number of beds, in which case the requirements of the regulation will be minimum. Where preservation of life is the concern, regulations will emphasize a strong life-safety code together with requirements for extensive medical supervision and service. A goal of maintaining a high quality of life will result in regulations that address themselves to the provision of social work, activities, and rehabilitation programs. Usually any kind of service goal is enunciated in regulations through staff requirements. Most common is the mandated presence of a particular professional skill. This may be extended to require a certain ratio of professionals or their aides to a given number of residents.

To be constitutionally effective, particularly if the regulations are to be enforced by criminal sanctions, they must be written explicitly so that there is no ambiguity or vagueness. Furthermore, to be effective they must be enforceable. Thus a regulation which has a high cost to its compliance is difficult to enforce unless provisions are made to enable the provider to meet the cost.

Regulations, too, must be seen not only as the enactment of prohibitions but within the context of the entire system of regulation. The decision to regulate, the determination and then publication of the requirements are an initial step in the process. To the extent that the institutions being regulated participate in these initial steps, enforcement and compliance problems may be eased. Communication of the regulations and their understanding by the target institutions is not solved by publishing alone. An educational process is part of the enforcement picture.

Often regulations will be nullified not by those to whom they are directed, but by those charged with carrying them out. A public administrator faced with an acute shortage of nursing home beds will be loathe to enforce regulations which will result in the dimunition of available beds. A health system which seeks relief from the high cost of unnecessary use of acute hospital beds, will press to avoid enforcement of a program that will reduce the number of alternative skilled nursing home beds.

While regulation has had some effect on improving the physical environment in long-term care institutions, it has had little effect on the quality of life. To a large extent, this has reflected the lack of such purpose, the difficulty of developing clear criteria, and the unwillingness of government to accept the financial burden which enabling provider response would incur.

As the result of many investigations in New York City, the city stiffened its health code and enforcement procedures. A subsequent survey found "no improvement in the over-all operation." Thirteen years later a subsequent investigation replied, "we did the best we could, but we failed" (Hess). All this within the climate of a highly publicized, presidentially endorsed effort of federal emphasis on effective regulation of skilled nursing homes. The multiple federal, state, and local efforts of regulation are best summed up in the title of the series of reports by the Senate Special Committee on Aging, *Nursing Home Care in the United States: Failure in Public Policy.*

Reimbursement, as has been observed, is the carrot aspect of Governmental attempts to govern behavior. Funding, like regulations, reflects purpose and goals. In the final analysis, public budget analysis is a method of identifying societal values which are enunciated as goals.

Medicare, at its inception, attempted to reimburse for skilled nursing home care (extended care facilities) as part of the pattern of health care. In its administration, this purpose was never carried out. Medicaid, which is now the primary method of SNF reimbursement, pays for almost 55 percent of $9 billion nursing home costs. Medicare and the Veterans Administration are responsible for 5 percent. Thus, 60 percent of the costs of these long-term care institutions are publicly funded. In fact, Medicaid spends more money for nursing home care than for acute care in general hospitals. The Senate Committee observes that "despite the heavy Federal commitment to long-term care, a coherent policy on goals and methods has yet to be shaped."

The private insurance sector has demonstrated virtually no concern in this field. A review of the Health Insurance Institute's annual report in 1976 which serves "as a central source of information for the public in health insurance" has one passing reference to nursing home benefits as part of major medical expense insurance. In fact, the glossary defining major medical expense insurance makes no reference to nursing home benefits (Health Insurance Institute).

The goals of reimbursement reflect the quality of care desired. Thus, the same options mentioned above are present—life safety, extension of life, or quality of life. Since Medicaid is the major source of reimbursement, and is administered and funded through state programs, there may be fifty different options exercised for a large sector of SNF care funding. Despite the sizeable commitment of federal funds in the Medicaid program, the Senate Committee describes HEW as "reluctant to issue tight standards to provide patients with minimum protection. Congress, in 1972, mandated the merger of Medicare and Medicaid standards, with the retention of the highest standards in every case. However, HEW then watered down the prior standards" (Subcommittee on Long-Term Care).

While the Social Security Amendments of 1972 mandated payment of costs by states for nursing home costs by July of 1976, it appears that most states will restrict services they are willing to fund. Several major issues are involved in the methodology of payment. To establish uniformity, comparability, and even knowledge of expenses, uniform cost accounting and uniform cost reporting are initial steps which must be taken.

Once costs are satisfactorily obtained, it remains to be determined whether reimbursement should be in terms of the care given or by the needs of the individual resident. An attempt to compromise this issue is the current device of levels of care represented by the establishment of intermediate and skilled nursing facilities. One of the problems presented by this designation is its lack of responsiveness to the trajectory of the severely chronically ill who require intermittently different levels of care. If both levels of care are available in one institution or in several, does the provider shuttle the resident about to receive adequate care and reimbursement? On the other hand, a system geared to the individual needs would require substantially more bookkeeping and reporting with infinite problems of auditing—in short, a replication of Medicare's problems with in-patient hospital care. Extension of the PSRO methodology, utilization review, and applicant screening programs are a few of the mechanisms which may be relied upon for auditing purposes.

One other aspect of financing to which the long-term care system responds is the availability of construction funds. HUD financing has had a marked effect on the growth of proprietary beds. The new Health Planning and Resources Development Act replaces the Hill-Burton (Hill-Harris) program with Medical Facilities (MF) construction and modification funds. The Health Service Agency created by the Health Planning Act, through participation in the State Medical Facilities Plan process and by reason of their necessary approval of such construction before Medicare and Medicaid reimbursement (Sec. 1122 of the Social Security Act), may emerge as the control mechanism for all health care facility operation and construction. The role of private financing, whether from banks, local public health authority bonds, or other financial institutions, may also be subject to the new health planning system.

Summary

Whatever the regulatory or reimbursement authority, auspice, mechanism or instrument, in the final analysis, programs, public or private, will reflect the value system of our society. The funds we are willing to allocate to facilities and manpower will be a mirror of the priorities set for ourselves individually and collectively. The emphasis placed on defining the need for care, what the services should be, and how they are linked into a program of continuity of care, depends upon our commitment to the solution of these problems. To some degree, both the quality and quantity of care and the method of financing are part of the total resources available to our society. However, 8.6 percent of the gross national product and $134 billion would seem, if only in comparative international perspectives, to be sums capable of delivery through a responsive rational system of health care including long-term care. Beyond commitment there is competence. One without the other will compound the chaos and confusion which surrounds long-term care. Together, competence and commitment, energetically implemented, may bring us to a system of long-term care which meets the needs of the chronically ill.

Chapter 19

A Word to Family and Friends—and to the Older People Themselves

To Family and Friends

This book has been written primarily for the people whose daily work is with your older family members and friends when it is necessary to consider placing them in long-term care facilities and when they are actually receiving such care. The purpose is to communicate to those professionals the available knowledge about how to ease the stresses involved and how to enrich the lives of the older people. Throughout the book, I have emphasized that you too are deeply affected by what happens to those older people and that you, too, are entitled to services and consideration.

Some of the other sections of the book may be of interest to you. However, during the past twenty five years, we at the Philadelphia Geriatric Center have seen

thousands of relatives and friends who have had responsibility for caring for older people, for arranging for
their placement when they cannot do so, and *who continue to care* even when they cannot provide physical
care. There are some things I want to say directly to
you.

I know that when your elderly parent or other relative began to experience physical and mental disabilities,
your first efforts were to try to provide them with the
services they needed. This observation is not mine alone.
A good deal of research on a broad scale has been carried out that confirms that fact. It has been shown beyond question that when older people need help, as in a
health crisis, they turn to their children, and the children respond. They help their parents and they do so
willingly. If the person who needs help is fortunate
enough to be married, the spouse does everything he or
she possibly can.

As a matter of fact, 80 percent of the health services
given to older people are provided by families. You,
primarily those of you who are daughters and
daughters-in-law, help with cooking and shopping, take
your older relatives to the doctor, care for them when
they are ill and provide other services. You also give
them the affection and concern that mean even more to
them than such concrete help. Of course, it cannot be
said that such behavior always occurs. Families differ in
the quality of their relationships. Not all young parents
give their small children the same amount or quality of
care and affection. Family relationships do not change
suddenly simply because the people concerned have
grown older. The way in which older people and their
family members relate to each other and help each other
depends a lot on long-standing relationships.

Most older people never are admitted to an institution. When such care is needed, it may mean severe stress on their families. At this particular time in our history, adult children often are in a severe bind. You may be caught between the need to place the older person on the one hand, and your feelings of anxiety and even guilt on the other.

Why is that so?

You were brought up as children in a world that simply did not contain as many older people. Science has not done a great deal to extend the upper limits of life, but it has made discoveries that now permit many more people to survive the earlier stages of life and therefore to reach those upper limits. Families in the so-called good old days very occasionally were faced with the problems of a sick older person needing care. Families were not as scattered geographically and less frequently lived in small apartments in large cities. It therefore was often possible for a family to care for an occasional sick, elderly parent. There were not as many women who worked outside their homes. And, the "children" who provided care in those days were considerably younger than you are when your parent begins to need care. It is likely that if you have a parent requiring a great deal of care, you are well into middle age or even into the age bracket commonly called "aging" (sixty-five and over).

At the same time, your attitudes and values were formed when such conditions did not exist. It was assumed even as recently as twenty or thirty years ago that families could give all the care needed and that old people who had "good" adult children would not need institutional care. Furthermore, long-term care facilities nowadays have inherited the stigma attached to the different types of institutions that existed in those "good old days"—the homes for well aged who had no family, the county homes for those who had no place in society, or psychiatric hospitals for mentally ill.

As there came to be more and more older people

with disabilities who could not be cared for in their own homes or the homes of relatives, the myth grew that families were not fulfilling their responsibilities. The word "myth" is accurate because that notion simply did not fit the facts. There are many signs, however, that our society is finally recognizing what the researchers and practitioners have known for a number of years:

> Families are not "dumping" older people into institutions
>
> Families whose elderly members apply and are admitted to long-term care facilities most often have tried to avoid the admission even at great economic, personal, and physical cost to themselves
>
> There has been a lag in the creation of services to help families keep older people out of institutions
>
> Institutions are not necessarily bad places simply because groups of people live under one roof to get the care they need
>
> There are ways of making long-term care facilities decent places to live and there are many good facilities.

Those facts are particularly important in view of the scandals about nursing homes that we read about in the newspapers. It is up to all of us—government, the professionals, and citizens—to see to it that such places are not permitted to exist.

I have talked about these things with you because I know it is a painful experience to see a beloved elderly parent become disabled mentally or physically. It is an extremely difficult decision to make when institutional care is being considered. But is unfair to expect you to carry a burden of guilt for circumstances you cannot control.

People often ask "When should I place my parent in an institution?" There is no simple answer to that question, and certainly the answer is different for different people at different times. However, there are certain steps you can take when a problem arises. First of all, you should not assume that your relative's ailments are due to age and that therefore nothing can be done. It is not necessary to be so pessimistic. Many of the health problems experienced by older people can be treated effectively. It is important to arrange for a complete medical work-up by a physician genuinely interested in older people and knowledgeable about them. You don't want to miss any bets in seeing to it that the older person is functioning at his/her best possible level.

Secondly, you and your relative should have the benefit of expert professional social work counseling to help you think through the best possible plan. In general, there has been a lag in developing the various services older people and families need to help the old person remain in his/her own home when completely independent functioning is no longer possible. However, in recent years there has been considerable effort to develop such services (such as meal preparation, transportation, meals on wheels, homemakers, and home health services) and to create other kinds of living arrangements (such as high-rise apartment buildings for older people, some of which offer one or more services). If you talk the situation over with a professional who knows all such resources in your community, he/she may be able to help you get services that would avoid or delay the need for institutional care.

There are various places to obtain such counseling, and the place for you to go depends on what is available in your particular community. Some voluntary homes (usually under sectarian auspices) such as the one at the Philadelphia Geriatric Center, provide this kind of service. (The details of how it works at the PGC are spelled out elsewhere in this book). In your community you may be able to obtain the counseling at your family service agency, a referral and information center, a senior citizen's center, or other agency. If your relative is in a hospital that has a social service department you may be able to get such counseling there.

The skillful professional can also help you sort out your feelings about different plans. If you are an adult child, you may have conflict about dividing your energies between your spouse, your parent(s), and your own children. If you have sisters or brothers, there may be family disagreements about what to do. The demands on your time may be causing family friction between you and your husband or wife.

It is extremely important that the older person be involved in thinking about possible plans, and that you talk them over with him/her as completely as possible. He/she is an adult who has the right to plan for him/herself to the fullest extent of his/her ability. No one should be deprived of that right. Many people mean well but assume that an old person should be planned for as one would plan for a young child. Disability and old age do not make people incapable of sharing decisions that concern their lives.

The same principle applies to the honesty with which you share information with your relative. Some adult children who really care about their parents deceive them, mistakenly thinking that it is kinder to do so. Sometimes, when admission is arranged, they tell the older person he/she is going to a hotel or that the placement is only for a few days. Such misinformation is always discovered. The older person then feels he/she has been treated like a worthless object who has no part in controlling his/her own life. It makes it much more difficult to begin the process of adjusting to a new way of life.

Let's return to the decision-making process and assume that, after careful consideration, you and the elderly individual in question realize that placement must take place. How do you choose the facility? Here again, there are no easy answers. Many factors are at work. For many older people, it is extremely important to be in a facility that provides the religious and cultural environment to which they are accustomed. You will want a place close enough to where you live so that visiting is as convenient as possible. In any case, you should shop carefully and see several facilities before you make a decision. After all, this choice affects the rest of your relative's life.

How you can begin to narrow down the choice? If you are fortunate enough to have obtained good counseling, the professional may steer you to some homes that are appropriate. If counseling is not available, you can obtain lists of licensed homes from your local Social Security office or state or county public social services agency. These government offices will provide you with free booklets that spell out the criteria for the benefits of Medicare and Medicaid. Some counties and states have a Consumer's Handbook on Nursing Homes that contains valuable information about nursing homes in your community.

However, it is extremely important that you *visit the homes yourself before placing your relative* and that you *take the older person him/herself to see the home before making the decision*. If your relative is too disabled or ill to be taken to see the home, *you should describe it to him/her and talk over various possibilities in detail*. You should not assume that the older person does not have the capacity to participate in the process of selecting a facility even if he/she is sick or confused or forgetful. It is better to assume that he/she has more competence than is actually the case than to risk denying him/her every opportunity to share these explorations and decisions. Such discussions will help to prepare him/her psychologically for placement and will ease the transition. Your actions in this matter will be a way of saying to him/her: "You are a dignified adult human being, even though you are old and disabled. This is your life, and you have a right to have your say about where it is to be spent. I respect you and value your opinions and judgment. I want to make the best possible arrangements for you."

What do you look for in a home and what kinds of information should you have? You will be able to tell a lot about a home from your visit to it. It is a bad sign if the staff is impatient with your questions or is unwilling to let you visit to look around. Such behavior before placement is a good clue as to how you and your relative will be treated after placement. If you are told that visiting is permitted only during a couple of hours a day, it makes one wonder what is happening the rest of the time. What is there to hide?

Of major importance are matters such as cleanliness, adequate staff, wholesome and attractively prepared food, and comfortable rooms. You should make sure that the facility is licensed, meets all the safety requirements set by various governmental agencies, and has adequate medical care and trained nursing staff.

You and your parent have a right to expect service and care that goes beyond a decent physical environment and basic staff to maintain physical well-being. You want all of the staff to have courteous and respectful attitudes toward the people they serve. You will want your elderly relative to have social work services. And you will want the home to offer a variety of recreational and occupational activities so that the older person can use his/her time constructively and enjoyably and does not have to spend her waking hours doing nothing at all.

Do the staff people you see have friendly attitudes? Do they seem satisfied and cheerful as they go about their work? A woman who had run nursing homes for many years once told me that if she herself had to go into a home, she would look for a place that had a happy staff. Do the staff talk to the older people or only to each other? Do they address the residents respectfully as Mr. X., Mrs. Y., or Miss Z? Or do they call them by their first names or nicknames, as though they were children instead of dignified adults?

As you walk through the home look carefully at the elderly residents. Most of them should be out of bed, look clean and groomed, and be dressed. Very few residents of nursing homes are so acutely ill that they cannot be up in chairs or walking around. You may see a few who are in chairs with restraints. Sometimes this is necessary for the person's own protection. But if many people are being restrained, something is wrong. It may be for the convenience of the staff rather than for the welfare of the residents. Note whether there are activities going on which the residents seem to be enjoying. Ask to see a schedule of activities.

Do not hesitate to ask questions about any matters that concern you. Find out how medical care is provided and what arrangements the home has for medical emergencies or transfers to hospitals when necessary.

Financial matters should be discussed in detail. You will need to know whether the home is approved for Medicare and/or Medicaid, whether your relative is eligible for such coverage, and how the benefits relate to private medical or hospitalization plans carried. If your relative has funds and will be paying for care from those funds, you will want to know if the home will keep him/her for the Medicaid rate if his/her own money should be used up. Ask if the cost quoted is inclusive. You should know what extras there may be, for there is wide variation in the services homes include in the basic charge. Some charge separately for laundry, medicines, incontinent pads, dressings, special nursing procedures, or other items and services. If so, you want to know whether bills for extras are itemized. You will certainly read every word of any contract or agreement you are asked to sign and get legal advice if you do not fully understand it.

Often, in a family where there are several adult children, one of them seems to take most of the responsibility for helping the parent. If this is the case in your family and you are that child, keep your sister(s) and/or brother(s) as well as your parent informed about what is happening. Discuss these matters with them as fully as possible. This will, of course, vary from family to family. In general it is better for everyone to be aware of all stages of the planning process. Your parent's adjustment—and yours, too—will be easier if differences are worked out as you go along, rather than erupting when a decision comes as a surprise to a family member.

You and your relative have now selected the home to which he/she will move. If you think of it as moving to a new home, it will help you to help your relative make the transition as easy as possible. Discuss the date and time as much in advance as possible, repeating the discussion if necessary. Talk over what small possessions should be taken. Older people (like younger ones) have favorite possessions such as family pictures, a clock, a radio, a TV, plants, or other things. It is difficult to give up one's own home with the accumulated possessions of a lifetime. A special effort should be made to take along what the older person selects if it can possibly fit in his/her new room. This will help give him/her a sense of the continuity of his/her life—that a complete break with the past is not happening.

One of the main things to keep in mind is that decisions should be made (or shared) by the older person to the fullest possible extent. It is a mistaken "kindness," for example, to close your parent's house or apartment and dispose of its contents without consulting him/her. It is a psychological cruelty to give people the feeling that others, no matter how well-meaning, have taken away their right to make decisions that affect their own lives. Your parent may wish to give a favorite table to a son, a chair to a grandchild, a lamp to a daughter, or various items to cousin Lizzie, nephew Ed, or to a neighbor or friend who has shown him/her kindness.

The actual move is extremely important. Placing your parent in a home does not mean the end of your relationship with each other. You will want to help with the settling-in and to spend as much time with him/her as good judgment indicates for the first few days. Some homes make a special effort to orient the new resident: to explain various medical and nursing procedures that will take place; to tell about mealtimes, laundry, and other details of daily living; to show where various facilities are such as bathroom, dining room, phone and so on. You can help with orientation or do all of it if the home does not.

It is a good idea when leaving to tell your relative exactly when you will visit again. Your attitude should convey that the new living arrangement will not prevent you from doing things for him/her that you have done in the past. You have a future together. For example, you should think about the ways in which you helped your relative before placement in the home and plan to continue to do so in the same way as much as possible. Did you invite him/her for dinner once a week? take him/her shopping? Bring grandchildren visiting?

If you can, you should make such activities a part of your routine. Family contacts are enormously important to older people in long-term care facilities. It gives meaning to their lives and is something to look forward to if they can count on your Sunday visit, or dinner at your house on Wednesday, or other such events. Here again, your relative's health or condition may restrict activities. But do not assume that is so. Family happenings such as weddings, parties, even funerals, should include the older person. He/she needs to continue to be part of the family and its sorrows as well as joyful occasions.

Families often try to "protect" the older person by keeping the death of a family member secret or by not telling the older person about it till after the funeral. This is not really a favor. Unless there is an extremely important medical reason to withhold information, do not do so. Your elderly relative has the right to be a family member in good standing. If not told at once, he/she is deprived of the normal outlet for shared grief at the funeral. Or if the deceased relative had been a regular visitor to the older person, the latter may feel neglected and unloved when the visits cease.

Visiting, of course, can be hard for you emotionally. It is not easy to accept the mental and physical decline of your relative. But most people continue to visit anyway, knowing the pleasure it gives the older person.

A study was done at the Philadelphia Geriatric Center of relatives who visited those of our residents who were extremely confused and disoriented. We found, as might be expected, that the frequency of visits varied from family to family. Some children visited daily, some who lived at great distances visited only a few times a year. The vast majority visited regularly at least once a week. Visits were often supplemented by telephone calls. Most of the visiting relatives did special things for the older people—brought them clothes, flowers, money, took them for walks, and so on. Many older people were visited by sisters and brothers, grandchildren, and nieces and nephews as well as by their adult children.

It was especially interesting to learn that the old person in the home and the visiting relative talked about a wide range of topics. In some cases, the older people gave welcome advice when asked; they talked about past and future family events; recipes were handed down. There was also a good deal of discussion about the residents' health and life in the institution.

Talking with your relative is enormously important for both of you. When you really listen carefully to what he/she has to say (and listening can be difficult), it is a way of saying to him/her, "You are an important person to me and I care about you." The older person's self-esteem is enhanced. Everyone likes to talk about themselves. Telling someone about one's problems makes them easier to bear. You should talk to your relative as well as listen. When you tell him/her about what is happening in the family or community, it implies that he/she has a right to know, and it also serves the purpose of keeping him/her in touch with the world outside of the institution.

You undoubtedly have noticed that many older people talk more about the distant past than about recent events. This sometimes is due to the fact that when memory fails it is easier to remember distant events. It also relates to the fact that like all people, the elderly want to tell about times when they played important roles and about happenings that were significant in their lives.

Dr. Jack Weinberg, a very wise psychiatrist who has been interested in older people for many years, wrote an article called What do I say to my mother when I have nothing to say?* While he was talking about older people and their children in general, his comments apply as well to the older people who are in long-term care facilities and to their children. He states that listen-

---

*Weinberg, Jack, What do I say to my mother when I have nothing to say?, Geriatrics, November 1974, pp. 155-159.

ing to your parents can be valuable for both generations, and that it is good to encourage your parents to tell you about their past lives. "The account of any person's life and times is like a novel and worthy of attention," he said. You will have a better understanding and appreciation of your roots and identity. Dr. Weinberg suggests that you can look together at old photographs to stimulate these reminiscences. Grandchildren, too, should be given the opportunity to relate to the old people in this way, with mutual enjoyment resulting.

At the Philadelphia Geriatric Center, the executive vice president, Mr. Bernard Liebowitz, was aware that families often do not know what to talk about or do with the older people when they visit. He therefore instructed the department of human services to develop a booklet on the subject for families. The text of the booklet is given in Appendix A.

During the months or years your relative is in a home, there will be many occasions on which you will need or want to talk to staff people. You may want information about health matters. You may have complaints, for even the best-run institution depends on a variety of staff and people are not perfect. You should remember that you have both rights and responsibilities. You have the right to ask questions and be answered fully and courteously. You have the right to bring your concerns or complaints to the attention of those in charge. You also have a responsibility to check facts before jumping to conclusions about something you don't like. And you have a responsibility to continue to do your part in making your relative's life as comfortable and enjoyable as possible.

You may know that government regulations now require that homes have a resident's (or patient's) bill of rights. Be sure to ask to see it, and make sure that your parent has a copy. The one used at the Philadelphia

Geriatric Center is a good example of what such a document should say. It emphasizes the rights that speak to human dignity and self-determination and includes a statement of residents' responsibilities as well.

Finally, you know that as the years have passed your relative may have lost husband or wife, sisters, and/or brothers, friends, his/her own home, and some physical and/or mental capacities. You sense that therefore you are more important than ever to him/her. This is a tremendous responsibility. But you must remember that you also have a responsibility to your husband or wife, your own children, and to yourself. You must try to work things out as best you can without blaming yourself for what you cannot do. Each person must work out his or her own way of achieving a comfortable balance.

TO THOSE WHOSE HUSBAND OR WIFE NEEDS CARE IN A LONG-TERM FACILITY

The section you have just read was written for the family and friends of older people who require institutional care. Everything in it applies to you as well as to the adult children and other relatives. However, as more people survive to advanced old age, it is happening more frequently that one half of a marital couple needs care in an institution while the other does not.

The experience of placing a husband or wife is extraordinarily painful. Since most people in institutions are over eighty, the separation often takes place after a marriage that has endured for fifty years. It may be inconceivable to you to think about living apart from the person who has shared most of your life. For you, added to all the feelings other family members have, there is a special loneliness and sadness. Your whole way of life is affected. The adaptation you must make and the changes you experience are as great as those of your husband or wife.

In the main, you did not consider placing your spouse until the situation really became unmanageable, the well-being of your spouse and your own well-being were seriously threatened, and you were simply unable to provide the needed care. Despite such realities, you still may feel guilty. If you have been under severe stress, it is only human to feel a sense of relief as well.

When your spouse has been placed, there undoubtedly will be things about his/her situation that do not please you. You may feel that no one is giving exactly the kind of attention that you would give if you were able to do so, and that no one understands your husband's or wife's needs the way you do. Certainly that is true no matter how excellent the quality of care in the facility. You may find this frustrating, and you may spend many hours each day visiting, trying to give that care and meet those needs.

One thing to remember is that it is important for your spouse to make the best possible adjustment to the new living arrangement. No one can tell you exactly how frequently to visit or how long to stay. You must exercise judgment in deciding when your visits and attentions are in your spouse's best interests and when they may be preventing him/her from really adapting to the new way of life.

You must also remind yourself that you too are important. You will not be able to help your spouse if you are not refreshed by some recreation and rest or if you do not attend to your own health and well-being.

I wish very much that there were an easy formula by which I could comfort you in this difficult situation. You should be eased, however, by knowing that you tried hard in the past and that you are still doing what you can. That is all any of us can expect of ourselves.

To Older People Who Live in Long-Term Care Facilities

This book is about you. Most of it is written to be read by the many professionals responsible for your care. Its goal is to share with them knowledge about meeting your needs—how to ease the stresses of being admitted to and living in long-term care facilities, and how to improve the quality of your life.

You have been subjected to many stresses. You have needed to leave your own home and family and to adapt to an entirely new way of life and to many new people. Most likely you have health problems that mean that you are dependent on others for care. One of the hardest things to bear is that you have less control over your daily life and routines.

I cannot feel that this book is complete without saying a word to you.

No matter how fine a long-term care facility you live in, there is still an ingredient necessary if you are to live in the best possible way within your capacity for doing so. That ingredient is *your own participation*. You have a *responsibility* to share in your own care and services. No one can do it all for you.

You have many rights. Some of them are spelled out in the statements of resident's (patient's) rights that every facility is now required to have. You should ask the administrator (or social worker or nurse) for a copy of those rights.

With rights also come responsibilities, and you have a responsibility to participate in every aspect of your life in the institution. For example, you have a right to ask health personnel such as doctors and nurses questions about your condition and to receive full explanations about any treatments prescribed. You also have a responsibility to participate actively in any procedures or routines that will maintain or improve your health. In the same way, you have a right to programs of recreational activities so that your time can be used constructively and enjoyably. But the staff can only provide the opportunities. It is up to you to avail yourself of them.

Apart from your own role in participating in your own care, you undoubtedly see many ways in which the institution can be improved. After all, you and your fellow residents know better than anyone else what it is like to live there. You should not be shy about going to the administrator yourself or about getting together with others to talk your complaints and constructive suggestions over with him. He/she may not be able to do all the things you request, but you have a right to a courteous hearing and discussion and explanations.

At the institution where I work, we have cared for many thousands of older people. We have a deep respect for their strength and adaptability. You too have those qualities, and I have faith in your ability and willingness to use them.

I know very well that if it were possible you would have preferred to remain in your own home. But you can share in making your new home a better place to live, and in making your life more pleasant now and in the future.

To all of you—family members, friends, and residents of long-term care facilities—

Good luck and good wishes.

Sincerely yours,

Elaine M. Brody

Visiting Your Relatives at the Philadelphia Geriatric Center: A Note to Family and Friends of Our Residents

Welcome to our PGC family! When your relative lives at PGC, we consider that you, too, are part of our family. We know you are very much interested in your parent, relative or friend and will be visiting regularly. We want to do everything possible to make those visits as pleasant as possible.

We know that the daily lives of our residents are very different from your own activities. As a result, sometimes it is difficult to know how to begin a conversation or what to talk about, or do, during the visit. The purpose of this booklet is to make some suggestions so that you and your relative can enjoy your visits fully.

You will find two major themes:

    1. What to talk about with your relative
    2. What to do together with your relative

WHAT TO TALK ABOUT.   Talking with your relative is extremely important for you as well as the resident. When you really listen carefully to what a person has to say (and listening can be difficult), it is a way of saying "You are important to me and I care about you." It gives an older person's self-esteem a real boost. All of us like to talk about ourselves, and relating one's problems makes them easier to bear. Try to talk as well as listen.

When you describe what is happening in the family or community, it includes the resident and also helps to keep in touch with the world outside PGC.

You may have noticed that many older people talk more about the distant past than about recent events. Sometimes when memory is failing it is easier to remember distant events. Like everyone else, the elderly want to tell about times when they played important roles and about siginficant happenings in their lives. Experts agree that it is good to encourage older people to talk about their past lives.

Here are some specific suggestions about talking to your relative:

1. Encourage reminiscing. Review the value of your relative's life and achievements. You may bring photos and albums, scrapbooks, or familiar objects from home to share together. Even a complaint about your relative's current situation may be used as a way of recalling how things used to be. If, for example, your mother complains about the food, sympathize with her and remind her of the great blintzes she used to make. Perhaps she'll remember the recipe and you can make some for her and for your family.

2. Do not give advice unless asked. Residents may not want advice from their children. Instead, ask their advice or opinions about a family matter to help them feel they are useful family members.

3. Tell the resident what's happening in the family, the community, and the old neighborhood. Share problems as well as pleasant and exciting family events. Older people are not too fragile to deal with sad-

ness and death. Protecting them may make them feel left out, and they have a right to know.

4. Include your relative's friends and roommate in your conversations. This encourages relationships and helps your relative to see your genuine interest in the present environment. However, some time should be spent privately for personal conversations.

5. Empathize with your relative's feeling of distress. However, do not try to deny its existence or the resident's feelings. Even if your relative is upset about an event which did not really occur (for example, if she thinks her roommate took her dress, and you know it is in the laundry), it is not important to convince her that the dress is actually in the laundry. She needs your sympathy that sometimes things get lost and that it's hard living with a roommate. Listen to complaints. Don't feel your relative is angry with you. Often, a sympathetic ear is all that is needed.

6. Talk to your relative's social worker. Every floor has a social worker, and the social worker assigned to your relative will be happy to discuss with you how to make your visits more pleasant. We realize the importance to our residents of maintaining relationships with their friends and family.

WHAT TO DO TOGETHER

1. Bring newspapers or magazine articles. You and your relative may look at them together. Or you may read to a relative who is

visually handicapped. It helps to keep in touch with the world.

2. Play games your relative enjoys. You may bring and play cards, dominoes, scrabble, or other games you enjoy together.

3. Help decorate your relative's room. Bring photos, pictures, plants, wall hangings, or throw pillows, and decide together where they will look best. This is your way of accepting your relative's present home and indicating your interest in it.

4. Help your relative with personal grooming. You can file and polish nails, set hair, shave, and mend clothes. Looking better helps people feel better.

5. Assist your relative with correspondence. Encourage writing to friends and relatives. Those who cannot write, may dictate a letter to you. Help with phone calls, sending birthday cards, and gifts. Let the older person do as much as possible, independently, even if it is only pointing to the card or gift to be sent.

6. Bring others to visit. Your relative will enjoy seeing other members of the family and friends. Try taking photos, and send them along as a remembrance of an enjoyable visit.

7. Bring grandchildren and great-grandchildren. Older people and children enjoy each other. It is meaningful to children to know their roots. Often they are fascinated, not frightened, by the attentions of older people. If we have a positive and accepting attitude toward people who are physically or mentally impaired, children will accept them too.

8. Bring pets. But please, do so only if the older person likes animals and only when you can visit out of doors.

9. Talk with the floor activities worker. Your account of your relative's interests will help the workers develop a program tailored to the older person's individual needs. Look at the activities schedules that are posted at the nursing station. There are floor activities and mass activities for the whole Center. What ideas do you have for programming? Tell the activities worker about activities in which you can join your relative. This may also encourage him to participate when you are not there.

10. Visit other areas of PGC. Taking your relative to visit a friend on another floor, or the cafeteria, gift shops, synagogue, patios, library, and outdoor grounds will give much pleasure.

One way to become involved with your relative and his extended family here is to participate in some of the festivities and trips planned by PGC. You will be welcome to come along on special trips to assist your relative and his friends with transportation or meals. And for special events within PGC, such as Family Day, or Las Vegas night, it will be an enjoyable shared experience for you and your relative, if you manage a wheelchair (his own, or his friend's), or offer a strong and willing arm.

11. Take your relative for an outing. An older person really enjoys a drive in the car, dinner at your home, eating out, a visit to the old neighborhood, and attendance at family affairs. Wheelchairs and walkers can be

taken in the car, and a physical therapist or nurse will be happy to teach you how to assist your relative.

12. <u>Share your skills and talents.</u> If you have skills or talents such as playing a musical instrument, singing, or art work that you could share with your relative and some of his friends, your accomplishments will give rise to feelings of pride.

Finally, if any special problems should arise, feel free to talk with the social worker. The social worker is here for that purpose and will do his/her best to help you personally or put you in touch with appropriate other staff people.

Again, welcome! Come as often as you can. Your relative wants you, and we want you!

APPENDIX B

SOCIAL WORK SERVICES FORMS

Social History A: For Applicants

Note: This outline is a guide only. Information is gathered not for its own sake but in order to understand the client so as to design his/her program of care and treatment. Emphasis should be on continuing values, interests, and relationships that can provide a foundation for the program.

Name:
Birthdate:
Birthplace:
Date of Arrival in U.S.:
Description: Mobility, speech, dress, affect, and responsiveness.
Informants: Who provided social information (including applicant), relationship, and attitudes.
1. Childhood History: Significant relationships, experiences, and background.
2. Education:
3. Birthplace and when immigrated:
4. Significant Health History: Major health, impairing incidents (e.g. disease, accidents, and chronic disabilities), and social, behavioral and emotional impact.
5. Work History:

6. Living Arrangements: Past and current.
7. Financial Status:
8. Marital Relations: List marriages and note quality of relationships.

Spouse's Name	Date of Marriage	Spouse's Age at Marriage	Applicant's Age at Termin.	Reason for Termination

9. Children: Names, ages, quality of relationship to client.
10. Extended Family: Note significant relationships.
11. Non-Familial Relations: Range and number of friends and quality of relationships.
12. Organizational Memberships and Community Activities:
13. Recreation, Hobbies, and Interests:
14. Retirement: Date, reason, and reaction of client.
15. Old Age: Note particularly any significant changes from previous functioning levels, when they were noticed (that is, approximate age when significant change was noted) and the response to these changes by persons in the applicant's surroundings. The general areas of interest are: self-care; sensory perception; awareness of self, others, and the world; memory; personality; anticipation of death.
16. Current Social Functioning: (Note: Recent events and current functioning are included on outline for guidelines for recording and interview.)

Social History B: For Residents*

1. Name_____ 2. Current room #____
                                 3. Current roommate(s)__
4. Previous room changes and roommate changes
_____

   From_____ to_____ Date_____Reason_____
5. Functioning in the institution. Evaluate overall adjustment. Where problems exist, be specific. The
   specifics should include: the nature of any problems,
   the circumstances under which they are manifested,
   which persons (staff or residents) are affected by the
   problems, and their frequency. If resident displays
   particular assets and strengths, cite them and supply
   specifics.
   a. Overall adjustment
   b. Interpersonal relationships to other residents,
      staff, roommates
   c. Involvement in planned and unplanned activities
   d. Physical and mental functioning (note changes
      since admission)
   e. Intrapersonal status: morale, self-reliance, com-
      plaints, mood, responsiveness, withdrawal, sus-
      piciousness, depression, etc.
   f. Behavior: adherence to norms, need for safety
      supervision, self-control (temper outbursts, tear-
      fulness, assaultiveness, sexual acting-out, "man-
      agement problem"), social behavior.
   g. Method of dealing with problems.
6. Interpersonal relationships outside the institution
   (with family and friends). Significant people (names
   and relationships); frequency of contacts; means of
   contact (i.e. visits to Home, visits to outside; letters,

_____

*This form is a supplement to Social History A to be used in up-dating his-
tory at any point after individual has been in the long-term care facility for a
time.

phone calls); resident's reaction to these contacts; problems, if any, arising from contacts.

7. Family functioning in relation to client and institution. (Include evaluation of family's adjustment to client's institutionalization and care).

Long-Term Care Inquiry Form

Date   Tel _____   Worker   Add'l file_____Yes

        Walk____Date   _____No

        Other____Prev

               Inq

Appl   Inq

Name   Name

Str   City   Str   City

Tel   Sp   Tel   Rel

Age	Health: Phys	Info
M F		To call
____	Mental	Appt
M S	A D L	Ref
D W	Reason for Inquiry	Rej
Sep		Financial PA
Child		SS
S		Pen
D		Sav
Comments		Other

Outline for Dictation of Initial Interview

INITIAL CONTACT. (1) Date, (2) names and addresses of applicant and family members, (3) age of applicant, (4) marital status.

Method of contact, source of referral, previous contacts with agency.

APPEARANCE & PERSONALITY. Speech, dress, affect, responsiveness, interests. Motivations toward change in physical and social functioning.

REASON FOR APPLICATION. Precipitating and contributory factors.

ALTERNATIVES CONSIDERED. Efforts to date to deal with problem.

CURRENT SITUATION. Present living arrangement, children's circumstances, etc.

BACKGROUND INFORMATION (Life-style and brief social history).

    1. Parents, siblings, relationships, socio-economic status.

    2. Education and work history.

    3. Reaction to stress situation, past and present. (See p. 330 for detailed social history).

FAMILY STRUCTURE AND RELATIONSHIPS

    1. Quality of relations with spouse, children

    2. Responsible members (i.e., who takes major responsibility for helping applicant in daily life and in planning).

HEALTH

    Physical status

    Mental status

    Emotional status

    Functional capacities (capacity for self-care, help needed)

ATTITUDE OF APPLICANT AND FAMILY TO-WARD ADMISSION

What do they see in favor of admission and what against.

FINANCIAL INFORMATION

RECOMMENDATIONS & STATUS

Applications given (active or deferred)?

Referrals made

Estimated placement (in terms of care needed) in receiving facility

Plans

Special Medical Authorization

This authorizes release to the Home ——————— of any medical information it requests from any doctor, hospital, clinic, nursing home to whom I am or have been known. This authorization includes psychiatric history and treatment as well as any other form of medical treatment, medical or nursing history or care received.

_____

Signature of Applicant

_____

or Signature of Responsible Agent

Witnessed by:

1._____

Name and Address

2._____   Date _____

S. Worker _____

Social Worker's Checklist

_____
(Applicant's Name)   (Age)

_____
(Date of Application)

_____
(Present Address)   Tel _____

Own Home _____ N.H. _____

_____

1. Application _____   Date_____
2. Medical Authorization _____
3. Medical History_____
4. Hospital Reports:
   a. _____
   b. _____
   c. _____
5. Chest X-ray _____
6. Kahn-Goldfarb _____
7. Physical Self-Maintenance _____
8. Instrumental Activities of Daily Living _____
9. Behavior/Adjustment Scale _____
10. Psychiatric Evaluation _____
11. Medical Transfer _____
12. Financial Arrangements: _____

13. Social Service Chart Summary_____
14. Recommended are of facility: Skilled_____ In-
    termed. _____
          Floor_____
15. Date Application completed _____

16. Medicaid Card—give to social worker at pre-admission interview. Hospitalization, Blue Cross and Blue Shield card—give information to social worker at pre-admission interview.

Name   Date   Classification   Worker

PHILADELPHIA GERIATRIC CENTER

Behavior and Adjustment Classification (Includes Mental and Emotional Functioning)

(Instructions below)

1. Mental Functioning; Planning and Decision-making.
   A. Intact mental functioning; capable of full participation in planning and exercising good judgment in decision-making.
   B. Mental functioning substantially intact; capable of participating in planning and decision-making with only minor dependence on others.
   C. Occasional memory lapses, but is oriented as to time, person, place; may have always had limited intellectual capacities; capable of participating in planning but may be slow in grasping content or must have some support from others in decision-making.
   D. Have memory defects but can function in daily living routines with some personal supervision and help; not disoriented; may have always been somewhat dependent on others due to retardation; capacity for planning and decision-making requires considerable help from others.
   E. Memory loss and disorientation sufficiently severe so that round-the-clock nursing care and supervision are required; totally dependent on others for planning and decision-making; may always have been severely retarded.
   F. Total disorientation and disorganization requiring mental hospital care.

2. Personal Adjustment—disturbing or disabling subjective symptoms, e.g., anxiety, depression, phobias, paranoid ideas.
   A. Free of above subjective symptoms.
   B. Mild subjective symptoms may be present but do not significantly impair functioning.
   C. May have mildly disturbing or disabling subjective symptoms.
   D. May have moderately disturbing or disabling subjective symptoms.
   E. May have severely disabling or disturbing subjective symptoms but do not endanger self or others.
   F. Mental impairment and/or psychosis which endangers self or others. Requires mental hospital care or treatment.
3. Behavior patterns which relate to capacity for group living, e.g., habits, grooming, disturbing behavior.
   A. Free of disturbing or disabling character traits; personal habits, grooming, and dress reflect good hygiene and interest in personal appearance.
   B. Mildly disturbing character traits which do not significantly impair capacity for group living; acceptable personal habits and hygiene.
   C. Mildly disturbing character traits which are not too disabling; continues to have interest in appearance and maintains acceptable hygiene with some supervision.
   D. Moderately disturbing character traits, but still within limits of tolerance in group living; needs considerable supervision and help for personal grooming and care.
   E. Incapable of conforming to socially acceptable standards of personal hygiene, dress, etc.; character traits create severe problems in management.
   F. Character traits and behavior unmanageable in group living; requires sufficient control and man-

agement so that commitment to security institution required.

4. Social Adjustment; existence of satisfactory or inadequate interpersonal relations with family, friends, e.g. excessive withdrawal, hostility, manipulation of others or dependence on others.

  A. Maintains active and satisfying relationships with family and friends, initiating contact when appropriate.

  B. Adequate social relationships with family and friends but may be less active in sustaining them.

  C. May have had adequate interpersonal relationships in the past but currently showing some diminution of interest or minor problems in this sphere; may historically have had minor problems.

  D. Needs considerable encouragement and/or stimulation in interpersonal relationships; may have life pattern of moderate disturbance in this sphere; less apt than formerly to be interested or concerned about others.

  E. Unable at present to maintain personal relationships except minimally; may have had life-pattern of severe distrubance.

  F. Pathology sufficiently severe in sphere of interpersonal relationships so as to require maximum management and control in mental hospital.

Explanation: This classification system encompasses four different aspects of behavior or functioning, which are designated by the Arabic numerals one through four as follows:

    1. Mental functioning; ability to participate in planning and decision-making.

    2. Personal adjustment; subjective symptoms: e.g. anxiety, depression, phobias, sleeping or eating problems, paranoid ideas.

    3. Behavior patterns which relate to capacity

for group living, e.g. habits, grooming, disturbing behavior.

4. Social adjustment; existence of satisfactory or inadequate interpersonal relations with family, friends, e.g. excessive withdrawal, hostility, manipulation of others or dependence on others.

Within each group there are six degrees of the level of function in that sphere. These gradations include the dimension of needing help (dependency) or supervision. They are designated by capital letters A through F, which describe the level of functioning in any sphere as follows:

A. Independent

B. Can function independently with minor support.

C. Requires moderate support and/or supervision.

D. Can function in relation to daily living routines only in protected or supervised setting.

E. Requires round-the-clock nursing and medical service in a highly supervised setting.

F. Requires mental hospital or maximum security care.

Instructions: One capital letter (A, B, C, D, E, or F) should be circled in each of the four groups (1, 2, 3, or 4). The overall classification will be a capital letter, and will be determined by the lowest letter circled. Thus, in classifying any client, four capital letters will be circled (one in each group). For example, if the circled letters should be 1A, 2C, 3B, 4D, the classification is D.

Physical Self-Maintenance Scale*

Subject's name_____Rated by S.W._____ Date ____
Circle one statement in each category A-F that applies to subject.

Informant _____

A. Toilet
   1. Cares for self at toilet completely, no incontinence.
   2. Needs to be reminded or needs help in cleaning self, or has rare (weekly at most) accidents.
   3. Soiling or wetting while asleep more than once a week.
   4. Soiling or wetting while awake more than once a week.
   5. No control of bowels or bladder.

B. Feeding
   1. Eats without assistance.
   2. Eats with minor assistance at meal times and/or with special preparation of food, or help in cleaning up after meals.
   3. Feeds self with moderate assistance and is untidy.
   4. Requires extensive assistance for all meals.
   5. Does not feed self at all and resists efforts of others to feed him/her.

C. Dressing
   1. Dresses, undresses, and selects clothes from own wardrobe.
   2. Dresses and undresses self with minor assistance.
   3. Needs moderate assistance in dressing or selection of clothes.

*Adapted by Brody, Elaine & Lawton, M. Powell from Langley-Porter Physical Self-Maintenance Scale, Philadelphia Geriatric Center, 5301 Old York Road, Philadelphia, Pa. 19141

   4. Needs major assistance in dressing but cooperates with efforts of others to help.
   5. Completely unable to dress self and resists efforts of others to help.

D. Grooming (neatness, hair, nails, hands, face, clothing)
   1. Always neatly dressed, well groomed, without assistance.
   2. Grooms self adequately with occasional minor assistance, e.g. shaving.
   3. Needs moderate and regular assistance or supervision in grooming.
   4. Needs total grooming care, but can remain well groomed after help from others.
   5. Actively negates all efforts of others to maintain grooming.

E. Physical Ambulation
   1. Goes about grounds or city.
   2. Ambulates within residence or about one block distant.
   3. Ambulates with asistance of (check one)
      a. another person   b. railing
      c. cane   d. walker   e. wheelchair
   4. Sits unsupported in chair or wheelchair but cannot propel self without help.
   5. Bedridden more than half the time.

F. Bathing
   1. Bathes self (tub, shower, sponge bath) without help.
   2. Bathes self with help in getting in and out of tub.
   3. Washes face and hands only, but cannot bathe rest of body.

4. Does not wash self but is cooperative with those who bathe him/her.
5. Does not try to wash self and resists efforts to keep him/her clean.

PHILADELPHIA GERIATRIC CENTER

Instrumental Activities of Daily Living Scale*

Subject's Name   Rated by   Date
                           S.Worker
Agency   Informant

Circle one statement in each category A-H that applies to subject.

A. Ability to use telephone
    1. Operates telephone on own initiative—looks up and dials numbers, etc.
    2. Dials a few well-known numbers.
    3. Answers telephone but does not dial.
    4. Does not use telephone at all.

B. Shopping
    1. Takes care of all shopping needs independently.
    2. Shops independently for small purchases.
    3. Needs to be accompanied on any shopping trip.
    4. Completely unable to shop.

C. Food Preparation
    1. Plans, prepares and serves adequate meals independently.
    2. Prepares adequate meals if supplied with ingredients.
    3. Heats and serves prepared meals, or prepares meals but does not maintain adequate diet.
    4. Needs to have meals prepared and served.

---

*Developed by Elaine M. Brody and M. Powell Lawton—Philadelphia Geriatric Center, 5301 Old York Road, Philadelphia, Pa. 19141

D. Housekeeping
1. Maintains house alone or with occasional assistance (e.g. "heavy work-domestic help").
2. Performs light daily tasks such as dish-washing, bed-making.
3. Performs light daily tasks but cannot maintain acceptable level of cleanliness.
4. Needs help with all home maintenance tasks.
5. Does not participate in any housekeeping tasks.

E. Laundry
1. Does personal laundry completely.
2. Launders small items—rinses socks, stockings, etc.
3. All laundry must be done by others.

F. Mode of Transportation
1. Travels independently on public transportation or drives own car.
2. Arranges own travel via taxi, but does not otherwise use public transportation.
3. Travels on public transportation when assisted or accompanied by another.
4. Travel limited to taxi or automobile with assistance of another.
5. Does not travel at all.

G. Responsibility for own Medications
1. Is responsible for taking medication in correct dosages at correct time.
2. Takes responsibility if medication is prepared in advance in separate dosages.
3. Is not capable of dispensing own medication.

H. Ability to Handle Finances
1. Manages   financial   matters   independently

(budgets, write checks, pay rent, bills, go to bank), collects and keep track of income.

2. Manages day-to-day purchases but needs help with banking, major purchases, etc.

3. Incapable of handling money.

Mental Status Questionnaire (Goldfarb-Kahn-Pollack)

NAME_____

ROOM NO._____

DATE_____

Please write resident's own words, if any question about correctness.

Give no hints.

Repeat question as often as necessary, but do not re-phrase, except to translate into Yiddish, if necessary.

1. What is the name of this place?
   (Home for Aged, H.J.A., Jewish Home for Aged, Old Folks Home)

Answer: _____

2. Where is it? (Philadelphia)

Answer: _____

3. What is today's <u>date</u>? (day of week not acceptable)

Answer: _____

4. Month? Answer: _____

5. Year?   Answer: _____

6. How old are you? (If family history indicates birth-date uncertain, credit if estimate is within two years of age given by family.)

Answer: _____

7. When were you born? (Month) Answer:_____

8. Year? Answer: _____

9. Who is the President of the United States?

Answer: _____

10. Who was President before him?

Answer: _____

Comments: _____

_____   _____

_____

Score: _____ Rater:_____

Outline for Completion Summary

Name _____

Age _____ Date _____

Living Arrangement
 (note any special urgency in situation)
Personality and Modes of Adaptations of Applicant
 (support evaluation with concrete facts)
Motivation
Interests
 Response to stress, interpersonal losses, loss of
 independence, separations
Degree of control (ego function)
Customary defenses against anxiety
 Past experiences that have had special impact on
current adjustment (physical, social, psychological).
Intrafamilial Relationships. Members most active, degree
and quality of their participation in planning and procedures.
Financial Arrangements. (Spell out specifics)
Placement Evaluation.
1. Living habits
2. Type of roommate pref-
   erable
3. Room preferences and
   needs (e.g. willingness to
   share room, need to be
   close to bathroom or
   nursing station, etc.)

Community Agencies Involved
Current Status of Application
Placement and Reason.
Date of medical examination
Medical classification
Nursing recommendation
Behavior and adjustment score
Kahn-Goldfarb score
Permanence of disability

Outline for Social Service Chart Summary

NAME:
Birthdate
Date
Social Worker
M & D I
Floor
DATE OF ADMISSION
SOCIAL HISTORY (include religious affiliation)
REASON FOR ADMISSION
ACTIVITIES AND INTERESTS
FAMILY AND FRIENDS
HEALTH (include recent information obtained since pre-admission medical examination, significant illnesses, hospitalizations, changes in functional capacity)
PATIENT PROFILE
PLACEMENT AND REASON
PLAN (expected length of stay, discharge plan if any)

Family Involvement Form

To be given to new resident and family at pre-admission interview

NAME OF RESIDENT_____

NAME OF RELATIVE_____

(who is completing form)

Tele. # _____

ADDRESS _____

NAMES & ADDRESSES OF OTHER RELATIVES WHO HAVE CONTACT WITH RESIDENT

_____

_____

It is very important to the welfare of an older person that he/she feels that "life goes on" after admission to an institution. We know families want to participate with us in planning individual programming to enrich the lives of our residents. Activities shared with families give the older person a sense of continuity and closeness. We therefore are eager that you complete this form so that we can plan accordingly.

1.   a) What types of activities have you or other family members participated in with your relative in the past year? e.g. taking him/her out to dinner, going shopping etc. How often?

ACTIVITY	HOW OFTEN

2.   a) How do you and other family members plan to continue these activities after your relative moves to the Home?

_____

_____

b)   How often do you plan to visit? Please indicate the approximate time of day. (We understand that there may be changes in your schedule, but we do like to have some idea about your plans for participating).

_____

3.   a) Often when visiting, family members like to participate in activities together rather than sitting and talking alone. Are there activities here at the Home which you or other family members would like to participate in with your relative? (See Monthly Schedule, Please specify.)

_____

b)   Would you or other family members like to volunteer to help with activities or programs here as a way of helping your relative? (e.g. working in the library, assisting the floor activities worker.)

_____

4.   We are eager to present PGC residents with many opportunities for enjoyment and learning. Would you or members of your immediate family be interested in performing or teaching classes to PGC residents? (e.g. giving music or dance recital, teaching a Hebrew, art, or sewing class, entertaining at one of our annual events, etc.)
        No _____
IF YES, Please specify. _____

Resident Activities Form

To be administered to residents and/or family members by resident activities therapist shortly after resident's admission.

SECTION I

1. What kinds of spectator activities do you enjoy?

Sports _____Reading _____
Movies, plays_____Being read to _____
T.V. _____Listening to music _____
Radio_____Other _____
Cards _____

2. In what kinds of activities do you enjoy participating?

Sports _____Walking_____
Cards_____Letter writing_____
Games_____Automobile trips_____
Visiting with friends_____Going to the park____
Shopping & window shopping___Picnics_____

3. Hobbies and creative arts

Sewing or handwork ___Playing a musical instrument___
Crafts (please specify)___Singing _____
Gardening _____Dancing _____
Other _____

4. In what social, political, or religious clubs or other community activities have you enjoyed participating?
_____

5. Are there any activities which you no longer do, but which you might like to try again?

_____

6. Do any of your immediate family members have particular talents or skills? Please explain.

_____

7. Is there anything you always wanted to try but never got around to?

_____

8. Do you generally enjoy "people" activities or more solitary activities?

SECTION II

Please use this space for any additional comments, especially regarding the residents and family's attitude toward participation in activities.

Referral Form: *Resident Service to Hospital Service*

Name of Resident _____

Age_____

Room # _____

Admission date to PGC_____

Date of Hospitalization _____

From: Res. S.W. _____

To: Hosp. S.W. _____

1) Problem areas including anticipated adjustment to hospital _____

_____

2) Social Work approach to resident problems _____

_____

FAMILY INFORMATION

3) Name and telephone number of most active family member_____

Hours to be reached_____

Anticipated problems re: resident hospitalization

_____

_____

Referral Form: Hospital Service to Resident Service

Date of Discharge _____

From: Hospital S.W. _____

TO: Resident S.W. _____

1) Adjustment to hospitalization _____

_____

2) Health problems during hospitalization _____

_____

3) Family contact

_____

4) Recommendations for follow-up _____

_____

_____

Charting Outline for Interdisciplinary Conferences

To be filled out by coordinator at floor staff meeting

Name: _____   Date: _____

Name: _____   Date set for re-evaluation: _____

Specific Functional Disabilities	Potential for Changing the Disability (good, fair, poor)	Objectives for Treatment	Therapeutic Steps	Staff Assignments	Results in Terms of Specific Functional Change

Recommendation for Resident Room Change

Please check when you have filled in appropriate section. This form to be returned to Social Work Department after completed by medical and nursing departments.

Nursing _____
Medical _____
Social Work _____
Administration _____

Dept. initiating request for change:

___Medical   DATE INITIATED _____
___Nursing   RESIDENT _____
___Social Service   PRESENT ROOM # _____
___Administration   SUGGESTED FACILITY _____

Did resident request change_____ yes _____ no _____

All departments indicate reason for recommendation below.
Any department disagreeing, please indicate with red "X"

NURSING
Charge Nurse   Date   Director of Nursing   Date
_____

MEDICAL
Physician   Date   Medical Director   Date
_____

SOCIAL SERVICE
Social Worker   Date   Director, S.S.D.   Date
_____

ADMINISTRATION _____ Date ____

FINAL DECISION
        move _____
        not move _____
        reason: Date ____

ORDER TO MOVE

Check one:

Voluntary move _____

Necessary move _____

New Room # _____

Date of move _____

Administrator _____

Date _____

Finalized Room Change Form

Name of Resident _____

To be move from rm. #. _____ to rm. # _____

Members of family notified _____ date _____

Reaction of family member_____

_____

Resident notified of change—date _____

Reaction of resident _____

_____

Present resident social worker_____

Transferred to social worker_____

Comments _____

_____

_____

Social Work Transfer Summary

Name of Resident
Admission Date
Room Number
If resident is being moved, new room number

Reason for transfer of case

Brief history of stay
1. How resident sees problems, how staff sees problems
2. Adjustment since admission to roommate and staff
3. Social service contacts with residents and family since admission.

Problems Areas
How resolved
Reaction of resident and family
Which family members active and quality of relationship

Changes and Current Status in Health
Mental and physical functioning
Behavior

Hospitalizations

Previous Room Changes
Reason
Reaction of resident and family

Conferences
Case, Rehabilitation, Staff
Recommendations for continuing service

Social Worker's Worksheet

19
(month)   (year)

(worker)

No.	RECEPTION	APPLICATION	ACTIVE WAIT. LIST	DEFERRED	RESIDENT
1					
2					
3					
4					
5					
6					
7					
8					
9					
10					
11					
12					
13					
14					
15					
16					
17					
18					
19					
20					
21					
22					
23					

Social Worker's Monthly Report
Services to Applicants

Social Worker _____

_____ 19 _____
(month)   (year)

Name

(Last First)	Current Inquiry (date)	Prev. Inq. (date)	Reception	Appl. Rec'd. AWL-DEF.	Admitted (date)	Closed Application			Reason	Application Transferred		
						Withdr.	Rej.	Dec.		AWL to DEF.	from DEF. to AWL	Floor Placed
TOTAL												

INQUIRIES: Men _____ Women _____ Couples _____

RECEPTIONS: Men _____ Women _____ Couples _____

Total Current Case Load: A.W.L. _____ Deferred _____

Prepared by:
Director, Social Service

Monthly Report of
Status of Applications

__19__ __(Yr.)__
(Month)

APPLICANT'S NAME (LAST—FIRST)	DATE	WORKER	APPLIC REC'D	ADMIT-TED	APPLICATION CLOSED			TRANSFERRED		PLACE-MENT
					WITHDN	REJ DEC	REASON	FROM AWL TO DEF	FROM DEF TO AWL	
TOTAL:										

Monthly Social Service Statistics: Services to Applicants

	Month	Year

I. <u>Active Waiting List</u>
   A. Carried over from previous month _____
   B. New Applications
       1. From community   _____
       2. From York House   _____
       3. From YH via Friedman   _____
       4. From community via Friedman _____
                     Total Applications   _____

   C. Transferred from Deferred List   _____
   D. Transferred to Deferred List   _____
   E. Admitted to
       1. to Robinson   _____
       2. to Sley   _____

                     Total Admissions   _____
   F. Closed
       1. Withdrawn   _____
       2. Deceased   _____
       3. Rejected   _____
                     Total Closed _____

   G. Total Active Waiting List   _____

II. <u>Deferred Waiting List</u>
   A. Carried over from previous month _____
   B. New Applications   _____
   C. Transferred from A.W.L.   _____
   D. Transferred to A.W.L.   _____
   E. Closed
       1. Withdrawn   _____
       2. Deceased   _____
       3. Rejected   _____
                     Total Closed _____

F. Total Deferred List _____

III. A. Number of Inquiries _____
   B. Number of Reception Cases_____

IV. Placement Needs of Active Waiting List

	ROBINSON INTERMEDIATE CARE	ROBINSON SKILLED CARE	ROBINSON N.W.	S.W.	SLEY	TOTAL
MEN						
WOMEN						
COUPLES						
TOTAL						

COMMENTS:

SELECTED BIBLIOGRAPHY

Chapter 2

Brody, E. M. A million Procrustean beds. *The Geron-tologist* 13:4, 1973. 430–435.
Brotman, H. Data based on 1960 Census.
Cohen, E. S. Mental illness among older Americans. Washington: Paper prepared for U.S. Senate Special Committee on Aging, U.S. DHEW, 1961.
———. An overview of long-term care facilities. In Brody, E. M. and Contributors, *A Social Work Guide for Long-Term Care Facilities.* Washington: DHEW Publication No. (HSM)73-9106, U.S. GPO, 1974, 11-26.
HEW. *Patients in mental institutions,* Parts I-IV, Washington: 1964.
HRA. Nursing homes: An overview of national characteristics for 1973–74. *Monthly Vital Statistics Report* 23: 6. Supplement, Sept. 5, 1974.
Kastenbaum, R., and Candy, S. The 4 percent fallacy: a methodological and empirical critique of extended care facility program statistics. *Aging and Human Development* 4: 1973. 15-21.
Maeda, D. Innovative services for the elderly in Japan. Paper presented at 10th International Congress of Gerontology. Jerusalem, Israel: June, 1975.
Mathiasen, G. *The Social Work Year Book of 1960,* vol. 14. National Association of Social Workers, Inc., New York 1960. Section on Aging, p. 95 et seq.
Mendelson, M. A. *Tender Loving Greed.* New York: Knops, 1974.

National Center for Health Statistics. Advance Copy of Tables from 1973–1974 National Nursing Home Survey. Washington: PHS, U.S. DHEW, March, 1975.

Subcommittee on Long-Term Care of the Special Committee on Aging, U.S. Senate. *Nursing Home Care in the United States: Failure in Public Policy, Introductory Report.* Washington: U.S. GPO, 1976. 22.

Townsend, C. *Old Age: The Last Segregation. Ralph Nader's Study Group Report on Nursing Homes.* New York: Grossman, 1971.

Worthington, N. L. National Health expenditures, 1929–1974. *Social Security Bulletin* 38: 2, 1975. 3–20.

Chapter 3

Aldrich, C. K., and Mendkoff, E. Relocation of the aged and disabled: a mortality study. *Journal of American Geriatrics Society* 11: 1963. 185.

Blenkner, M. Environmental change and the aging individual. *The Gerontologist* 7: 1967. 101–105.

Bok, M. Some problems in milieu treatment of the chronic older mental patient. *The Gerontologist* 2: 1, 1971. 141–147.

Bourestom, N. C., and Pastalan, L. *Relocation Reports 1 and 2.* Ann Arbor: Institute of Gerontology, University of Michigan, 1972.

Brody, E. M. The mentally impaired aged patient: a socio-medical problem. *Clinical Medicine* 75: 1968. 49–58.

———. Follow-up study of aged applicants and non-applicants to a voluntary home. *The Gerontologist* 9:3, 1969. 187–196.

———. The etiquette of filial behavior. *Aging and Human Development,* 1:1, 1970. 87–94. In Scott, F. G., and Brewer, R. M., eds., *Perspectives in Aging,* Continuing Education Publication, Corvallis, Oregon: 1971.

————. Long-term care: the decision-making process and individual assessment. Proceedings, *Symposium on Human Factors in Long-Term Health Care,* National Conference on Social Welfare. Columbus: 1975.

————. Basic data requirements for geriatric institutions and services. *Medical Care* 14:5, Supplement, 1976. 72–82.

————, and Gummer, B. Aged applicants and non-applicants to a voluntary home: an exploratory comparison. *The Gerontologist* 7: 234-243, 1967.

————, Kleban, M. H., and Moss, M. Measuring the impact of change. *The Gerontologist* 14:4, 1974. 299–305.

Brody, S. New assessment mechanisms for the elderly. Paper presented at 10th International Congress of Gerontology. Jerusalem, Israel: June, 1975.

Camp, W. P. Planning for care and treatment of the mentally impaired aged. In Lawton, M. P., and Lawton, F. G., eds., *Mental Impairment in the Aged. Proceeding of the Institute on Mentally Impaired Aged,* Philadelphia Geriatric Center, 1965. 130–137.

Carp, F. Attitudes of old person toward themselves and toward others. *Journal of Gerontology* 22: 1967. 308–312.

Federal Register 39:12, Part III, Jan. 17, 1974. 2244.

Ferrari, N. A. *Institutionalization and Attitude Change in an Aged Population: A Field Study in Dissonance Theory.* Unpublished doctoral dissertation, School of Applied Social Sciences, Western Reserve University, 1962. Cleveland Ohio.

Freidsam, H. J., and Dick, H. R. *Decisions Leading to Institutionalization of the Aged.* Final report, Social Security Administration Cooperative Research and Demonstration Grant Program, Project # 037 (C1)-2-031, unpublished, 1963. 32 ff.

Goldfarb, A. I., Shahinian, S., and Turner, H. Death rate in relocation residents of nursing homes (abstract). *Gerontologist* 6:3, Part II 1966. 30.

Gottesman, L. E. The personal care assessment model. Project funded by State of Pennsylvania, Office for the Aging, Sept. 1974 to June 1976. Philadelphia Geriatric Center, 1974.

————, and Brody, E. M. Psycho-social intervention programs within the institutional setting. In Sherwood, S., ed., *Long-Term Care: A Handbook for Researchers, Planners, and Providers.* New York: Spectrum, 1975. 455–509.

————, Moss, M., and Worts, F. Resources, needs and wishes for services in urban middle class older people. Paper presented at 10th International Congress of Gerontology. Jerusalem, Israel: June, 1975.

Institute of Gerontology, University of Michigan-Wayne State University. *Preparation for Relocation, Relocation Report # 3.* Ann Arbor: 1973.

Jasnau, K. F. Individualized versus mass transfer to nonpsychotic geriatric patients from mental hospitals to nursing homes, with special reference to the death rate. *Journal of American Geriatric Society* 15:3, 1967.

Jones, E. W. *Patient Classification for Long-Term Care.* Washington. HEW, Health Resources Administration, 1973.

Lawton, M. P. The functional assessment of elderly people. *Journal of the American Geriatric Society* 29:6, 1971. 465–481.

————, and Brody, E. M. Assessment of older people: self-maintaining and instrumental activities of daily living. *The Gerontologist* 9: 1969. 179–186.

————, and Nahemow, L. Ecology and the aging process. In Eisdorfer, C. and Lawton, M. P., eds., *The Psychology of Adult Development and Aging.*

Washington: American Psychological Association, 1973. 619–674.

———, and Yaffe, S. Mortality, morbidity and voluntary change of residence by older people. *Journal of American Geriatric Society* 18: 1970. 823–831.

Lieberman, M. A. Institutionalization of the aged: effects on behavior. *Journal of Gerontology* 24: 1969. 330–342.

———, Prock, V. N., and Tobin, S. S. Psychological effects of institutionalization. *Journal of Gerontology* 23: 1968. 343.

Liebowitz, B. Impact of intra-institutional relocation: background and the planning process. *The Gerontologist* 14:4, 1974. 293–295.

Locker, R. and Rublin, A. Clinical aspects of facilitating relocation. *The Gerontologist* 14:4, 1974. 295–299.

Marlowe, R. A. Paper presented at annual meeting of Gerontological Society, Puerto Rico, Dec. 1972, as reported in *Geriatric Focus* 12:31, 1973.

Miller, D., and Lieberman, M. A. The relationship of affect state and adaptive capacities to reactions to stress. *Journal of Gerontology* 20: 1965. 492.

Patnaik, B. Lawton, M. P. Kleban, M. H., and Maxwell, R. Behavioral adaptation to the change in institutional residence. *The Gerontologist* 14:4, 1974. 305–307.

Pfeiffer, E. Multidimensional quantitative assessment of three populations of elderly. Paper presented at Annual Meeting of the Gerontological Society, Miami Beach, Fla., Nov. 5–9, 1973.

Sainsbury, P., and Grad, J. Evaluation of treatment and services. *The Burden on the Community*. London: Oxford University Press, 1962.

Subcommittee on Long-Term Care of the Special Committee on Aging, U.S. Senate. *Nursing Home Care in the United States: Failure in Public Policy, Introductory*

Report. Washington: US. GPO, 1974.

Yawney, B. A., and Slover, D. Relocation of the elderly. *Social Work* 18: 1973. 86–94.

Chapter 4

Executive Office of the President, Office of Management and Budget. *Catalogue of Federal Domestic Assistance.* Washington: U.S. GPO, 1975.

National Association of Social Workers. *Encyclopedia of Social Work 16th Issue.* Cf. articles on Aging, Homemaker service, Housing special groups, and Protective services for adults. New York: 1971.

Public Health Service, U.S. Department of Health, Education, and Welfare. *Coordinated Home Care Programs, 1964.* Washington: U.S. GPO., 1966.

Trager, Brahna. *Home Health Services in the United States.* A report to the Special Committee on Aging, United States Senate, 92nd Congress, 2nd Session. Washington; U.S. GPO, 1972.

U.S. Dept. of Health, Education, and Welfare, Social Security Administration. *Social Security Handbook, 5th Edition.* DHEW Publication No. (SSA) 73-10135. Washington: U.S. GPO, 1974.

Veterans Administration. *Veterans Administration Fact Sheet, IS-1.* Washington: U.S. GPO, 1975.

Chapter 5

Beattie, W. M., Jr., and Bullock, J. Unpublished preface to a counseling service. St. Louis: Health and Welfare Council of Metropolitan St. Louis, 1963.

Brody, E. M. The aging family. *The Gerontologist* 6:4, 1966. 201–206.

———. Follow-up study of aged applicants and non-applicants to a voluntary home. *The Gerontologist* 9:3, 1969. 187–196.

374 LONG-TERM CARE OF OLDER PEOPLE

————. A million Procrustean beds. *The Gerontologist* 13:4, 1973. 430–435.

————. Aging and family personality: a developmental view. *Family Process* 13:1, 1974. 23–37.

————. Basic data requirements for geriatric institutions and services. *Medical Care* 14:5, Supplement, 1976. 72–82.

————, and Gummer, B. Aged applicants and non-applicants to a voluntary home: an exploratory comparison. *The Gerontologist* 7:4, 1967. 234–243.

————, and Spark, G. Institutionalization of the aged: a family crisis. *Family Process* 5:1, 1966. 76–90.

Brotman, H. B. National population trends as of July 1, 1966. *Useful Facts No. 15.* Washington: U.S. HEW, 1967.

————. The older population revisited. *Facts and Figures on Older Americans No. 2* AoA, SRS, HEW, 1971.

————. *Every tenth American.* Mimeo, 1975.

DHEW, Public No. (OHD) 75-20013, AoA. *Statistical Memo No. 31: Estimates of the Size and Characteristics of the Older Population in 1974 and Projections to the Year 2000.* May 1975.

Eisdorfer, C., and Lawton, M. P., eds. *The Psychology of Adult Development and Aging.* Washington: American Psychological Association, 1973.

Friedsam, H. J., and Dick, H. R. Decisions leading to institutionalization of the aged. Unpublished final report, Social Security Administration Cooperative Research and Demonstration Grant Program, Project 037 (C1) 20-031, 1963.

Goldfarb, A. I. Current trends in the management of the psychiatrically ill aged. In *Psychopathology of Aging,* ed. P. H. Hoch and J. Zubin. New York: Grune and Stratton, 1961. 248–265.

————. Prevalance of psychiatric disorders in metropolitan old age and nursing home. *Journal of American Geriatric Society,* 10: 1962. 77–84.

————. The senile older person. *Selected Papers, 5th Annual Conference of State Executives on Aging.* Washington: U.S. HEW, 1965. 42–45.

Gottesman, L. E. *Report to Respondents.* Nursing Home Project. Philadelphia: Philadelphia Geriatric Center, 1971.

————, and Brody, E. M. Psycho-social intervention programs with the institutional setting. In Sherwood, S., ed., *Long-Term Care: A Handbook for Researchers, Planners, and Providers.* New York: Spectrum Publications, 1975.

————, and Hutchinson, E. Characteristics of the institutionalized elderly. In Brody, E. M., and contributors, *A Social Work Guide for Long-Term Care Facilities,* U.S. GPO, 1974.

Grintzig, L. *Selected Characteristics of Residents in Long-Term Care Institutions.* Long-Term Care Monograph No. 5, Washington: Research Division, Dept. of Health Care Administration, George Washington University, 1970.

Group for the Advancement of Psychiatry. *Psychiatry and the Aged: An Introductory Approach Report No. 59.* New York: 1965.

Jackson, H. Planning for the specially disadvantaged. In E. Pfeiffer, ed., *Alternatives to institutional care for older Americans: Practice and planning.* Durham: Center for the Study of Aging and Human Development, Duke University, 1973.

Jackson, J. Really, there are existing alternatives to institutionalization for aged blacks. In E. Pfeiffer, ed., *Alternatives to institutional care for older Americans: Practice and planning.* Durham: Center for Study of Aging and Human Development, Duke University, 1973.'

Lawton, M. P., and Nahemow, L. Ecology and the aging process. In Eisdorfer, C. and Lawton, M. P., eds.,

The Psychology of Adult Development and Aging. Washington: American Psychological Association, 1973.

Lowenthal, M. F., Berkman, P. L., and Associates. *Aging and mental disorder in San Francisco: A social psychiatric study,* San Francisco: Jossey-Bass, 1976.

National Center for Health Statistics. Unpublished data from the 1969 Survey of Institutions. U.S. DHEW, Washington: 1972.

National Center for Health Statistics, Advance Copy of Tables from 1973–1974 National Nursing Home Survey. PHS, U.S., Dept. of HEW, 1975.

National Health Survey. *Characteristics of Residents in Nursing Homes and Personal Care Homes.* U.S. June–Aug. 1969. Series 121, No. 19, HSMHA, National Center for Health Statistics, 1973.

National Institute of Mental Health, Biometry Branch, Statistical Note # 72, *Age, Sex and Diagnostic Composition of Resident Patients in State and County Mental Hospitals, U.S. 1961–70.* U.S. Dept. of HEW, 1972.

Neugarten, B. L. Adult personality: Toward a psychology of the life cycle. In Neugarten, B. L., ed., *Middle Age and Aging,* University of Chicago Press, Chicago: 1968. 137–147.

Neugarten, B. L., and associates. *Personality in Middle and Late Life.* New York: Atherton Press, 1964.

Pincus, A. Toward a developmental view of aging for social work. *Social Work* 12:3, 1967. 33–41.

Reid, O. M. Aging Americans: A review of cooperative research projects. *Welfare in Review,* 4: 1966. 1–12.

Rosow, I. The aged, family and friends. *Social Security Bulletin* 28:1965. 18–20.

Shanas, E. Family responsibility and the health of older people. *Journal of Gerontology,* 15:1960. 408–411.

———. Family relationships of older people. *Health Information Research Series* 20:1961.

————, and Associates. *Old People in Three Industrial Societies.* Chapter 2. New York: Atherton Press, 1968.

Spark, G., and Brody, E. M. The aged are family members. *Family Process* 9:2, 1970. 195–210.

Subcommittee on Long-Term Care of the Special Committee on Aging, U.S. Senate. *Nursing Home Care in the United States: Failure in Public Policy, Introductory Report.* Washington: U.S. GPO, 1976.

U.S. DHEW, PHS. *Long-Term Care Facility Improvement Study, Interim Report.* 1975.

Stotsky, B. A. Psychiatric disorders common to psychiatric and non-psychiatric patients in nursing homes. *Journal of American Geriatric Society,* 15:1967. 664–73.

Streib, G. F. Family patterns in retirement. *Journal of Social Issues,* 14:1958. 46–60.

Sussman, M. B. Relationships of adult children with their parents in the United States. In Shanas, E. and Streib, G., eds., *Social Structure and the Family: Generational Relations,* New York: Grume and Stratton, 1968. 62–92.

Townsend, P. The effects of family structure on the likelihood of admission to an institution in old age: The application of a general theory. In Shanas, E. and Streib, G., eds., *Social Structure and the Family: Generational Relations.* Englewood Cliffs: Prentice-Hall, 1965. 163–187.

Chapter 10

Brody, E. M., and Kleban, M. H. Intermediate housing for the elderly: first year progress report. Supported by NIMH and AoA, Grant # 19936, May, 1972.

Brody, E. M., and Kleban, M. H. Intermediate housing for the elderly: second status report and some preliminary information on the nature of the population. Supported by NIMH and AoA, Grant # 19936, April 1974.

Brody, E. M., Kleban, M. H., and Liebowitz, B. Living arrangements for older people. *American Institute of Architects Journal* 59:3, 1973. 35–40.

Brody, E. M., Kleban, M. H. and Liebowitz. Intermediate housing for the elderly: satisfaction of those who moved in and those who did not. *The Gerontologist* 15:4, 1975. 350–356.

Gottesman, L. E. Need, cost, and effects of home services for the aged. AoA grant # 93-P-57436/3, Philadelphia Geriatric Center, mimeo, 1973.

Kleban, M. H. Architecture and behavior: the mentally impaired aged. NIMH Grant # MH 16139, Philadelphia Geriatric Center, mimeo, 1969.

Lawton, M. P. Supportive services in the context of the housing environment. *Gerontologist* 9:1969. 15–19.

Lawton, M. P. Prosthetic architure for mentally impaired aged. HEW, HSMHA Grant # HS00100-HSR, Philadelphia Geriatric Center, mimeo, 1969.

Liebowitz, B., and Brody, E. M. The Philadelphia Geriatric Center: many options to meet many needs. *Journal of the American Hospital Association* 49:1975.

Sherwood, S., Greer, D. S., Morris, J. N., and Sherwood, C. C. *The Highland Heights Experiment: A Final Report.* Washington: U.S. GPO, 1973.

Subcommittee on Long-Term Care of the Special Committee on Aging, U. S. Senate. *Nursing Home Care in the United States: Failure in Public Policy, Introductory report and 9 supporting papers.* Washington: 1975.

Waldman, A. Non-institutional living arrangements for the aged—fact or fiction. In *Selected Papers, 5th Annual Conference of State Executives on Aging* 56–58. Washington: U.S. DHEW, 1965.

Part III

Aldrich, C. K., and Mendkoff, E. Relocation of the aged and disabled: A mortality study. *Journal American Geriatric Society* 11:1963. 185–94.

American Hospital Association. *Meeting the Social Needs of Long-Term Patients.* Chicago: 1965.

American Hospital Association. *Essentials of Social Work Programs in Hospitals.* Chicago: 1971.

American Hospital Association. *Winds of Change.* Chicago:1971.

Ball, E. L. Recreation: How to organize and conduct a successful program. *Professional Nursing Home* 5:1963. 44–46.

Barton, M. G. Group counselling with older hospital patients. *The Gerontologist* 2:1, 1962. 51–56.

Beattie, W. M., Jr. Responsibility of the long-term facility to the long-term patient. *Hospitals* 38:17, 1964.

———. The design of supportive environments for the life span. *The Gerontologist* 10:3, 1970.

Bennett, R. The meaning of institutional life. *The Gerontologist* 3:3, 1963.

Blank, M. Recent research findings on practice with the aging. *Social Casework* 52:6, 1971.

Blenkner, M. Environmental change and the aging individual. *The Gerontologist* 7:1967. 101–105.

———, Bloom, M., and Nielsen, M. Protective services for older people. Report on a controlled demonstration. *Social Casework* 52:8, 1971.

Brody, E. M. The aging family. *The Gerontologist* 6:4, 1966.

———. The mentally impaired aged patient: A sociomedical problem. *Clinical Medicine* 75:6, 1968.

———. Follow-up study of applicants and non-applicants to a voluntary home. *The Gerontologist* 9:1969. 187–96.

————. Serving the aged: Educational needs as viewed by practice. *Social Work* 15:4, 1970. 42–51.

————. Aging. National Association of Social Workers, *Encyclopedia of Social Work*. Washington: 1971.

————. Long-term care for the elderly: Optimums, options, and opportunities. *Journal American Geriatric Society* 9:6, 1971.

————. A million Procrustean beds. *The Gerontologist* 13:4, 1973. 430–435.

————. Aging and family personality: A developmental view. *Family Process* 13:1, March 1974. 23–37.

————. Long-Term Care: The Decision-Making Process and Individual Assessment. Invited paper prepared for Symposium on Human Factors in Long-Term Care sponsored by the National Conference on Social Welfare and the Division of Long-Term Care, Bureau of Health Services Research, U.S.P.H.S. San Francisco: 1975.

————. Basic data requirements for geriatric institutions and services. *Medical Care* 14:5, 1976. 72–82.

Brody, E. M., and Brody, S. J. Aging and social work: the decade of decision. *Social Work,* 1974. 544–554.

————, and Cole, C. The deferred waiting list of a voluntary home. *The Gerontologist* 11:3, 1971.

————, and Contributors. *A Social Work Guide for Long-Term Care Facilities.* NIMH, U.S. GPO, Washington, D.C. DHEW Publication No. (HSM)73-9106, 1974.

————, and Gummer, B. Aged applicants and non-applicants to a voluntary home: An exploratory comparison. *The Gerontologist* 7:4, 1967. 234–243.

————, Kleban, M. H., and Liebowitz, B. Living arrangements for older people. *Journal of American Institute of Architects,* 1973.

————, Kleban, M. H., and Liebowitz, B. Intermediate housing for the elderly: Satisfaction of those who moved and those who did not. *The Gerontologist*

15:4, 1975. 350–356.

———, Kleban, M. H., and Moss, M. Measuring the impact of change. *The Gerontologist* 14:4, 1974. 299–305.

———, and Liebowitz, B. Long-term care: The institution and the community. In *Medical World News, Geriatrics,* 1973. 76–78.

———, and Silverman, H. A. Individualized treatment of mentally impaired aged. *Social Work Practice.* New York: Columbia University Press, 1970.

Brody, S. Comprehensive health care of the elderly: An analysis. *The Gerontologist,* 1973. 412–418.

Bronson, E. P. An experiment in intermediate housing facilities for the elderly. *The Gerontologist* 12:1, 1972. 22–26.

Brotman, H. B. The demography of aging and mental illness and impairment. Paper prepared for the Staff College, NIMH, 1975.

Brudno, J. J. Group program for new residents of a home for the aged. *Journal American Geriatric Society,* 10:9, 1962.

Cath, S. H. Some dynamics of middle and later years. *Smith College Studies in Social Work* 32: 1963.

Central Bureau for the Jewish Aged. *The Social Worker's Use of Group Approaches in Work With the Aged.* New York: 1966.

Central Bureau for the Jewish Aged. *Workshop for Group Activity Workers in Institutions for the Aged.* New York: 1969.

Central Bureau for the Jewish Aged. *The Significance of Group Activity Program for the Institutionalized Aged.* New York: 1970.

Cohen, E. S. Recreation in the nursing home. *Professional Nursing Home,* 1962.

Eisdorfer, C., and Lawton, M. P., eds. *Psychological Processes of Aging.* Washington: American Psychological Association, 1973.

Erikson, E. H. *Childhood and Society.* New York: W. W. Norton, 1950.

Flack, H. S., and Kane, M. K. *It Can't Be Home: Social and Emotional Aspects of Residential Care.* Rockville, Maryland: NIMH, 1971.

Farrar, M., and Hemmy, M. L. Use of nonprofessional staff in work with the aged. *Journal National Association of Social Workers* 8:3, July 1963.

————, Ryder, M. B., and Blenkner, M. Social work responsibility in nursing home care. *Social Casework* 45:9, 1964.

Feil, N. W. Group therapy in a home for the aged. *The Gerontologist* 7:3, 1967. 192–195.

Frankel, F. H., and Clark, E. Mental health consultation and education in nursing homes. *Journal American Geriatric Society* 17:1969. 360–365.

Friedman, S. The resident welcoming committee: Institutionalized elderly in volunteer services. *The Gerontologist* 15:4, 1975. 362–367.

Fulton, R. *Death, Grief, and Bereavement: A Chronological Bibliography 1843–1970.* Minneapolis: Center for Death Education and Research, University of Minnesota, 1970.

Gelwicks, L. E. Design can brainwash the chronic care patient. *Modern Hospital* 102:1964. 106–11.

Gerontological Society. Research and development goals in social gerontology. A report of a special committee. *The Gerontologist* 9:4, 1969.

Glaser, B. G., and Strauss, A. L. *Awareness of Dying.* Chicago: Adline, 1965.

————. *Time for Dying.* Glencoe: Free Press, 1968.

Goldfarb, A. I. Contributions of psychiatry to the institutional care of aged and chronically ill persons. *Journal Chronic Disease* 6:5, 1957.

————. The senile older person. *Selected Papers, 5th Annual Conference of State Executives on Aging.* Washington: U.S. DHEW, 1965.

————, Fisch, M., Shahinian, S. P., and Turner, H. Chronic brain syndrome in the community aged. *Archives General Psychiatry*, 18:5, 1968. 739–745.

Gossett, H. M. Restoring identity to socially deprived and depersonalized older people. *Adding Life to Years*. Bulletin of the Institute of Gerontology, State University of Iowa 15: Supplement # 4, 1968. 3–6.

Gottesman, L. E. Extended care of the aged: Psychosocial aspects. *Journal Geriatric Psychiatry* 11:2, 1969.

————, and Brody, E. M. Psycho-social intervention programs within the institutional setting. In Sherwood, S., ed., *Long-Term Care: A Handbook for Researchers, Planners, and Providers*. New York: Spectrum, 1975. 455–509.

Group for the Advancement of Psychiatry. *Death and Dying: Attitudes of Patient and Doctor*. Symposium # 11, 1965.

Group for the Advancement of Psychiatry. *Psychiatry and the Aged: An Introductory Report*. Report No. 59. New York: 1965.

Hayflick, L. The strategy of senescence. *The Gerontologist*, 1974. 37–45.

Hearings before the Special Committee on Aging. *Death With Dignity*. U.S. Senate, 92nd Congress, 1972.

Hemmy, M. L. Social and psychological needs of persons living in homes for the aged and nursing homes. Paper presented at Catholic Conference of Services for Aging, Institute on Accreditation, St. Louis, Missouri, February 18, 1965.

Institute of Gerontology, University of Mich-Wayne State University *Preparation for Relocation*. Relocation Report #3. Ann Arbor: 1973.

Ishizaki, ·D. Families: Hindrance or help. *Proceedings of Conference, Family Involvement in Long-Term Care*. Minneapolis: Sister Kenny Institute and Minnesota Department of Health, 1976.

————, and Howmiller, J. Community organization as the method of choice by a county worker assigned to nursing homes. Paper presented at 24th Annual Meeting of the Gerontological Society, Houston, Texas, mimeo, October 1971.

Jackson, H. Planning for the specially disadvantaged. In E. Pfeiffer, ed., *Alternatives to Institutional Care for Older Americans: Practice and Planning*. Durham: Center for the Study of Aging and Human Development, Duke University, 1973.

Jackson, J. Really, there are existing alternatives to institutionalization for aged blacks. In E. Pfeiffer, ed., *Alternatives to Institutional Care for Older Americans: Practice and Planning*. Durham: Center for Study of Aging and Human Development, Duke University, 1973.

Jasnau, K. F. Individualized versus mass transfers for non-psychotic geriatric patients from mental hospitals to nursing homes, with special reference to the death rate. *Journal American Geriatric Society* 15:1967. 280–84.

Kahana, E. Matching institutional environments to needs of the aged: A conceptual scheme. In J. Gubrian, ed., *Late Life: Recent Developments in the Sociology of Aging*. Springfield, Ill.: Charles C. Thomas, in press.

Kalish, R. A. A continuum of subjectively perceived death. *The Gerontologist* 6:1966. 73–76.

————. ed. *The Dependencies of Old People*. Ann Arbor: Institute of Gerontology Occasional Papers, 1969.

Kaplan, J. Observations on the somatic and psychosomatic significance of group activity on older people. *Mental Hygiene*, 1954. 640–646.

————. The social care of older persons in nursing homes. *Journal American Association of Nursing Homes*, 1954.

————. Evaluation techniques for older groups. *The American Journal of Occupational Therapy* 12:5, 1959.

221–226.

———. New theories affecting geriatric social institutions. *Geriatrics* 17:1962.

———. An analysis of multiple community services through the institution for the aged. *Geriatrics* 19:1964.

———. Individualizing group variations. *The Gerontologist* 10:2, 1970.

———. The social worker in the long-term care facility. *Hospital Progress*. St. Louis, Mo: Catholic Hospital Association, 1970.

———. Book review of Brody, Elaine M., and contributors, *A Social Work Guide for Long-Term Care Facilities. The Gerontologist*, 1975. 80.

Kastenbaum, R. J. The mental life of a dying geriatric patient. *The Gerontologist*, 7:1967. 97–100.

———. Multiple perspectives on a geriatric death valley. *Community* Mental Health Journal 3:1, 1967.

———. Future direction of nursing homes in meeting the mental health needs of the elderly. *Journal Geriatric Psychiatry* 1:2, 1968. 226–34.

———. While the old man dies. In A. H. Kutscher, ed., *Psycho-social Aspects of Terminal Care*. New York: Columbia University Press, 1971.

———, and Candy, S. E. The four percent fallacy. *Geriatric Focus* 12:3, 1973.

Kleban, M. H., and Brody, E. M. Prediction of improvement in mentally impaired aged: Social worker ratings of personality. *Journal Gerontology*, 27:1, 1972.

Kubie, S. K., and Landau, G. *Group Work with the Aged*. New York: International University Press, 1953.

Kübler-Ross, E. *On Death and Dying*. New York: MacMillan, 1969.

Lawton, A. H. Medical and psychological aspects of a treatment program for the mentally retarded aged.

The Gerontologist 6:1966. 139–42.

Lawton, M. P. Social rehabilitation of the aged: Some neglected aspects. *Journal American Geriatric Society,* 16:1968. 1346–63.

——— Assessment, integration, and environments for older people. *The Gerontologist* 10:1, 1970.

———. Institutions for the aged: Theory, content, and methods for research. *The Gerontologist* 10:1970. 305–312.

———. The functional assessment of elderly people. *Journal American Geriatric Society* 19:1971. 465–481.

———, and Brody, E. M. Assessment of older people self-maintaining and instrumental activities of daily living. *The Gerontologist* 9:1969. 179–86.

———, Carp, F. J., McGuire, M. C., Schooler, K. K., Hamnovitch, M. B., Peterson, J. E., and Lipman, A. Housing for the elderly: A symposium. *The Gerontologist* 9:1, 1969.

———, and Nahemow, L. Ecology and the aging process. In C. Eisdorfer and M. P. Lawton, eds., *The Psychology of Adult Development and Aging.* Washington: American Psychological Association, 1973.

———, and Yaffe, S. Mortality, morbidity and voluntary change of residence by older people. *Journal American Geriatric Society* 18:10, 1970.

Lieberman, M. A. Relationships of mortality to entrance to a home for the aged. *Geriatrics,* 1961.

———. Observations on death and dying. *The Gerontologist* 6:1966. 70–72.

———. Institutionalization of the aged: Effects on behavior. *Journal of Gerontology* 24:1969. 330–340.

———, Prock, V. A., and Tobin, S. S. Psychological effects of institutionalization. *Journal of Gerontology* 23:1968. 343–353.

Liebowitz, B. Impact of intra-institutional relocation,

special report from the Philadelphia Geriatric Center. Background and the planning process. *The Gerontologist* 14:4, 1974. 293–295.

———, and Brody, E. M. Integration of research and practice in creating a continuum of care for the elderly. *The Gerontologist* 10:1, 1970.

———, and Brody, E. M. The Philadelphia Geriatric Center: Many options to meet many needs. *Hospitals* 49:1975. 101–106.

Linn, M. W., and Gurel, L. Initial reactions to nursing home placement. *Journal American Geriatric Society* 17:1969. 219–223.

Liton, J., and Olstein, S. C. Therapeutic aspects of reminiscence. *Social Case Work* 50:5, 1969.

Living Arrangements of Older People: Ecology. In "Research and Development Goals in Social Gerontology," *The Gerontologist* 9:4, 1969.

Locker, R. Elderly couples in institutions. *Social Work* 21:2, 1976. 149–150.

———, and Rublin, A. Clinical aspects of facilitating relocation. *The Gerontologist* 14:4, 1974. 295–299.

Lowenthal, M. F. *Lives in Distress*. New York: Basic Books, 1964.

———, Berkman, P. L., and Associates. *Aging and Mental Disorder in San Francisco: A Social Psychiatric Study*. San Francisco: Jossey-Bass, 1967.

Lowy, L. The group in social work with the aged. *Social Work* 7:1962. 43–50.

———. Roadblocks in group work practice with older people: A framework for analysis. *The Gerontologist* 7:1967. 109–113.

Lucas, C. *Recreational Activity Development for Aging in Homes, Hospitals, and Nursing Homes*. Springfield, Ill.: Charles C. Thomas, 1956.

Manaster, A. The family group therapy program at Park View Home for the Aged. *Journal American Geriatric*

Society 15:3, 1967.

Margulies, M. S. Classification of activities to meet the psycho-social needs of geriatric patients. *The Gerontologist* 7:1967. 93–96.

Marlowe, R. A. Paper presented at Annual Meeting of Gerontological Society, Puerto Rico, December, 1972 as reported in *Geriatric Focus* 12:31, 1973.

————. Effects of Environment on Elderly State Hospital Relocatees. Presented at 44th Annual Meetings of the Pacific Sociological Association, Scottsdale, Arizona, May 3, 1973.

Mayadas, N. S., and Hink, D. L. Group work with the aging, an issue for social work education. *The Gerontologist* 14:5, 1974. 440–445.

Morris, R. Aging and the field of social work. In Riley, M., Riley, J. W., and Johnson, M. E., eds., *Aging and Society, Vol. 2: Aging and the Professions.* New York: Russell Sage Foundation, 1969.

National Association of Social Workers. *Utilization of Personnel of Social Work: Those With Full Professional Education and Those Without.* New York: 1962.

————. *Social Group Work With Older People.* New York: 1963.

National Conference on Social Welfare. *Human Factors in Long-Term Health Care.* Columbus: 1975.

National Health Survey. *Characteristics of Residents in Nursing Homes and Personal Care Homes.* U.S. June-August 1969, Series 121, No. 19, HSMHA, National Center for Health Statistics, 1973.

Neugarten, B. L. Adult personality: Toward a psychology of the life cycle. In Neugarten, B. L., ed., *Middle Age and Aging.* Chicago: University of Chicago Press, 1968. 137–147.

————, and associates. *Personality in Middle and Late Life.* New York: Atherton Press, 1964.

Noam, E. *Homes for the Aged: Supervision and Standards; A*

Report on the Legal Situation in European Countries. Washington: U.S. DHEW, Administration on Aging, U.S. GPO, 1975.

Novick, L. J. Occupation therapy and social group work in the home for the sick aged. *American Journal Occupational Therapy,* 15:5, 1961.

Oklahoma State Health Department. *Social Work Training Manual for Nursing Home Personnel.* Oklahoma City: 1968.

Patnaik, B., Lawton, M. P., Kleban, M. H., and Maxwell, R. Behavioral adaptation to change in institutional residence. *The Gerontologist* 14:4, 1974. 305–307.

Pearson, L., ed. *Death and Dying: Current Issues in the Treatment of the Dying Person.* Cleveland: Press of Case Western Reserve, 1969.

Pincus, A. Toward a developmental view of aging for social work. *Social Work* 12:3, 1967.

———. Reminiscence in aging and its implications for social work practice. *Social Work* 15:3, 1970.

Posner Institute. *Dynamic Factors in the Role of the Caseworker in Work With the Aged.* Sponsored by Central Bureau for the Jewish Aged, Carnegie Endowment Center. New York: 1961.

Riley, M. W., and Foner, A. *Aging and Society, Vol. 1: An Inventory of Research Findings.* New York: Russell Sage Foundation, 1968.

Romney, L. S. Extension of family relationship into a home for the aged. *Social Work* 7:1, 1962.

Rosen, B., Anderson, T. E., and Bahn, A. Psychiatric Services for the Aged: A Nationwide Survey of Patterns of Utilization. Paper presented at 44th annual meeting of American Ortho-psychiatric Association, Washington, March 1967.

Rosen, T. The significance of the family to the residents' adjustment in a home for the aged. *Social Casework,* 1962.

Rosow, I. Intergenerational relationships: Problems and proposals. In Shanas, E., and Streib, C. eds., *Social Structure and the Family: Generational Relations.* Englewood Cliffs, N.J.: Prentice-Hall, 1965.

Shanas, E. Family responsibility and the health of older people. *Journal of Gerontology* 15:1960. 408–411.

———. Measuring the home health needs of the aged in five countries. *Journal of Gerontology* 26:1971. 37–40.

———, and Streib, F., eds. *Social Structure and the Family: Generational Relations.* Englewood Cliffs, N.J.: Prentice-Hall, 1965.

Shanas, E., Townsend, P., Wedderburn, D., Friss, H., Milhoj, P., and Stehower, J. *Old People in Three Industrial Societies.* New York: Atherton Press, 1968.

Shore, H. Group work program development in homes for the aged. *Social Service Review* 26:2, 1952.

———. The application of social work disciplines to group work services in homes for the aged. *Social Service Review* 36:4, 1952.

———. Social services in the extended care facility. *Professional Nursing Home.* 1966.

———. Working with relatives. *Geriatric Care,* 1969.

———, and Leeds, M., eds., *Geriatric Institutional Management.* New York: G. P. Putnam Sons, 1964.

Simon, A. The geriatric mentally ill. *The Gerontologist* 8: 1968. 7–15.

Spark, G. M., and Brody, E. M. The aged are family members. *Family Process* 9:1970. 195–210.

Stotsky, B. A. Psychiatric disorders common to psychiatric and non-psychiatric patients in nursing homes. *Journal American Geriatrics Society* 15:1967. 664–673.

———, and Levely, S. The interdisciplinary responsibilities of public health and mental health in nursing homes. *Nursing Homes* 9:1967.

Swenson, W. Attitudes toward death in aged population. In Tibbits, C., and Donahue, W., eds., *Social and*

Psychological Aspects of Aging. New York: Columbia University Press, 1962.

Symposium: Care and rehabilitation of the geriatric patient. *Journal American Geriatric Society,* 17:1969. 1132–1156.

Texas Association of Homes for the Aging. *Manual on Volunteer Services in Homes for the Aging and Nursing Homes.* Austin: 1970.

Townsend, P. *The Last Refuge.* London: Routledge and Kegan Paul, 1962.

————. The effects of family structure on the likelihood of admission to an institution in old age: The application of a general theory. In Shanas, E. and Streib, G., eds., *Social Structure and the Family: Generational Relations.* Englewood Cliffs, N.J.: Prentice-Hall, 1965.

Turner, B., Tobin, F., Sheldon, S., and Lieberman, M. A. Personality traits as predictors of institutional adaptation among the aged. *Journal of Gerontology* 27:1, January, 1972.

U.S. Department of Health, Education, and Welfare, Public Health Service. *A Guide for Social Services in Nursing Homes and Related Facilities.* PHS Publication No. 1878. Washington: Superintendent of Documents, U.S. GPO, 1968.

U.S. Department of Health, Education, and Welfare, Public Health Service. *Activities Supervisor's Guide: A Handbook for Activities in Long-Term Care Facilities.* PHS Publication No. 2021. Washington: Superintendent of Documents, U.S. GPO, 1969.

U.S. Public Health Service Publication No. 1459. *The Aging Person: Needs and Services. Working With Older People, Vol. III: A Guide to Practice.* Washington: Superintendent of Documents, U.S. GPO, 1970.

U.S. Department of Health, Education, and Welfare. PHS, *Long-Term Care Facility Improvement Study:*

Interim Report. Washington: 1975.

U.S. Department of Health, Education and Welfare PSS, Office of Nursing Home Affairs. *Long-Term Care Facility Improvement Study: Introductory Report.* Washington: U.S. GPO, 1975.

U.S. Senate Special Committee on Aging, Subcommittee on Long-Term Care. *Nursing Home Care in the United States, Failure in Public Policy: Introductory Report.* Washington: U.S. GPO, 1974.

Waldman, A. Non-institutional living arrangements for the aged: Fact or fiction. *Selected Papers, 5th Annual Conference of State Executives on Aging.* Washington: U.S. Department of Health, Education, and Welfare, U.S. GPO, 1965.

Wasser, E. *Creative Approaches in Casework with the Aging.* New York: Family Service Association of America, 1966.

Wax, J. Developing social work power in a medical organization. *Social Work* 13:62, 1968.

Weinberg, J. Interpersonal relationships in multigeneration families. *Living in the Multigeneration Family.* Institute of Gerontology, University of Michigan-Wayne State University, 1969.

Weisman, A. D. *On Dying and Denying: A Psychiatric Study of Terminality.* New York: Behavioral Publications, 1972.

————, and Kastenbaum, R. The psychological autopsy. *Community Mental Health Journal,* Monograph Series, No. 4, New York: Behavioral Publications, 1968.

Yawney, B. A., and Slover, D. Relocation of the elderly. *Social Work* 18:1973. 86–94.

Chapter 17

APA Hospital and Community Psychiatry Service. *Reality Orientation.* Washington: undated.

Atkinson, S., Fjeld, S. P., and Freeman, J. A. An intensive treatment program for state hospital geriatric patients. No. 2: Further progress and results. *Geriatrics* 10:1955. 111–117.

Atthowe, J. M., and Krasner, L. Preliminary report on the application of contingent reinforcement procedures (token economy) on a "chronic" psychiatric ward. *Journal of Abnormal Psychology* 73:1968. 37–43.

Ayllou, T., and Azrin, N. H. The measurement and reinforcement of behavior of psychotics. *Journal of Experimental Analysis of Behavior* 8:1965. 357–383.

Barns, E. K., Sack, A., and Shore, H. Guidelines to treatment approaches: modalities and methods for use with the aged. *The Gerontologist* 13:4, 1973. 513–527.

Bennett, R., and Eisdorfer, C. The institutional environment and behavior change. In Sherwood, S., ed., *Long-Term Care: A Handbook for Researchers, Planners, and Providers.* New York: Spectrum, 1975.

Burdock, E. I., Elliott, A. E., Hardesty, A. S., O'Neil, F. J., and Sklar, J. Biometric evaluation of an intensive treatment program in a state mental hospital. *Journal of Nervous and Mental Diseases* 130:1960. 271–277.

Donahue, W. An experiment in the restoration and preservation of personality in the aged. In W. Donahue and C. Tibbetts, eds., *Planning the Older Years.* Ann Arbor: University of Michigan Press, 1950.

———, Hunter, W. W., and Coons, D. A study of the socialization of old people. *Geriatrics* 8:1953. 656–666.

Folsom, J. C. Reality orientation for the elderly mental patient. *Journal of Geriatric Psychiatry* 1:2, 1968. 291–307.

Goodall, K., Who's who and where in behavior shaping. *Psychology Today,* 6, 1972.

Goodall, K., Margaret, age 10, and Martha, age 8—A simple case of behavioral engineering, *Psychology Today,* 6, 1972.

Gottesman, L. E. Milieu therapy of the aged in institutions. *Gerontologist* 13:1973. 23–26.

———. Nursing home performance as related to resident traits, ownership, size and source of payment. *American Journal of Public Health* 3:1974. 269–276.

———, and Brody, E. M. Psycho-social intervention programs within the institutional setting. In Sherwood, S., ed., *Long-Term Care: A Handbook for Researchers, Planners, and Providers.* New York: Spectrum, 1975.

———, Coons, D., and Donahue, W. Milieu therapy and long-term geriatric patients. Final report to Gerontology Branch, Division of Chronic Disease, Public Health Service, Washington: HEW, 1966.

———, Bourestom, N. C., Donahue, W., and Coons, D. Milieu treatment of the older mental patient: A final report. Project supported by NIMH Grant # MH14894, May, 1972.

Hawkins, R. P., Stimulus/Response: It's time we taught the young how to be good parents (and don't you wish we'd started a long time ago?), *Psychology Today,* 6, 1972.

Jones, M. *The Therapeutic Community.* New York: Basic Books, 1953.

Krasner, L. Behavior therapy. *Annual Review of Psychology* 22:1971. 483-532.

Letcher, P. B., Peterson, L. P., and Scarbrough, D. Reality orientation: a historical study of patient progress. *Hospital and Community Psychiatry* 25:12, 1974. 801–803.

McClannahan, L. E. Therapeutic and prosthetic living environments for nursing home residents. *The Gerontologist* 13:4, 1973. 424–429.

Mishara, B. L., and Kastenbaum, R. Free and earned

wine as environmental enrichments for chronic institutionalized geriatric mental patients. Northville State Hospital, unpublished paper, 1971.

Pappas, W., Curtis, W. P., and Baker, J. A controlled study of an intensive treatment program for hospitalized geriatric patients. *Journal of American Geriatric Society* 6:1958. 17–26.

Phillips, D. F. Reality orientation. *Hospitals* 47:1973.

Psychology Today 6. Articles by Goodall, K., and Hawkins, R. P., on behavior modification, 1972.

Rechtschaffen, A., Atkinson, S., and Freeman, J. A. An intensive treatment program for state hospital patients. *Geriatrics* 10:1954. 28–34.

Sherwood, S., ed. *Long-Term Care: A Handbook for Researchers, Planners, and Providers.* New York: Spectrum, 1975.

Sklar, J., and O'Neil, F. J. Experiments with intensive treatment in a geriatric ward. In P. H. Hoch and J. Zubin, eds., *Psychotherapy of Aging.* New York: Grune and Stratton, 1961.

Subcommittee on Long-Term Care of the Special Committee on Aging, U.S. Senate. *What Can be Done in Nursing Homes: Positive Aspects in Long-Term Care,* Supporting paper # 6. Washington: U.S. GPO, 1975.

Chapter 18

Health Insurance Institute. *Source Book of Health Insurance Data, 1975-76.* New York.

Hess, John L. Literally, it is business as usual in the nursing homes, *The New York Times Week in Review:* March 7, 1976.

Subcommittee on Health and Long-Term Care, Select Committee on Aging, House of Representatives,

94th Congress. *New Perspectives in Health Care for Older Americans.* January, 1976.

Subcommittee on Long-Term Care of the Special Committee on Aging, United States Senate. *Nursing Home Care in the United States: Failure in Public Policy.* Washington: U.S. GPO, 1974. 6.

Name Index

Subject Index